D1585816

The
Fragmented
State

To Lesley

The Fragmented State

THE POLITICAL GEOGRAPHY OF POWER

RONAN PADDISON

Basil Blackwell

First published 1983
Basil Blackwell Publisher Limited
108 Cowley Road, Oxford OX4 1JF, England

British Library Cataloguing in Publication Data

Paddison, Ronan
  The fragmented state.
  1. Balance of power   2. World politics
  I. Title
  325.1'12   JX1318

  ISBN 0-631-19580-7
  ISBN 0-631-13087-X Pbk

Typesetting by Katerprint Company Limited, Oxford
Printed in Great Britain by T. J. Press, Padstow

Contents

Introduction

Political geography has one of the longer traditions among the different branches of the geographical discipline. Classical scholars were aware of the interrelationships between geography and the organization of political institutions, notably the city-state, and though contemporary opinion might be critical of this early legacy its influence was still apparent among political philosophers of the Enlightenment. However crude, the determinist's argument as it developed in the latter part of the nineteenth century — that the environment has a definite influence in shaping political relationships — became part of conventional wisdom. Because of the centrality of politics to the organization and control of societies, the determinist's paradigm was fraught with its own dangers. Ratzel's Laws of the Spatial Growth of States were the harbinger of a crude form of analysis that was to lead the subject into ill-repute.

Political geography has advanced since the dark days of *Geopolitik*. Both methodologically and even more through detailed empirical work, a research momentum has been maintained, though as a possible criticism of the subject there are grounds for arguing that it has become too empiricist and too diffuse. Political geography could certainly not be accused of being a narrow field of enquiry. Looking specifically at the subject's research frontiers, a recent review (Anon., 1982) identified some 21 fields, grouping these, firstly, into studies in which the spatial environment has an influence on political relationships, secondly, into those where political processes are viewed as having a spatial impress and, finally, into those concerned with methodology and theory, that is providing the theoretical and conceptual frameworks within which politico-geographical relationships need to be examined. Studies in the first two groups admit, quite correctly, that geography and politics interact: in looking for the influence of the former we could examine how ethnicity or the *de jure* spatial organization of the state affects its functioning, and of the latter how politics influences the spatial patterning of social wellbeing, a question that helps integrate the political viewpoint into the mainstream of human geography.

Nor is it just a case of political geographers being concerned with a very wide range of topics that fit only very loosely together. To these different fields we need to add the different perspectives from which the subject is analysed. Political geographers differ from one another in the different emphases they place on the need for theory (let alone what theory), in the level of their analysis pursued and in the ideological frameworks within which they operate, which will generate key assumptions about how the political world functions.

Such eclecticism has its advantages and disadvantages. Since the subject generally is enjoying something of a mini-renaissance, we could argue that the multiplicity of different perspectives will help to enrich the field. Countering this, such differences, particularly as they become reinforced, could undermine the potential for any integration. This is, of course, a not unfamiliar problem to human geography or the social sciences more generally. Perhaps these differences are most stark between the growing number of political geographers utilizing Marxist arguments and those whose stance is implicitly liberal or, even more, atheoretical.

The 'common core' that yet allows for a multiplicity of perspectives has much to recommend it. For political geography, there is much to be said for this core being the state. In a number of respects the state is the fulcrum of political life: its agents and institutions mediate the essential tasks of control and allocation; it is the dominant actor among the formal levels of political institution, from local to supranational; the winning of state power has been the driving force behind the quest for self-determination, a movement that, first within the developed world and, more recently, within the Third World, has underlain the dissolution of empires and the progressive subdivision of the world map into an ever greater number of sovereign political units. Analysing the state enables the political geographer to come to terms with those questions of conflict and consensus, of power, that should occupy a central position within the field.

Arguing that the state might act as a 'common core' for the political geographer, a plea that has its historical precedent, does not preclude the study of the subject from a variety of perspectives. There is all the more reason to be catholic rather than blinkered in our approach when political geographers search for theories of the state.

This book is concerned with one aspect of the state, the role and functioning of regional and local — or sub-state — government. The network of sub-state governments into which the national territory is divided constitutes part of the political apparatus of the state; it performs a number of functions that help the state to function. Perhaps most visible among these functions are the outputs of local public policy-making, the goods and services that are provided by the local public sector. A less tangible function, though no less real for liberal democratic theory, is the ability of local government to act as the means by which spatially differentiated sets of preferences for goods and services can be democratically controlled.

We shall examine two major themes raised by the existence of sub-state government, both of which relate to the distribution of power within the state. The first of these deals with the diffusion of power between national and sub-national governments. The notion of power — which can be defined simply as the ability or capacity to produce desired effects — is basic to understanding how political processes operate. Within virtually all states there is an explicit spatial division of power between national and sub-national governments, though the variety of political institutions through which power is diffused — that is, where decision-making powers over the allocation of resources is located — means that local autonomy is greater in some countries than in others. Federalism is one type of political institution usually associated with considerable local autonomy, more than in unitary states with their higher degree of centralization.

In chapters 3 and 4, both the federal and the unitary state are analysed largely from the viewpoint of the interaction between the national and the regional governments. In the federal state the separate states or provinces into which the national territory is divided constitute the regional governments. Their existence in the classic federal state (such as the United States or Australia) is a measure of the political bargain struck between two levels of government, whose origin is rooted in historical claims to local autonomy. Federalism is a constitutional expression of the amalgamation of political territories into a larger unit without coercion, in contrast to the historical experience of a number of the unitary states with which we shall be concerned, particularly those in Western Europe where there have been demands for regional autonomy. These demands, arising especially from differences of ethnicity, have encouraged the formation of more decentralized forms of government that are in effect 'quasi-federal'.

While demands for greater regional autonomy represent attempts to gain access to power, in chapters 5 and 6 we shall look at some of the implications of the dispersal of power to sub-state governments, parti-cularly in relation to their function as service providers. In this sense power is seen as the means by which to influence how public goods and services are provided. The service function, the second theme of this study, enables us to look at several different modes of analysis — the systems model, to explain inter-jurisdictional variations in public service provision, and alternative theories underlying unequal service provision within jurisdic-tions, specifically the city. Services need to be paid for, and in our discussion we shall take up some of the fiscal implications of service provision in the fragmented state. One of these follows on directly from the act of dividing the state, which leaves a mismatch between fiscal resources and needs among governments ('rich' and 'poor' jurisdictions) occasioning the necessity for some fiscally compensating measure(s). These effects of fragmentation are especially severe in the metropolitan areas of the US, particularly in the older urban centres of the North and North-East, where they contribute to the fiscal crisis of the central city.

In the final chapter we shall return to the question of central–local relations more directly to look at how the territorial framework of local government is reorganized and at the barriers to reform. Though characteristically a question that most of the industrial nations have considered, it will be argued that for various reasons — national and local, partisan and organizational — reorganization is more often gradualist than comprehensive. The way in which reorganization has been considered links up with the service theme of chapters 5 and 6; underlying many attempts at local government reorganization has been the drive by central governments to ensure the efficiency (or effectiveness) of service provision.

At several points in this introduction we have suggested that local government should not be considered in isolation from the state. Local government is very much part of the state, though which part varies with different theories of the state. In chapters 1 and 2 we shall flesh out some of the general points, firstly by discussing the nature of the state and of local government and, secondly, by looking at some of the basic concepts raised by the territorial distribution of power within the state.

Acknowledgements

Few authors work in such isolation that the finished product requires no acknowledgement of the help they have received. This book is no exception. I should like to express my gratitude to my colleagues and students in the Geography Department of Glasgow University, and to the university generally, for providing the environment which made this work possible. Discussions with political geographers and political scientists too numerous to mention have been a considerable source of ideas and inspiration. John Davey, of Basil Blackwell, has been all that an author would wish of an editor – encouraging, especially when the task seemed a long one. Equally, in the final stages Nicola Harris dealt patiently with a long list of queries and changes. Finally, to my wife, for ensuring the necessary peace at home, I owe especial thanks.

For permission to reproduce figures the author and publishers are grateful to the following: Fig. 2.9 from A. F. Leemans, *Changing Patterns of Local Government*, 1970, International Union of Local Authorities, the Hague; Fig. 3.5 from M. Hechter, *Internal Colonialism*, 1975, Routledge & Kegan Paul and University of California Press; Fig. 4.3 from D. J. Elazar, *American Federalism*, 1972, Harper & Row; Fig. 6.1 from C. J. Smith, 'Neighbourhood effects on mental health', in D. Herbert and R. J. Johnston (eds), *Geography and the Urban Environment*, 1980, John Wiley; Fig. 7.1 from R. Honey, 'Alternative approaches to local government change', in A. D. Burnett and P. J. Taylor (eds), *Political Studies from Spatial Perspectives*, 1981, John Wiley.

1

Politics, Space and the State

This chapter introduces some of the basic concepts with which we shall be concerned in this book. After a discussion of the role of the state, the increasing scope of government activity and the meaning of power, two particular themes are considered. The first deals with the ways in which local government fits into the wider context of the state. Two basic models are introduced — emphasizing variously consensus and conflict — and it is argued that both are useful in helping to explain the spatial division of power within the state. The second theme brings in the question of space and its relevance at empirical and theoretical levels to our analysis. The chapter concludes by looking broadly at the factors that commonly underlie the pattern of political centralization and decentralization within the modern industrial state.

THE STATE AND POLITICAL POWER

One of the more striking accompaniments of the emergence of the modern industrial state has been a marked increase in the volume and scope of government activity. The usual, if somewhat crude, measure of this involvement is the ratio of government spending to the Gross National Product, itself a measure of the total amount of goods and services produced in a country. In the less developed world outside the socialist bloc these ratios are usually small, less than 10 per cent in countries such as India and Pakistan. In the United States, by contrast, whose statistics are comparable to other non-socialist developed countries, federal, state and local expenditures represent one-third of the GNP. In some of the industrial nations where redistributive programmes, notably through welfare spending, are more developed, as in the Scandinavian democracies, the ratios are closer to 40 per cent.

At earlier stages in the development of the state, maintenance of law and order and the collection of taxes were the prime functions of governments. In the early modern period in Europe, the state and the institutions necessary to its maintenance were allied to what Finer (1975) terms the 'extraction–coercion cycle', the means by which standing armies might be controlled and maintained. Today the state is responsible for the supply of a growing array of services some of which, such as the defence of the national territory, it is argued, are more efficiently provided by the public rather than the private sector. Besides acting as a supplier of public goods, the state acts as a regulator — providing and maintaining the framework within which the market economic system can operate — and as the forum within which the competing claims of different interest groups can be resolved (Clark and Dear, 1981). In most of the advanced industrial nations the state has also adopted a role as social engineer, aiming to structure society within a desired set of normative goals. This has led the state towards intervention in the socio-economic structure to meet some defined level of distributive justice, a role that it has seen as necessary to counterbalance the inequalities created by the market system.

While in the industrial democracies state intervention within the economic and social order has become of undeniable significance, there is considerable debate about the nature and proper scope of government activity, both of which concern the role of the state. Theories of the role of the state vary from those who argue that the state is (and should be) a relatively passive actor within the overall framework of socio-economic activities to those who argue, using Marxist arguments, that its central function is the support of the capitalist economic system. To the political geographer the importance of these different interpretations lies in the accompanying theoretical approaches that they generate. Very broadly these can be divided into two main types: orthodox and liberal perspectives and the radical viewpoint. While the former view the modern democratic state as a means to gain consensus or as a means to check the excesses of the capitalist system, albeit generally within a framework that accepts the *status quo,* radical perspectives question the existing system, seeking to unravel how the state is able to perpetuate the interests of the dominant class.

According to the political scientist David Easton (1965), a political system such as the state functions to 'authoritatively allocate values'. This implies that the outputs of the political system are to be considered as rewards that will meet the interests of either individuals or groups within society; it also implies that the decisions of the political machinery are both binding and established through legitimate channels of negotiation. Such rewards might be a subsidy to the economically marginal hill-sheep farmer or financial incentives to aid a depressed region. Both of these cases can be examined in terms of their geographical effects and though in fact the spatial incidence of such benefits is often of secondary, or even less, importance to the decision-maker — notable exceptions will be the politician anxious to cultivate his local vote (Johnston, 1979) or, as we shall see later, attempts by the centre to placate peripheral discontent — this interaction between political processes and spatial structure remains one of the central concerns of the political geographer (Muir and Paddison, 1981).

Such cases can serve to illustrate another basic theme in political geography: that our unit of analysis is fundamentally the political area at different levels of spatial resolution. The question of regional development assistance brings in its train such problems as which regions are to be favoured by selection, how their boundaries are to be fixed and what kinds of incentives are to be offered within the different areas. It brings together actors representing different national and regional political units. Because political life is so widely organized along territorial lines, the impact of these processes on the political area, whether at micro- or macro-level, is of enduring significance.

It is easy to see from these illustrations that the state, and what it does, is and should be of critical concern to the political geographer. If the state is omnipresent, then the question of the sources of political control and allocation is fundamental. Put thus, this oversimplifies what is inherently a notoriously difficult concept to define and articulate. Power is one of a number of concepts with which political scientists have traditionally been preoccupied, which is hardly surprising since it forms one of the central supports to their discipline. Where, at minimum, politics is to be defined as to do with 'relationships of control and compliance between individuals and groups of individuals or agencies in society' (Potter, 1975, 173), power plays a central part.

Though opinions differ as to its possible definition, a widely held view is that a power relationship exists where A is able to get B to do something that the latter would not otherwise do (Weber, 1948; Dahl, 1957). Notice that this definition makes power a relational concept between individuals, groups or agencies and that, basically, there should be a conflict of interests between the parties resulting in one of the parties acceding to the wishes of the other.

How A is able to bring about this change depends upon the strategies it adopts. One method is through force or coercion. Though crude, it can be effective in ensuring compliance and if it is used only as an ultimate sanction it is a strategy that is frequently linked with the state. There are, however, more subtle methods by which power relationships can be maintained: through dominance, manipulation or persuasion. In this way we can see how power is a broad concept and how it has become virtually interchangeable with such concepts as force, coercion, persuasion, etc. (La Palombara, 1974).

This view of power is a relatively simple one and certainly does not exhaust the ways in which parties interact in power relationships. According to the general definition given above, one party is able to force the other to adopt a policy over an issue — say, to compel sub-national governments to adopt a particular education plan — because of the use the 'dominant' unit makes of its resources, for example its constitutional authority or its financial 'buying power'. But power relationships can also be maintained through what Bachrach and Baratz (1970) define as non-decision-making, the ability to thwart B's wishes by simply preventing these from being entered on the political agenda. In other words, dominant groups or agencies 'make the rules' by which the political game is to be played and not unnaturally do so to their own advantage. Thus, in an enlightening study of which cities in America were adopting pollution controls, Crenson (1971) shows that failure to do so was related to the power wielded by big industry within the urban areas. Obviously the study of power relationships through non-decisions carries with it a number of problems for the empirical researcher — many non-decisions, for example, will defy discovery — and most researchers have looked at it in terms of policy-making within the local political scene (Wolfinger, 1971; Newton, 1972).

Power within a political system can be described and analysed in a variety of ways. Dahl (1968) discusses several headings, including magnitude, scope and domain. (The domain of a power relationship means the degree to which the relationship between the controlling and responsive actors is reinforced by being extended over a variety of fields.) His fourth measure, the distribution of power, is the one with which we shall be most concerned. To Dahl, distribution raises such questions as whether power is dispersed so that control is exercised democratically, the alternative being some form of oligarchic rule, and 'was power disproportionately allocated spatially so that (for example) political elites were drawn more from one region than they were from others?' Distribution is something that varies between societies and within the same society at different points in its development. Thus, outside the socialist bloc, competitive and more democratized polities are associated with economically advanced nations, though this association is more in the way of being a general tendency than a law-like relationship.

The distribution of power can be construed in two main ways: who has power and where power is located in a geographical sense. In terms of who has power, distribution refers to whether power is concentrated or dispersed. Political scientists view the question of who has power within the community (local or national) from three theoretical perspectives: pluralist, elitist and Marxist. The first argues that power is widely diffused to individuals, groups and between agencies and that, although these are not equal in the sense of their influence, if we look at a specific issue this diversity of interests is readily apparent within the policy-making processes. To the pluralist the opportunity to participate in these processes is an avenue potentially open to each citizen. To the elitist school (as also to the Marxists) political power is concentrated. In Floyd Hunter's study of the community power structure (1953), in which he pioneered the reputational approach by which to discover 'who governs', it is the economically and socially prominent members of the community — the elite — who are key actors. These input biases are, not unexpectedly, matched by similar biases in outputs; once dominated by particularistic interests, the political machine can help to perpetuate the inequalities that are the hallmark of the elitist-dominated society. Marxists would agree that political power is monopolized by the few, but they would argue that it is used to perpetuate the interests of the capitalist class. To Marx the state existed merely as 'a committee for managing the common affairs of the whole bourgeoisie' and though, as we shall see later in this chapter, recent interpretations have modified this somewhat crude view, power relationships within the capitalist state are skewed to favour particular groups.

Power can also be distributed geographically. Distribution in this sense refers to the extent and manner of decentralization within the state, particularly to different types of sub-national governments. (It could also refer to the 'spatialization' of national politics — the extent to which separate localities are represented within national political institutions.) Though until recently the question of the spatial division of power has been somewhat overlooked, particularly by political geographers, it is as universal as it is enduring. Virtually all states, and certainly the advanced industrial liberal democracies with which we shall be primarily concerned, are confronted by the problem of how to organize power spatially within the state. Because the environment within which this spatial organization operates frequently changes, the 'proper' spatial division of power remains an item on the political agenda, albeit one whose priority varies, as the case of local government reform in different countries illustrates.

A spatial division of power arises because of the commonly recognized need to divide the function of governing within the state between national and sub-national governments. The latter, such as local government, would have certain powers and duties, quite often those stipulated by the central (or national) government, and the financial and other resources with which to meet these responsibilities. Note that this describes the apportioning of governmental responsibilities between different territorially defined jurisdictions and is in fact the spatial division of power*s*; but, as this division is associated with the establishment of a multiple set of power centres, we can also talk meaningfully about the spatial organization and distribution of power.

These two aspects of the distribution of power complement one another and we shall need to look at both at various points in our analysis. The question of where power is located feeds into the problems of central–local relations and regional and local autonomy. The issue of who has power will be more closely scrutinized when we come to look at the distribution of public services within the city. This is based on the assumption that it is through studying distributional outcomes that we can assess who benefits from public service provision, and thus who has power.

Local and regional governments form integral parts of the political machinery by which the state is governed. While there is good justification for considering sub-state governments as miniature political systems in their own right (Stanyer, 1976), an understanding of their working would need to take into account their position within the wider construct of the state.

For the political geographer a certain problem enters at this juncture, which is that, where justifiably the state should occupy the central place within the discipline, there are a variety of theories within which analysts have come to terms with the state. 'Problem' may not be the right word for our purposes, however; political geographers might take their cue here from political scientists and urban sociologists who argue for theoretical eclecticism (Dunleavy, 1980b; Saunders, 1979). Nevertheless, these alternatives do provide substantively different approaches to understanding the state. As an example we might contrast analyses of local government, firstly in liberal terms and secondly according to recent Marxist analysis.

According to the liberal viewpoint, the real value of local government is rooted in the extension of the democratic principle to the locality. As Dilys Hill has expressed it:

> In England local government has long been defended as a vital and integral part of democracy. Local self-government is valued because it is just . . . Local representative institutions enable a larger number of people to take an active part in democracy. Local self-government is also a part of the state through which services are brought to people in their home communities, subject to local opinion and with the benefit of local knowledge. (Hill, 1974, 20)

Local representative government is aimed at establishing the goals of liberty, equality and fraternity, though according to one leading authority on English local government its value is more as a service provider than in terms of these more encompassing goals (Sharpe, 1970). But even if local government is effectively only a service provider to its citizenry, the advantage of local democracy, it is argued, is that ultimate influence over how these services are provided resides in the ballot box. This meets much of current political science thinking in that democracy is seen as a means for deciding the competition for power and rewards.

Pluralist explanations of the state — of both national and local politics — are closely linked with this liberal explanation. Power is seen as legitimately centred in the elected representatives of the locality and it is through the ballot box and electoral competition, together with the activity of an extensive range of interest groups, that local institutions will be made responsive. To the pluralist the state is essentially neutral between the interests of different classes and groups. Politics is a relatively open and democratic process and even if the majority do not readily participate their potential to do so is a brake on the system being used to perpetuate biases.

Marxist accounts of the state (and of the local state, the term coined for sub-national governments) begin from a radically different position and proceed to ask a different set of questions. Far from being neutral the state is seen as working in the interests of the dominant capitalist class so that the activities of the state become integrally bound with the need to foster capital accumulation. Marxists are divided themselves about the nature of state intervention. According to the instrumentalist interpretation, state policies are directly aimed at maintaining the interests of the economically dominant class. This view has been substantially modified by the structuralists, who argue for the 'relative autonomy' of the state — that is, state policies are not so inevitably geared to capitalist interests, and indeed may be antithetical to the short-term interests of capital (Castells, 1978). More important to the structuralist argument, the state seeks to ensure the overall cohesiveness of the social formation, providing a stable framework within which capitalism will be fostered.

Marxist accounts of the local state (Saunders, 1979; Duncan and Goodwin, 1982) tend to treat it as a simple extension of the national state. One of the few detailed empirical studies, Cockburn's (1977) analysis of the inner London borough of Lambeth, allows us to see the kind of approach and questions such an account generates. Thus the task of the local state is seen partly as ensuring the reproduction of the conditions under which capital accumulation can occur, for example through welfare services helping to ensure reproduction of the labour force. One of her particular arguments concerned the origin of community development and the use to which it was put by the borough as a means of encouraging participation. The need to foster local participation but direct it through legitimate channels had become real following a breakdown in confidence in the formal democratic machinery and the appearance of direct action and protest movements. Participation through community development programmes was effectively a 'sop' to the working class, ensuring that local public debate would be channelled towards 'transitory factors', such as the quality of public services, rather than the more fundamental sources of inequality in a capitalist society. Indeed, the emphasis on community by the borough was an exercise in mystification, an attempt to argue that conflict is spatially rather than class based. The overall objective of the community development strategy was to be interpreted as contributing to the environment in which local business interests were accommodated and could prosper. Furthermore, because community development pro-grammes were directly encouraged by central government, the borough council was acting as the arm of the national government.

From these brief descriptions of the liberal and Marxist formulations of local government, one or two basic differences are apparent in their approaches. A key difference is obviously in the neutrality of the political machinery, though in more recent structuralist accounts this argument has become more subtle insofar as the (local) state has to give the illusion of neutrality (to class interests) in order to ensure social and political stability (Offe, 1975). A second difference is in the importance attached to local democratic processes and the ability of local government institutions to be responsive to popularly expressed demands. A third difference is that Marxist accounts of the state have tended to treat it as an undifferentiated whole, that is, they have not recognized any separate existence for local government. Also, where Marxist accounts have recognized different levels of government (as in Cockburn's analysis), there is a tendency to see the local jurisdiction merely as an agent of central government. This agency interpretation effectively undermines the concept of local auton-omy. Pluralists and liberals, on the other hand, argue that for a variety of reasons local democratic government is a more or less autonomous institution depending on the nature of the relationships, constitutional and other, between it and the central government. Finally, liberal and Marxist interpretations differently emphasize consensus and conflict. In the plural-ist/liberal explanation the political machinery is seen as a means of establishing consensus, which in turn will underwrite the overall stability of society. In a way this stability becomes a prime goal of the state, and it is this aspect that Marxists take exception to. Their analysis highlights conflicts arising from the contradictions inherent within the capitalist mode of production.

The state and the localities: an 'integrationist' framework

Political systems, such as the state, are continually confronted by problems that threaten their ability to govern effectively. Some of these problems, the most intense, may lead to territorial dismemberment, others to aspatial outcomes such as the replacement of one regime by another basing itself on a different ideology.

The argument of the integrationist framework is that the spatial organization of power within the state can be viewed as part of the more general processes by which the state becomes integrated into a coherent set of institutions that is able to meet certain critical but typical crises that arise in the course of its development. The general thrust of the model is in helping to explain how the state becomes a stable, politico-territorial form. Sub-national governments are part of the process by which this integrationist objective is achieved.

Political scientists working within the field of comparative developmental politics have constructed an overall framework within which to examine the processes underlying political development (Binder *et al.*, 1971). They identify five problem (or crisis) areas that influence how political development unfolds within societies undergoing modernization (see table 1.1). In the first place, though, arising from the strains imposed by the transition to a modern society, political development can be reduced to the contradictions posed by 'the rising demands for equality (popular participation, similar standards of material well-being), a greater need for capacity

TABLE 1.1   Political problems and the territorial division of power

Problems	Defining features[1]	Examples related to the territorial division of power
Identity	Mutual sentiments by members of a territorial group towards government.	National identity: existence of nation-state. Sub-national identities: complementary to or competitive with national identity.
Legitimacy	Acceptance of government decisions because of the 'rightness' by which they are derived.	Do some spatially segregated groups question the authority of government? generally? or only over specific, particularly territorial, policies?
Participation	Who contributes to decision-making.	Are any regions/localities/population (e.g. class) groups relatively advantaged or disadvantaged within the formal decision-making machinery, e.g. separate regions within national executives; class groups within local government councils.
Penetration	Effectiveness of government control.	Central government ensuring its policies are executed through the establishment of field service apparatus. Controls by central government over local jurisdictions to ensure 'national policies'.
Distribution	Extent to which decisions distribute/redistribute material benefits within society.	Fiscal transfers between 'rich' and 'poor' areas. Service delivery patterns.

[1] Definitions abbreviated from Verba (1971, 299)

(efficiency and wide-ranging interventionalism) and an inexorable tendency towards greater differentiation (epitomised by progressive specialization and the territorial division of labour)' (Binder *et al.*, 1971, vii). These key factors tend to conflict with one another: the need for greater efficiency is frequently considered to be at odds with the democratic ideals embodied in the equality dimension, while systems of social stratification arising from the progressive differentiation of society impose strains on both capacity and equality. It is to these three principal components of political development that the five problem areas are addressed. These concern identity, legitimacy, participation, penetration and distribution, each of which will be encountered by the typical state and to which solutions will need to be engineered. Simplified definitions of each of the problem areas are listed in table 1.1, together with examples affecting or related to the territorial division of power.

Before outlining how this set of questions can be useful to the political geographer examining the territorial basis of government within states it is necessary to enter some qualifications. Using any model constructed to understand some other or wider process has its obvious dangers. Most fundamentally this conceptual framework was devised to study processes more all-embracing than are of interest here. On the one hand, the analysis is directed towards the state, whereas the thrust of our argument is intra-state and therefore only relates to part of the totality of political arrangements; while on the other, as political scientists, Binder *et al*, survey a whole suite of issues, both spatial and aspatial. Indeed, the spatial argument is only one argument among many to the political scientist and often relatively less important than social, economic or other conditions. In fact this is not and should not be a problem to the political geographer; politically determined spatial outcomes will inevitably be influenced by the wider socio-economic conditions in which these processes occur. The other point — that we are concerned here more with the intra-state level — can also be largely countered. As we have emphasized earlier, local governments are in one sense of the state; that is, they are used by the state to meet the kinds of problems described in table 1.1. What is equally true, however, is that this schema is potentially applicable to analysis of the state in general.

One other qualification is that, in contrast to this study, Binder and his colleagues constructed the framework with the specific aim of understanding political development. With the exceptions of the chapters dealing with unitary and federal states, the concerns here do not revolve around the problems of modernization. However, enough evidence exists to suggest that these problems are of continuing significance to the industrial state even though of a differing order of magnitude possibly from experience earlier in the evolution of the state. A simple example from within the United Kingdom might help to illustrate this point. Although, overall, the legitimacy of the state is accepted, specific decisions can bring this into question. Thus a decision in 1980 to impose a surcharge on electricity consumption in the offshore islands of West and Northern Scotland, to offset higher production costs, provoked a strong reaction to the legitimacy of the decision, on the grounds of some pre-defined notion of territorial equity. Similarly, the establishing of political equality in the form of universal suffrage gave rise to internal crises in many countries; but, as the work by Taylor and Johnston (1979) shows, the problem of equality is a continuing one in that it is only in the exceptional country that 'one man, one vote, one value' is true. Electoral redistricting to meet the demands for such equality, or rather contribute towards it, occasions recurrent political crises in a substantial number of the industrial democracies.

In many respects, legitimacy occupies a central position among the five problem areas, since problems arising from one of the other areas, particularly those of identity and participation, are likely to lead to a legitimacy problem. A number of the other interrelationships shown in figure 1.1 are also worth emphasizing, for example the mutual interaction between who participates (territorial collectivity, social class group, etc.) and both territorial identity and questions of the distribution of rewards. In other cases the links between the problem areas are more indirect as, for instance, between identity and distribution problems.

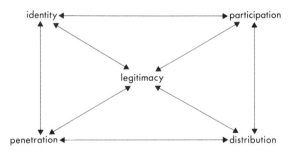

FIGURE 1.1   Interrelationships between the problem areas (from Binder *et al.*, 1971)

For the political scientist a fundamental question raised by this schema is whether there is any 'ideal' sequencing of the problems through which the political system should proceed. In *Crises and Sequences* the authors suggest a plausible evolution as that of identity–legitimacy–penetration–participation–distribution. Once national unity is established then the means for meeting legitimacy problems will be eased and so on, finally leading to the position where distribution problems can be tackled. (In fact, a comparison of cross-national experiences shows that actual historical progressions tend to be more complex than this unilinearity suggests, offering a fertile field for future politico-geographical research (Grew *et al.*, 1978).)

Rather than seeing these problem areas in any strict historical progression we shall be looking more at their interaction. Thus in seeking to explain regional autonomy movements within centralized states (chapter 3) and the emergence of peripheral ethnic nationalism, these problem areas, or crises, overlap and reinforce one another. The re-emergence of peripheral politics is in part linked to a crisis of (national) identity; it is also a questioning of the legitimacy of the state, which is in turn linked to the failure of the state effectively to penetrate the periphery or to distribute the rewards of economic development equitably within the national territory (or be effective in influencing this distribution).

While these problems can be seen to interact, their influence varies depending on whether we are looking at regional government (or demands for regional autonomy by an ethnic minority) or local government. Local governments (for example) do not generate identity crises for the state, or central government; regional autonomy demands, on the other hand, can. The penetration of the central government and its ability to control or influence the policy-making processes of sub-state governments will differ according to the constitutional relationships linking the centre with the localities. Constitutionally, we would expect the states within a federation to enjoy greater autonomy from central control than would local governments within a unitary state.

The competition for local power

These five problem areas identify typical problems confronted by the state. At best, however, their identification provides only a skeletal framework within which to understand the distribution of power within the state. A specific omission is the failure of the framework to link the question of the distribution of power with any of the theoretical approaches discussed previously. Before returning to these we need to reintroduce some basic ideas relating to power.

Closely allied to how power is distributed are the concepts of conflict and competition. Just as power relationships presume a conflict of interests, so is there competition for positions of power between groups (social classes, ethnic minorities in the multi-ethnic state, pressure groups, etc.) as well as between actors representing geographical collectivities. The reasons for this competition are two-fold and follow from the recognition that power is both an end and a means to an end. As an end in itself, the acquisition of power is important because of the status it gives to the individual, group or locality. 'Home Rulers', community control groups and, at a different level, nationalist movements all seek power partly because of the recognition that it bestows. Local autonomy becomes, then, a means by which status for the geographical collectivity is enhanced (Hartle and Bird, 1971). But the quest for power is also often based on an understanding that the act of gaining power can lead to material gain — that, in other words, those in positions of power have command over resources enabling the interests of the group or a locality to be protected and furthered. (This bland assumption will need qualifying in a number of ways; for example, local autonomy presumes that the jurisdiction will have adequate fiscal resources.)

This competition for power (or for the access to power) takes place in a variety of arenas. Some are explicitly spatial, as when the competition is between actors representing institutions accountable to or for *de jure* territories, such as national and local governments. Such competition arises very often because of a conflict of interests between the two levels of government, the one representing what it considers the national interest, the other the local interest. (These terms need treating with caution, for what is considered the national or local interest may be more representative of factional or partisan viewpoints.) Another general type of conflict for greater access to power occurs when a *de facto* territorially segregated group attempts to wrest some measure of local autonomy from an existing *de jure* government — for example when an ethnic minority attempts to gain local autonomy from the state, or the separation of a suburb from a metropolitan jurisdiction, where in neither case do the existing institutional arrangements (if any) give sufficient recognition to the separate interests of the group. A third, very common type of conflict occurs between different classes or interest groups. Spatial delineation is not so immediately important or so apparent in inter-group conflict; nevertheless, like all political activities, it takes place in space and may result in a discernible spatial outcome.

It is by looking at the nature and the outcomes of this competition, whether for greater access to power or for the rewards that power brings, that we can usefully bring in some of the ideas posited by the different theories of the state. For example, is access to power relatively dispersed between groups and localities as pluralist accounts would argue or is it more concentrated and biased as, from their different perspectives, elitist, corporatist and Marxist theories would argue? To the extent that there are separately distinguishable regional groupings within the state — by reason of their economic structure or perhaps their ethnic composition — do these enjoy separate political recognition, through regional autonomy, or is political control more concentrated within institutions and groups located within a core region, and how adequately do national political institutions represent regional interests?

Fundamentally political geography studies the interactions between space and political processes. This begs the questions about the ways in which space is important to the fragmented state and why, the answers to which can be reduced to two main aspects — the influence of space in an organizational sense and, following on from this, territoriality as a principle binding people to localities. A third factor that we need to discuss at this juncture is the 'ambiguity of space', the extent to which space *per se* is a valid theoretical construct underpinning the functioning of the state.

Space as a politically organizing factor

Either implicitly or explicitly space is of abiding importance to political institutions. As far as their organization is concerned it is an explicit relationship. Externally, states are delimited by internationally recognized boundaries marking the limits of their territorial sovereignty; and the importance to be attached to these is readily apparent where, for one reason or another, such recognition is absent. Internally, too, the organization of the state is space-bound. The functions of government — service delivery, regulation and control — are commonly administered through a structured set of government units. These will act as the media through which the policies of local, as well as central, governments can be implemented.

Using territory directly as an organizing factor belies the complex range of types of territorial government. A territorial division of the state can be dictated by, if for no other reason, the simple need to deliver services on a more local basis rather than by the centre; such localization combines the potential advantage of local democratic control. Both factors can be clearly traced in the general-purpose local government unit administering a range of services. But such a unit differs in a number of respects from the general-purpose regional governments characteristic, by definition, of the federal regime but also of a growing number of other countries. In some countries this much more complex larger unit represents a substantial portion of the national territory, and reflects territorial political schisms powerful enough to threaten the unity of the state. Since 1945 there have been violent reminders of the forcefulness of political regionalism in countries such as Canada, Spain and Belgium. In spite of what political scientists had been suggesting, the task of fully integrating the component regions of the state remains a problem within the industrial nations as well as in the newer nations of the Third World (Esman, 1977).

The common denominator of different types of sub-national government is their territorial definition: they all constitute examples of what Cox

(1973) terms 'legally-bounded spaces'. They differ, howeve
the scale of operation. It will be convenient for us to recogni
spatial levels on which sub-national organization focuses, the
regional, even though in practice, particularly when making
comparisons, such terms become rather 'loose' in their
regional we shall mean an area intermediate between the locality
(municipality, commune, district) and the state. Clearly this allows for
considerable variation between countries, which makes direct cross-
national quantitative comparisons difficult.

There is a more fundamental difference between these levels than that of
scale alone. Decentralization to local government, for example, usually
involves the running of services that it is considered more suitable to
operate locally but within legislative guidelines determined by the central
government. Regional-level government, on the other hand, can be
distinguished by the involvement of more far-reaching 'balance of power'
questions between the national government and the regions, in which the
sub-national governments may have legislative competence in their own
right and hence wider powers of autonomy. These state–regional questions
are paramount in federal countries. In countries that historically have been
more centralized, the substantial shifts of power from the central authority
to the region implicit in this form of government have been avoided.

The territorial principle

Why should territory be of such importance to the organization of the
state? The idea of territoriality, the organization of space into discrete
areas that at least in part are considered as 'exclusive' by their occupants,
provides one, if in some ways contentious, starting point. Though
territoriality has been considered a basic principle linking social groups or
communities with a specific locale, its political implications are less clear.
Jones and Eyles (1977), arguing from a socio-geographic viewpoint, show
that the value of territory arises from the way in which it caters for the
three needs of identity, security and stimulation. The first two of these, in
particular, are commonly provided by the political territory, though the
manner and extent of this varies according to type of unit. Thus, to the
state, security is measurable in military–defensive terms, but within the
local suburban jurisdiction (for example) security takes on a different
meaning — the safeguarding of local values. Sommer (1969) has suggested
an interesting explanation of the phenomenon, arguing that, collectively,
territoriality segregates sub-groups, thus reducing potential conflict, while
ensuring the integrity of the larger group. It is an argument that political
theorists have applied to explaining the advantages of decentralization
within the state.

The way in which the territorial 'principle' is translated into political ɔrganization appears to be strongly influenced by cultural factors. Within Western society, the precise division and subdivision into tight political spaces reflects Western ideas on property, 'in which pieces of territory are viewed as "commodities" capable of being bought, sold or exchanged at the market-place' (Soja, 1971, 9). The nation-state, with its emphasis on territorial sovereignty and precisely demarcated boundaries, was a European concept. If political territoriality in the Western tradition is tied to the importance of property, then attachment to these 'spaces' carries with it a sense of identity. Social geographers have been at pains to show that one of the differences between human and animal territoriality is the importance of the 'sense of place' (Gold, 1976); humans typically develop identities with territories that are the product of cultural acquisition, memory, previous experiences and the like. Such links are often translated into loyalties, expressions of which in a political sense are apparent at various levels in the hierarchy of political units in a willingness to defend the territory. Suburban jurisdictions divided along class lines and anxious to safeguard community values highlight ideas that are reflected more generally in Home Rule, States Rights and other similar movements.

The idea of political territoriality has been more contentious when it involves drawing direct correspondences with animal behaviour. Territoriality is one of the basic principles with which ethology operates, though as a human phenomenon it is important to remember that it is only being used in an analogous sense. Among animals, though not within all species, territoriality — owning and defending a slice of territory — may be instinctive, but it is an oversimplification to argue that it is similarly so among humans. Political and other geographers have hesitated in making such direct comparisons, not least because though there are 'similarities in form and function . . . motivations differ markedly' (Soja, 1971, 31). Thus the defence of territory has provoked more complex patterns of response in the human world: not only is man willing to join alliances to safeguard his interests but he is capable of bartering to the point, if necessary, of forgoing parts of the territory in order to protect the integrity of the majority. Equally, to argue that political territoriality is 'natural' in some way ignores the part played by the state, in particular, in developing identities with the national territory.

This argument can be turned around; that is, the importance to governments of the territorial principle lies in its potential use for fostering allegiances to a particular area. As we have seen, the question of identity is one that typically confronts the state early on in its development. Indeed, establishing such identities can be seen as essential for the state because of its contribution to social reproduction; attachments to the territorial state become part of the process by which the reproduction of the labour force is ensured.

It is widely recognized that citizens commonly identify with a hierarchy of spatially defined territories, from the home area (embracing the immediate locale) through to the national territory itself. Some might even profess a degree of association with an international grouping of states. Not unexpectedly, the intensity of association varies with the type of political territory, a point made by Bergman (1975) citing the evidence of an American Gallup Poll survey (figure 1.2). Primary identities were noticeably stronger to the national and immediate local territories than they were to the state or to the regional grouping of states.

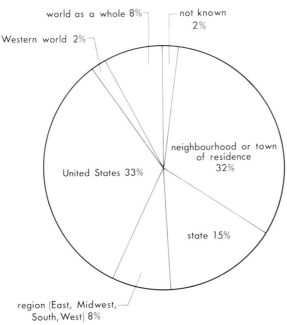

FIGURE 1.2   American levels of affective integration (areas with which citizens identify most strongly)
(from *European Community*, 1973, 12, cited in Bergman, 1975)

These associations will usually differ between citizens of different age and class. Table 1.2 illustrates the results of a survey in a small market town in the south of the Irish Republic. A greater sense of identity was generally felt towards the local town, though this was more pronounced among the working class and, though less marked, among middle-aged inhabitants. These differences of primary orientation reinforce the distinction between 'localists' and 'cosmopolitans' that sociologists have made.

Governments, both national and local, that are able to harness the support implicit in these expressions of association will be in that much stronger a position to resist threats to their territorial base and, more generally, to their own stability. Because their own policies will be able to

TABLE 1.2   Local and non-local identities in an Irish country town[1]

| | Greatest attachment towards | | |
	Mallow town %	County Cork %	Don't know %
All sample	58	38	4
By age:			
21–35	57	43	0
35–60	69	31	0
60+	25	50	25
By social group:			
Professional	30	60	10
Intermediate	80	20	0
Manual	62	34	4

[1] Based on the question about which geographical area — the local town or county — the respondent felt he/she belonged to. 147 completed questionnaires.
Source: Survey by the author in 1972

foster and build upon the association, there is a circularity to the process. National governments, in particular, actively encourage what Duchacek (1970) has termed territorial socialization — the forging of identities with political territories. This will be produced both visibly through such iconographic symbols (Gottman, 1952) as the national flag, anthem and the like and more covertly through the biasing of information, as in the education system, which often favours the state at the expense of neighbouring territories. Sub-national governments also employ symbols, though not so widely, to foster association, the more obvious examples being the component states of federal countries. In a different vein the grandiose town hall, a measure of the locality's apparent wealth, equally acts as a symbol linking the citizen with his local government.

So far it has been suggested that space is of relevance, and of value, as an organizing agent; to be more precise, power can be meaningfully divided territorially within the state between various levels of *de jure* governments. However, territory is not the only means through which the processes of government are, or can be, organized (Tarrow *et al.,* 1978; Fesler, 1949). Organization on the basis of function provides one alternative. Indeed, political scientists have more usually considered the question of distributing power in functional terms, for example in terms of allocating duties among officials in the capital city, constituting what Maass (1959) describes as the capital division of powers, in contrast to its areal counterpart. The tasks of central government administration are normally divided functionally among a number of ministries (trade, housing, social services and the like), but the interests of specific regions and localities are not separately recognized in cabinet or other executive positions of the

national administration — with the important
countries where, by definition, territorial interests
expression within the central (or national) goverr
   There are other reasons why a functional rathe
may be more appropriate in analysing politico-g
Both sociologists and political scientists have arg
be a major factor in the functioning of the modernizeu ͺ
main societal cleavages within industrial societies will be basͺͺ
economic rather than spatial differences: 'we can almost say that a peuͺ.
is as much advanced as territorial divisions are more superficial' (Durkheim, 1964, 187). This is obviously a substantive point — particularly to
the political geographer because of its apparent dismissal of the spatial
factor — and one to which we shall return.

From our present perspective, it can be seen that, while functionally
based divisions have undeniably become more prominent, territory
continues to be a force around which political organization can be
meaningfully structured. Perhaps a good example is the organization of
popular representation within elected assemblies. To a number of observers the continued use of territory as the basis of representation is
anachronistic. In his treatise, *Representative Government,* John Stuart Mill
proposed that representation should be organized so as to accommodate
the emerging functional divisions within society. However, more than a
century later only a handful of countries actually organize their national
elections on the basis of a single constituency. The territorial constituency
has persisted, albeit quite possibly because no other wholly effective
substitute has been found.

As Tarrow (1978) suggests, however, the case of the elected assembly
shows that the functional organizing principle can co-exist with its
territorial counterpart. On the one hand, representation is based on
constituencies so that within the rule-making processes the interest of the
locality will be represented. But these processes will equally be influenced
by functionally organized interests — for example trade union groups,
farming lobbies — whose reference to any geographical unit is not in itself
of any importance.

The relationships between politics and geography are two-way. The *de
facto* division of space into different types of areas — nodal city or
economically homogeneous regions, socio-economically defined urban
neighbourhood, etc. — influences the political compartmentalization of
space; the resulting *de jure* arrangements contribute to and reinforce these
spatial differences. Territory is an organizing agent, and the division of the
state into local units compounds the differences between localities. These
interrelationships are captured in the political scientists' term 'localism',
the set of influences the local environment has on the policy-making
behaviour of the local elected politician and bureaucrat. Thus, as Young

amer (1978) argue, political leaders in the higher-status outer
opolitan London borough were influenced by their image of the
lity they represented, a factor that contributed to their resistance to
eir territory being a reception area for working-class population to be
rehoused from inner London. Territorial fragmentation gives greater
emphasis to these localist impulses, not infrequently having divisive social
consequences, particularly in metropolitan areas.

These interrelationships between territory as an organizing agent and
the influence of political processes on territorial differentiation probably
differ cross-nationally, though we lack sufficient information. The
influence of territory on political life appears to be especially important in
some countries. Based on Italy, J. Pratt (1980) describes a society in which
local (communal) territory origins play a crucial political and administrative part in the life of the individual; even the Communist Party, though by
proclamation organized along workplace lines, is actually divided territorially, breaking down villages and city into residential sections. This tends to
confuse class and space loyalties, a point to which we shall turn in the next
section.

Before concluding this section, however, we might ask whether locality,
expressed through political territoriality, is not an inevitable feature of the
contemporary state in spite of what some sociologists have suggested. Our
evidence so far has pointed to its ubiquity, but only implicitly to its
inevitability. Explicit evidence, not surprisingly, is difficult to find, though
some support is found from the case of Israel. Israel provides a rare
opportunity to look at a state in which institutionally the territorial
dimension is only weakly developed, and is absent altogether in that the
members elected to the national assembly (the Knesset) do not represent
separate constituencies. Working within a state that is politically highly
centralized, the system of local government is weak (for example, the
budgets of the local municipalities are decided largely by the centre).

Ideological reasons help explain the underplaying of spatially represented interests. The Israeli state was in large measure to be grounded in
principles that had governed the organization of Jewish communities in the
pre-state period. These 'communities . . . [had been] organised on
ideological lines. The constituent units were not territorially based but
consisted of transterritorial parties or "movements" that functioned as all-
encompassing civil societies, providing their members with virtually all the
domestic and local services normally provided by governments' (Elazar,
1978, 4).

If in terms of its political institutions Israel has consciously subordinated
the territorial dimension, there are signs that this may change. Several
attempts, for example, have been made to reorganize the electoral system
so that it is structured on a constituency basis (Waterman, 1981). This
reflects the growing importance of territory in national political life, which

can be ascribed to two interrelated factors. On the one hand, the development of the state has become accompanied by growing socio-economic disparities between the core (Tel Aviv/Haifa/Jerusalem) and peripheral regions. Some political geographers have linked the centre–periphery problem to the political under-representation of the periphery. According to Gradus (1982), looking at the spatial distribution of the Knesset's members since 1949, the northern and, particularly, the southern peripheries were systematically under-represented. The absence of any strong constituency base prevented the emergence of porkbarrel politics (whereby largesse is distributed in order to gain political favours) while tending to ensure that the centre was disproportionately favoured by public investments and the like. On the other hand, the territorial factor is becoming stronger as place loyalties emerge in the separate areas of the state. Given that much of the state's population comprises recent immigrants, these emerging territorial loyalties are interesting evidence in their own right and probably partly relate to awareness of the differences in spatial wellbeing within the state. They too will tend to encourage the transition from, in Elazar's words, 'the ideological to territorial democracy'.

Space as an independent variable

Space may be of direct, though not exclusive, value from the viewpoint of organizing the national territory, but we need to be more circumspect when examining the independent significance of space within the functioning of the state. The argument encapsulated in the quote above by Durkheim tends to undermine the value of examining the internal working of modern industrialized states from a spatial viewpoint. At most space will be only a secondary factor overshadowed by other mainly socio-economic processes. As one student has remarked in the expressive term 'spatial fetishism', human geographers have been guilty of overemphasizing the independent significance of space so that the 'relationships between social groups or classes are analysed as a set of relations between areas' (Anderson, 1973, 3). Thus within social geography criticism has notably been directed against the analysis of spatial distributions of welfare differences without recourse to the societal context from which they are derived.

These arguments about the independent significance of space have been recently rehearsed within the field of urban politics (Saunders, 1980; Dunleavy, 1980a). One particular theoretical approach, pioneered by the American political scientist Oliver Williams, has sought to make spatial location *the* focus of urban politics: urban politics is the 'means by which space and place are socially controlled and allocated in order to facilitate or limit accessibility' to desired outputs of the political system (O. Williams,

1971, 36). In the fragmented American metropolis, which Williams uses as his testing ground, suburban jurisdictions have by a variety of methods captured desirable facilities and excluded the less desirable (see chapter 5). The problem with this approach, however attractive to the political geographer, is that it tends to lend space too much significance as an independent variable. All political processes take place both in space and within a societal context, and it is difficult to separate out the influence of space.

To argue for the significance of space independent from the wide-ranging suite of social, economic and political processes that take place within it may be a difficult position to sustain theoretically. Saunders has put it more emphatically:

> If the level of health care, the quality of schooling, the rate of unemployment . . . or whatever differs between Surrey and Tyneside, or between Brixton and Chelsea, or between Protestant and Catholic areas of Belfast, this is because of differences in the class, race or religion of the inhabitants of these areas, in which case it is class, race and religion, rather than space, which constitute the theoretical keys to analysis. (Saunders, 1980, iv)

Nevertheless, territorially based political conflict becomes more salient where spatial divisions coincide with class or ethnic divisions. This is apparent at both regional and local levels when there are demands for autonomy by regional ethnic groups or conflict over resource allocation between local jurisdictions. In this sense, space is a contributory factor: quite apart from the fact that such processes are taking place in space, it is because these class or ethnic differences are identifiable with distinct areas that space becomes an integral part of the explanation.

Related to the problem of overemphasizing the significance of space is the danger political geographers face in anthropomorphizing the political areas that form the focus of their analysis. If political geography is concerned with the interaction between political processes and space, our primary concern here is with different types of political area within the state. Thus we shall be examining the demands for regional autonomy within centralized states, the interaction between states and provinces within federal countries, and so forth. But it is not regions that seek autonomy or federal states that compete for power with the national government; it is politicians representing these units. Furthermore, in anthropomorphizing the political area, we overlook internal diversity and assume that the area acts as a single entity, whereas there are separate interests within these areas that need recognition and that, to a greater or lesser extent, have a political voice. Thus geographical units such as the South East of England conceal internal differentiation, such as different class interests, that affects political relationships and further confuses the part played by the spatial factor.

CENTRALIZATION AND DECENTRALIZATION: AN OVERVIEW

One of the very pronounced tendencies within the industrial state is the apparently inexorable trend towards centralization. This might bring into question the importance of looking at sub-national government rather than the state were it not for the fact that strong decentralizing pressures are also evident, that lend weight to territorial divisions within political life. Moreover, within the liberal democracy, decentralization has ideological foundations integrally bound up with the make-up of the state. In this introductory chapter we might usefully conclude by reviewing some of the major factors underlying political centralization and decentralization as a backcloth to our later analyses.

The expansion of government activity in the industrial state has usually been accompanied by the progressive centralization of the polity. Symptomatic of this centralization has been the steady urbanizing of the population and its cultural standardization, leading to an expected decline in territorially based cleavages, and therefore territorial political conflicts, within the state. Politically, this centralization has been signalled in a variety of ways: by the transfer to a higher and sometimes national tier of government of functions that even at the beginning of the present century were provided by local jurisdictions; by the relative growth in stature of the national government measured by their spending patterns vis-à-vis lesser governments; and more generally by the increasing emphasis popularly focused on the central organs of government. Even in the federal state, with its 'guaranteed' diffusion of power, centralization has steadily moved the political focus towards the national government and, in the case of the American president, to specific offices within the central government.

Political centralization in the industrial state can be traced to a variety of causes (Sharpe, 1979). As figure 1.3 shows, some of these underpin the general trend towards centralization characteristic of the modernized (and modernizing) society, while others are more specific to the way in which the political system operates. This distinction, however, is by no means clear-cut and there are strong relationships between the two sets of factors. Moreover, although these factors are to be associated with centralization, paradoxically some also help explain the trend underlying decentralist moves within the state.

It is widely accepted that improvements in transport and communication technologies have been instrumental in fostering centralization. Faster modes of transport have been vital to what Janelle (1968) terms the time–space convergence — distance becoming less of a barrier. This

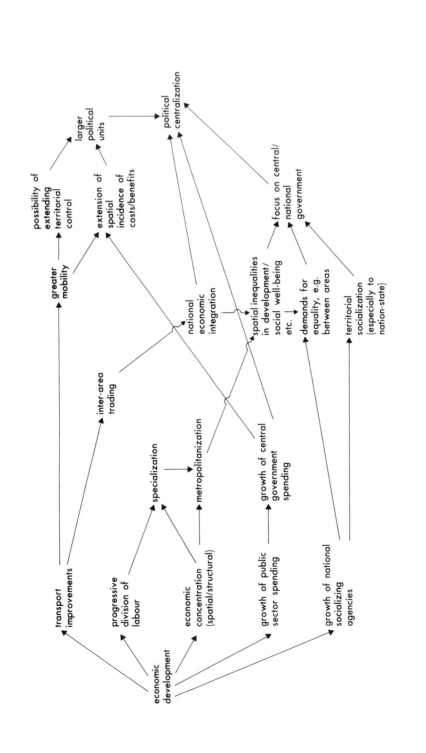

FIGURE 1.3   A simplified model of the factors influencing political centralization

stimulated the reorganization of space. Economically this was spelt out by changes in the spatial pattern of production towards a more concentrated distribution, and in increasing locational differentiation and areal specialization. Politically such changes were to have an impact on the ability to coordinate and control space. The feudal state, even though in some notable cases it might have covered territorially extensive areas, consisted of a formally linked but otherwise loosely integrated set of territorial collectivities. A shrinking world has enabled man to administer larger political areas more effectively and to mobilize support more universally.

Increased mobility has also fostered centralization by extending the spatial incidence of the costs and benefits attached to the goods and services that sub-national governments deliver, leading in turn to pressures to reorganize political territories over larger areas. One basis on which local governments are predicated is the matching of the delivery of those public goods with the territorially defined populations likely to benefit from the service; that is, given that the benefits of a service (for example, fire protection or air pollution control) are local and that they are spatially identifiable, the boundaries of the jurisdiction should be drawn correspondingly.

Political centralization is also influenced by the wider societal changes involved in the modernizing process. The steady absorption of different regions within the national economy has helped in binding the state politically, though some take this further, arguing that national economic integration is an inevitable precursor of the politically integrated state. This question apart, political integration has in many countries accentuated the ascendancy of the national government over the sub-national jurisdictions.

Although modernization works to bring the component parts of the state together into an economic whole, in the capitalist state the benefits of economic development are not distributed evenly. This can lead to demands for redistributive measures by the central government and thus influence the patterns of centralization and decentralization within the state. Political geographers can begin to explain these trends by the centre–periphery model (Gottman, 1980). Certainly one of the defining features of the centre–periphery model, the domination of one unit by another, has political as well as economic connotations.

One other way in which the processes of economic development impinge on political centralization is in the recurrent pressures to enlarge the administrative areas within which the state is organized. In the United States these pressures have been seen as a challenge to the federal structure, since the states have been 'forced' into inter-state compacts, while piecemeal attempts to overcome the problem of metropolitan fragmentation have typically been associated with proposals simplifying the territorial structure and the centralizing of control. Though there are a variety of reasons to explain this trend, a recurrent factor is the importance attached to planning and administering services over larger areas.

It can be argued that some of the factors that have underlain the trend towards political centralization also help to explain the reverse pattern. In the most advanced societies, increased mobility, the progressive division of labour and economic specialization and concentration are factors that contribute to the alienation and stress characteristic of the post-industrial society: 'increasing differentiation of individuals and the increasing scale of society's control organisations have combined with greater mobility to alienate individuals and produce stress' (Janelle, 1975, p. 108). One reaction to this has been the demand for more participation and decentralization. This demand has assumed a number of guises, from the community control movement in the United States to neighbourhood environmental lobbies to demands for greater participation on the factory floor (in French parlance *autogestion*). One of the more striking features of the decentralist movement is that it has become so widespread within the industrial states.

Spatial inequalities in economic development and social wellbeing can, under certain conditions, likewise lead to demands for local autonomy, and, where they are overlain by ethnic differences, to demands for separatism. Decentralist trends can then be the harbinger of territorial disintegration. As Ronen (1980) suggests, looking at the interplay between nationalism and state formation, there is no obvious final number of sovereign states that will constitute the international system. In reality, therefore, there are both centralizing and decentralizing tendencies at play and in the next chapter we shall take up some of the broad questions that this raises.

2
Territory and Power: Some Basic Concepts

In nearly all states the task of governing is distributed among a hierarchy of national and sub-national governmental units. The exceptions include the very smallest states — for example, the European micro-states, such as Monaco and Andorra, together with small island-states such as Malta — in which presumably their size is sufficient to enable the centre to provide services that would otherwise be managed by more local forms of government. As far as the sub-national governments are concerned, the territorial distribution of power is associated with the duty to fulfil certain prescribed functions, either purposefully delegated from the political centre (or national government) or existing, as in federal countries, as of right in state or provincial governments.

In this chapter we shall start our discussion by outlining the major types of territorial power distribution. This leads on to two substantive issues, the measurement and correlates of political centralization within sovereign states and the political, economic and other criteria on which the centralization, or the decentralization, of power is predicated.

TYPES OF TERRITORIAL POWER DISTRIBUTION

De jure power is territorially distributed within sovereign states by a number of methods. Though it is a distinction that, as a simple dichotomy, we shall have to qualify, the commonly made division between federal and unitary states is a convenient starting point for analysis.

In at least one respect, that of the formal distribution of sovereignty, there is a major difference. In the more centralized unitary state sovereign political power is undivided, being vested within the various organs of the central power. In federal countries, by contrast, recognition is given to two distinct layers of government, the one national, the other sub-national, neither of which in theory is considered the subordinate in the partnership.

The difference between federal and unitary states mirrors the contention that power is distributed according to two basically contrasting processes

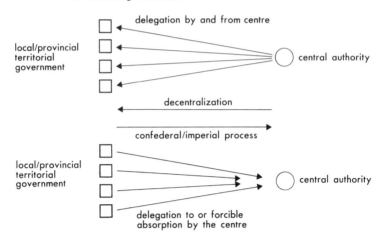

FIGURE 2.1   Decentralization and territorial association (from
Duchacek, 1970, 113)

(figure 2.1). In the association or union of hitherto separate political communities, either voluntarily as in federal unions or as a result of coercion in the case of imperialism, the movement of power is effectively 'upwards' to some territorially larger unit. In the converse process — the decentralization of authority — power is delegated from a central authority to lesser jurisdictions within the polity, albeit often with safeguards to allow some measure of control by the national government over the local administrations (Duchacek, 1970).

There are also different levels of the decentralization of power. Within the process of governing we can distinguish between political institutions responsible for rule- (or law-) making and those responsible for the implementation of decisions. In between are the decision-making bodies whose task is the interpretation of laws made by some higher body of government. The term 'decentralization' is usually associated with decision-making powers in which the responsible organ of government has some discretion about how the directions from the central power (national government) are to be interpreted and implemented, while 'deconcentration' refers to the implementation of decisions within local areas of the state, normally under closer supervision of the higher organs of government. In the highly centralized state, rule-making and much decision-making, if not the administrative implementation of decisions, will be concentrated within the centre or national government. Conversely, in the less centralized polity — including those organized within federal principles — even rule-making powers will be more spatially diffused.

A crude assessment of the differences between countries in the territorial distribution of power can be made by locating them on a centralization–decentralization spectrum (see figure 2.2). The extremes of the spectrum are total decentralization, resulting in the complete dispersal of power and the break-up of the state, and total centralization, implying the retention of all power within the central authority, that is, in the national capital. (Total centralization could also imply the absolute concentration of power within a dictatorship or some political elite.) Fesler (1965, 371) has discussed the implications of both: 'Total decentralisation would require the withering away of the state, whereas total centralisation would imperil the state's capacity to perform its functions.' Neither would be acceptable to the state, the one because it would spell the balkanization of its territory, the other because it would be an inefficient and undemocratic method of governing.

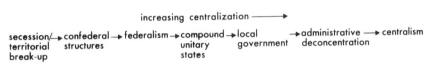

FIGURE 2.2   The basic 'centralization–decentralization spectrum'

According to figure 2.2, federalism is the most explicitly decentralized form of government. However, insofar as the term decentralization carries with it the implication of power being transferred from the centre to the periphery, Elazar (1979) has suggested in preference the term 'non-centralization'. Within the classic federations of the developed world, if less so in the more recent experiments with federalism, especially in the Commonwealth, such as India, Pakistan and Nigeria (Watts, 1966), power has not been decentralized from some central (national) body to sub-national governments. Rather, in the United States, Switzerland and Australia in particular, much of the impetus for the political union came from the original units of the federation, resulting in a national government with specified powers of control and regulation. Thus we should not see the national, state and local governments in a hierarchical relationship: 'there are no higher or lower power centres, only larger or smaller [territorial] areas of political decision-making and action' (Elazar, 1979, 15).

Though federally organized states are inherently less centralized than their unitary counterparts (or at least should be), this should not be interpreted as meaning that the unity of the former is any less real. One of the hallmarks of the federal constitution is, as the popular description of the American compact suggests, 'an indestructible union of indestructible units' (Texas v. White, 7 Wallace 700 (1869)). Yet the Supreme Court's ruling came shortly after the Civil War, which had exposed how federal unions can harbour fissiparous tendencies. In more recent times, federal breakdown, either total or through the secession of individual units, has been confined to the less developed countries, including the West Indies, the Central African Federation and the secession of Singapore from Malaysia (Dikshit, 1975; Hicks, 1978). In such countries, whatever the other causes of federal failure (Franck, 1968), localist sentiments have outweighed loyalties to the wider area. Demands for the independence of Quebec, particularly following the electoral successes of the Parti Québecois in the 1970 elections, provide the major exception to the stability of the industrial federations.

In the unitary state, power is decentralized primarily to various forms of local government, where the relationship with the national government is hierarchical. Local governments typically are associated with distinct, legally bounded spaces and are responsible for discharging functions that the higher (central) power considers more appropriate organized locally. In this sense local government is to be seen as a device by which the centre organizes its political hinterland. Yet it would be erroneous to suggest that the way in which government is structured, both spatially and functionally, lies exclusively within the control of the centre. We need to distinguish between this essentially *constitutional* viewpoint and the *political* environment within which the relationships of national and local governments are set. For instance, the central government may find it difficult for political reasons — the existence of relatively powerful local political bases resisting change, for example — to restructure local government spatially according to its own preferences (Gourevitch, 1978).

TABLE 2.1   Types of local government

| | Functions | |
Representativeness	Multi-purpose	Special-purpose
Representative	France: communes England: counties	US: school board
Non- or semi-representative[1]	France: *arondissements*	UK: joint planning boards in National Parks

[1] Semi-representative means that membership of the body is by indirect election.
Source: Adapted from Humes and Martin (1970, 28)

Local governments are of different types. Primarily their task is the provision of public services within a defined area for which they are able to raise local taxes. Within this basic definition they can be multi-purpose or special-purpose, representative or non-representative (see table 2.1). The main type is the multi-purpose, representative authority. The origins of this type of local government within European states can be traced to medieval forms of urban government, but it was during the nineteenth century — encouraged by the needs of the rapidly expanding urban populations and aimed at meeting demands for local participation — that multi-purpose governments were established on a representative footing, on the basis, that is, of the suffrage of the majority of the local populace.

One of the problems apparent in attempting to classify states as either federal or unitary is that there is a sizeable and growing number of countries that do not fit into either type. Some political scientists have suggested that retaining the dichotomy between the two types has tended to blinker analysis of the way in which the forms of government operate and that it is probably better, as Bulpitt (1971) has suggested, 'to take our territorial systems of government as we find them'. For our purposes it will be convenient to recognize a third type of state intermediate between the truly federal and unitary polities, which Elazar (1975) terms 'compound unitary'. These are states that have devolved substantial, in many cases rule-making, powers to sub-national governments, in which they have adopted federal-like practices.

Compound unitary states are more accurately divided into two types. There are those (C1 in figure 2.3) whose federal-like practices stem from the establishment of regional governments, which are vested with legislative powers and/or functional responsibilities that in unitary states would normally be considered the prerogative of the central government. Regional devolution of this type is often only granted to parts of the state and in particular, where it is more generally associated with multi-national states, to ethnically distinct minority homelands. Examples are found in both the developing (Sudan, Burma) as well as the developed world (Italy, Spain). Insofar as regionally recognized units such as Sicily, Wales or Scotland are as 'indestructible' (Duchacek, 1970) as Queensland or Alberta, this 'quasi-federal' devolution does reflect qualities similar to federally organized countries.

The second type of compound unitary state is associated with the federacy, a form of 'political association which permits relatively small communities to maintain their cultural identity through separate political organization while retaining ties — economic, political, military and so on — to a larger more powerful nation-state' (R. M. Stevens, 1977, 177). Offshore islands, which are relatively small communities by comparison with the power to which they are associated, provide the most frequent examples, though some of the European micro-states have sought such umbrella associations with their neighbouring powers. Typically they are geographically peripheral to the dominant state, are by definition small and, at least in the case of the more historically established federacies (as in the UK), have most often been created by the voluntary seeking of association by the lesser power rather than by imposition by the central power. As more recent examples illustrate — notably the Azores and Madeira, which were granted local autonomy by post-Salazar Portugal —

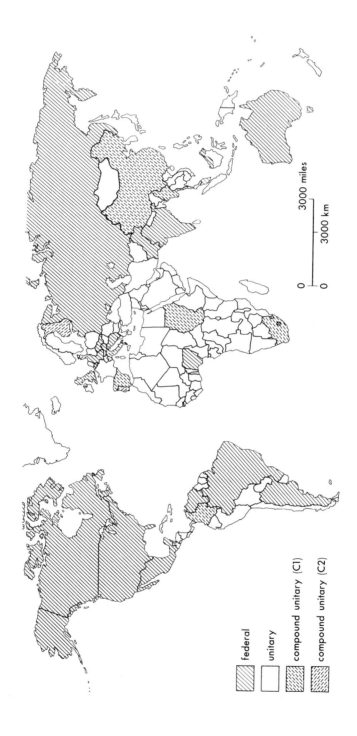

federal

unitary

compound unitary (C1)

compound unitary (C2)

FIGURE 2.3   Federal, unitary and compound unitary states

3000 miles

3000 km

0

0

TABLE 2.2   Federacies in Western Europe compared with the power with which they are associated

Federacy	Associated power	Population of federacy[1]	Multiple of dis-proportion[2]	Area of federacy (sq. kms)	Multiple of dis-proportion
Aaland	Finland	20,500	223	1,481	205
Andorra	France	20,550	2,264	465	1,186
Azores	Portugal				
Faroe Islands	Denmark	38,681	128	1,399	31
Guernsey	UK	51,351	999	78	3,109
Isle of Man	UK	56,248	912	572	424
Jersey	UK	65,000	789	116	2,091
Liechtenstein	Switzerland	21,350	294	160	258
Madeira	Portugal				
Monaco	France	23,400	1,988	0.2	2,758,003
San Marino	Italy	17,000	3,201	61	4,938

[1] Population at various dates, 1960–72.
[2] Measures how many times larger is the associated power than the federacy.
Source: Adapted from R. M. Stevens (1977)

the federacy model provides the means by which small, peripheral distinct communities can be politically recognized within the state.

Figure 2.3 summarizes our argument so far. In a formal, constitutional sense, some 18 countries in the world are federal and, with the noteworthy exception of China, include the more populous states of the international system. Unitary states are much the most numerous type and are found in distinct clusters, notably in Africa, the Middle East and South East Asia. Compound unitary states — and it should be noted that countries like the United Kingdom include both regional devolution and federacy — are more geographically spread with a single major cluster in Western Europe.

It remains to describe deconcentration. Typically this is associated with a field service unit through which a specific service is locally administered. Unlike local government, field services generally lack the element of democratic control and the degree of autonomy. They act as the administrative outpost of some headquarters organization, often a central government department, which is responsible for the overall management of the service. The field service is of importance in that it is a vehicle by which central government is able to penetrate the state, ensuring that policies decided nationally are implemented locally. Their use is not limited to national governments, however; local governments also deconcentrate to field services. Furthermore, in most capitalist states the 'mixed economy' has become increasingly significant, and there has been a growth of territorially organized field services administered by semi-government or para-state bodies such as nationalized industries or by public agencies such as UK National Tourist Boards.

The territorial imprint

The configuration of *de jure* territorial governments within the state is more complex than our previous discussion suggests. This is partly because of the large number of sub-national governments. In the United States, local governments alone exceeded 79,000 in 1977 and to this should be added various other spatially decentralized units of government, federal and state field service units, mini-town halls and so on. We can best illustrate the types and range of sub-national government by looking briefly at specific countries. Australia, the Republic of Ireland and Denmark have been chosen to represent the three types of federal, unitary and compound unitary state (see figure 2.4).

Australia The principal sub-national governments are the six component states of the federation, the boundaries of which are sovereign. The states had been more or less defined — with the exception of the short-lived Central Australian state — by the time of federation in 1900, prior to which each had existed as a separate colony. In the pre-federation period colonial government was strongly particularistic so that when federalism was established it produced relatively powerful states and a national government that was less so. Even though federal powers, especially those of finance, have become more centralized, the states still occupy a comparatively powerful position in comparison with the other English-speaking federations (table 2.3).

TABLE 2.3   Relative share of public sector expenditure by national and sub-national governments

	Australia (1969–70) %	Canada (1969) %	US (1967–68) %	GB (1970) %
National government	50.0	37.2	58.9	65.3
State/province	42.6	41.2	15.7	N.A.
Local government	7.4	21.6	25.4	34.6

N.A. – not applicable
Source: National government publications

Each of the component Australian states operates as a unitary authority within its own territory. Local government, the principal form of decentralization within states, is consequently under their control. As table 2.3 illustrates, Australian local governments are relatively unimportant, being responsible for less than ten per cent of public sector expenditure. Several reasons account for this: the lack of financial resources and of either a

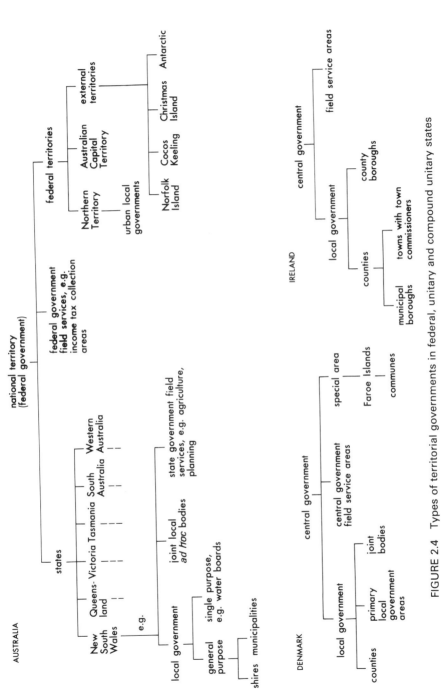

FIGURE 2.4 Types of territorial governments in federal, unitary and compound unitary states

history of community identity or local independence, and the existence of strong state governments (AGPS, 1976). The colonial period in Australia's development was characterized by high levels of urbanization so that local government, normally established by voluntary incorporation, was mainly confined to the cities and towns. This was particularly the case in New South Wales where less than one per cent of the state area had been incorporated by the time of federation. A general system of local government in New South Wales (except for the sparsely-populated western sector) had to be imposed by the Sydney government in 1905 so that necessary 'works and services', especially roads, were provided.

Partly because they are the separate responsibility of each state, but also because of the irregularities in population distribution, Australian local governments exhibit great diversity in relation to characteristics such as population and territorial size. Relative to the size of the national population (14.6 million in 1980), there are a large number of local governments (nearly 900; compare this with 400 in England with a population of 46.5 million in 1980). Obviously this means that a large number of authorities, mainly rural ones, are small: 53 per cent have populations of less than 5,000 (1973), though the proportion varies from 43 per cent in Victoria to 70 per cent in South Australia. Metropolitan local governments, by contrast, have populations ranging from 10,000 to 70,000. Functional responsibilities of local government differ between states, too, though the provision of basic services such as local roads, sanitation and street lighting remains the mainstay of their activities.

Federations also typically include special governmental areas. Though integral parts of the state, these have different constitutional arrangements from the component states. They include federal territories, which are administered directly by the national government. The federal capital (Canberra) falls into this category, as does the Northern Territory, a sparsely populated and economically underdeveloped area that until recently has not been considered viable as a separate state. The Northern Territory has not always been governed by the national government — for a period until 1911 it was controlled by South Australia; the argument for its control as a federal concern is partly to be attributed to the greater financial resources of the national government and to apparent misman-agement by the overseeing state.

Superimposed upon the network of state and local governments and federal territories are the administrative units related to the field services, mainly of federal and state government departments. Many of the federal government field services use the state boundaries as their primary division, for example those administering social security programmes or that are used as the basis for the collection of statistics (the compilation of a population census being a responsibility of the federal government).

Ireland   The Republic of Ireland is a small, unitary state. It was formed by the partition of the island in 1922, a division effected partly along ethno-religious lines so that the Irish Republic was left as an ethnically homogeneous state. Decentralization within the state is divided simply between devolution to various types of local government and deconcentration to field service units.

The structure of local government is based on the pre-1972 English model. This consists of general-purpose county councils responsible for physical planning, roads (though not trunk routes, which are administered by central government), libraries and a number of other services. The four largest urban centres — Dublin, Cork, Limerick and Waterford — also act as county authorities and are called county boroughs. The smaller urban centres function as 'lower-tier' authorities and are divided into two types: the larger towns are municipal boroughs, while the smaller towns have town commissioners, a difference that is reflected in the range of functions that each discharges. For a number of functions, particularly that of physical planning, the counties are amalgamated into *ad hoc* regional bodies, whose status, in contrast to the constituent counties, is advisory.

We shall examine the spatial structure of field service units in a later chapter. With few exceptions, however, all central government ministries deconcentrate the mundane operation of services such as the administration of social welfare and education to territorial units. Alongside these exist the field service structure of semi-state bodies, for example those for the railways and tourist development.

Denmark   As a small country the chief vehicle for decentralization in Denmark is local government, which is composed of two tiers, the county and commune. In 1976 their numbers were 14 and 277 respectively. The local government structure was radically reshaped by a process of reform, beginning in 1967 when there were 1,097 authorities. Local government in the capital city, Copenhagen, as in a number of other countries, has a different structure, functioning as a single governmental area supervised by a central government appointee, the 'overpresident'.

In common with several other West European countries, Denmark is more accurately described as a compound unitary state (type C2 in the classification above). It incorporates two territories, the Faroe Islands and Greenland, that are governed as federacies. The Faroe Islands were granted devolution by the Danish government under the Home Rule Act of 1948. The Act included provision for the election of a local parliament (Lagting) whose legislative competence was to extend mainly to economic questions. Control over foreign policy and defence are retained by central government, together with education and social welfare, functions that in the federal countries are normally controlled by the state or provincial governments. Greenland, as a colonial holding of Denmark, has been given local autonomy following a local referendum in 1978 testing opinion about whether the territory should become fully integrated with the metropolitan power or not.

Summary   Power is dispersed territorially within states to various types of institutions and at various levels. The main types include devolution, either constitutionally as in federal countries or to local governments as in more centralized states, and administrative deconcentration. The two basic levels are regional and local, though in practice the hierarchy of sub-national units is more complex and G. Smith (1972) has offered a more detailed typology: (1) national government, (2) federal state units, (3) regional government or administration in unitary states, (4) upper-tier local government, e.g. province, (5) intermediate government administration, e.g. sub-regional unit, (6) lower-tier local government, e.g. commune or municipality, (7) sub-communal units, e.g. parish council. Though no country has representatives belonging to every level, the 'spread' varies between countries. Denmark has a spread typical of the more centralized countries with representatives from levels 4, 5, 6 and 7. Federations, in contrast, will normally have a wider span, Australia having representatives from 2, 3, 5, 6 and 7.

POLITICAL DECENTRALIZATION: ITS MEASUREMENT AND CORRELATES

The extent to which power is spatially diffused varies between countries. Some, such as France, are popularly described as strongly centralized, though this is challenged in recent studies (Ashford, 1982) and is anyway changing with the new (1981) socialist regime. Others, notably federal countries, are characterized by much less centralization. Power in this context is closely concerned with the ability to make authoritative decisions over the allocation of resources. Two questions are pertinent here: how can decentralization be measured (B. C. Smith, 1980) and, presuming an answer to this, what, if any, are the influences of the social and economic environment of the polity on the extent to which political power is located in sub-national governments?

The measurement of decentralization

There are several methods by which decentralization can be assessed (Clark, 1968), though none is totally satisfactory. Ideally such a measure would assess quantitatively the independent decision-making powers of individual levels of government — national, regional and local — in such a manner as to afford direct comparison between countries. Power itself is a difficult concept to quantify and one indicator on which political scientists have normally relied is the level of government that pays for particular services. The functional responsibilities of national and sub-national governments can also be used as the basis for assessing decentralization. Certain functions remain the natural preserve of national governments — defence and national security, foreign affairs, broad economic questions of money supply and stabilization. In other fields, however, there is much greater variation between countries; in some, central governments administer services that in others are entrusted to local governments.

Stephens (1974) devised a more complex measure of decentralization. By restricting his analysis to the United States, it was possible to avoid the considerable data problems that cross-national comparisons encounter. He examined the differences in local autonomy between the 50 states on the basis of the relative financial and functional responsibilities of state and local governments and the distribution of public service employees (weighted for type of employment according to its labour intensity) between the two levels. Each state was then classified according to its position on the centralization–decentralization spectrum (figure 2.5).

It is not certain that, by devolving functions to lesser governments, the national government will not continue to influence or control how these services are delivered, so it becomes difficult to distinguish the separate importance of the different layers of government. Clark (1971) devised a composite index to measure the influence of extra-community actions, especially those of the federal government, on the local decision-making process. Good (1978) also utilizes the idea that locally devolved powers may still be influenced by national governments to assess the extent of effective autonomy in the newly created Italian regional governments. The 15 regions were given legislative competence in a wide variety of fields, but each bill has to be approved by the government commissioner, an agent of the national government, who is empowered to refer the legislation to central government. The ratio between laws enacted and laws vetoed by central government was used to calculate a veto rate for each region. The rate varied between 20 per cent in the northern regions to over 30 per cent in the south, reflecting differences mainly in the extent to which regions were seen by the centre to be exceeding their powers. Clearly, cross-national comparisons are precluded from such analyses.

In spite of a number of drawbacks, fiscal variables have been most frequently used as a measure of political decentralization. One advantage of their use is that it is possible to make cross-national comparisons. Basically fiscal centralization is measured by the proportion of total government revenues and/or expenditures accounted for by the central government. In the following analysis we shall examine only expenditures, giving a measure of the relative importance of national and sub-national governments in the output of public goods and services. Besides providing

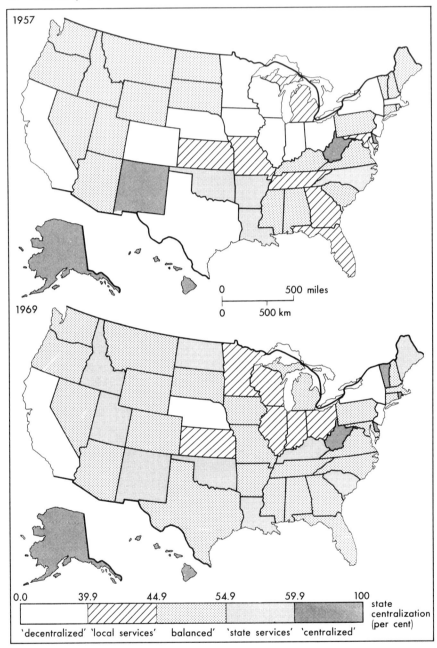

FIGURE 2.5   State–local centralization in the United States, 1957 and 1969
(adapted from data in Stephens, 1974)

the basis for direct comparison between countries, the fiscal ratio can be used to explore quantitatively the types of environmental variables that influence decentralization.

Prior to discussing spatial variations in centralization it is necessary to point out the limitations of the fiscal ratio: the major assumption underlying its use is that the spending sub-national unit has the major, if not the exclusive, influence over how expenditure should be allocated. In most countries, sub-national governments do not enjoy such power, particularly where, as in the case of local government, they are considered the subordinate bodies. Moreover, in most countries, local services rely on fiscal subsidies from higher levels of government. In industrial societies the pace of urban growth has generally outstripped the fiscal abilities of local governments to meet the provision of those services for which they have been delegated responsibility, so that in the United Kingdom, for example, over 60 per cent of local expenditure derives from central government transfers. The point at issue, on which it is easy to over-generalize, particularly when comparing countries, is the extent to which local autonomy is eroded by the dependence on fiscal subsidies from higher levels of government. Central government control will be most apparent in particular situations — such as projects involving major capital expenditure (highways, hospitals, etc.) where the distribution of funds becomes a matter of national policy (Prud'homme, 1977) — or, more generally, when the fiscal transfer is tied, as in a specific or conditional grant. The evidence from a wide cross-section of countries of inter-jurisdictional variations in the quality of public services equally suggests that local autonomy (or discretion) is a salient factor in spite of fiscal dependence. We might conclude that fiscal measurements are relevant as indicators of local autonomy, though recognizing that this is rarely an exclusive control.

The correlates of variations in centralization

Fiscal centralization varies substantially between countries (figure 2.6). In four countries (West Germany, Netherlands, Japan and Sweden) it is less than 40 per cent, while in 15 states over 90 per cent of expenditure is accounted for by the central government. The values peak bi-modally: those within the lower peak (40–49%) include only three less developed countries (Brazil, Uruguay and Colombia) in contrast to the upper peak (90–100%), which is composed exclusively of Third World countries.

Differences in fiscal centralization can be related to the variations in physical make-up (physical features, etc.), and in the social and economic conditions that distinguish individual countries. In this sense political centralization can be considered a response to the environment in which the political system operates (Easton, 1965). In a cross-national study of 45 countries, Viera (1967) investigated the strength of association between

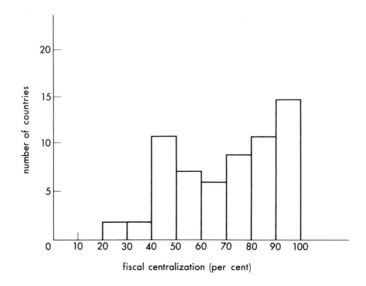

FIGURE 2.6   Fiscal centralization
(from Viera, 1967)

devolution and variables measuring economic–technological development, territorial and demographic size, population density, the number of sub-national governments and the age of the state. Figure 2.7 illustrates the major factors associated with centralization and some of the interrelationships between them.

Economic wealth   Centralization differs markedly between developed and less developed countries. In industrialized countries the average fiscal ratio is 43.4 per cent, while in developing countries it is 75.3 per cent. There are several reasons for this (Sharkansky, 1976). In the poorer country, the centralizing of decision-making will ensure greater control over limited resources. Further, the character of the political system in many Third World countries is authoritarian rather than liberal–democratic, so that, besides a high degree of centralization, power is concentrated within relatively few hands. Less developed countries also tend to be younger states. The age of the polity has a strong positive correlation with decentralization, implying that a unified state is a precondition for the dispersal of power. This is most apparent in Africa where the average centralization ratio (among 16 countries) is 83.1 per cent. Only in Nigeria and, to a lesser extent, Sudan, both of which are characterized by other correlates of centralization (large size, cultural diversity), are the ratios significantly lower.

Size The size of the national polity has frequently been linked with decentralization and, more specifically, with particular forms of government. *Ceteris paribus,* small size will favour centralization. Conversely, as K. W. Robinson (1961, 2) has argued, 'countries of large areas and small population, or even rather large population concentrated in widely scattered areas are obviously suitable for [a federal] form of government.' In some countries such as Australia, federalism has been considered a more suitable form of government because of the sheer size of the country and its population distribution. Size also influences decentralization through economic factors (Oates, 1972). In a small country, because of scale economies, there will be cost-savings to be gained in centralizing decision-making, while in a larger and more populous country the localities making up the state will be of sufficient size to generate their own scale economies and, in this sense, warrant local autonomy.

Though intuitively attractive as an explanatory factor, it is easy to oversimplify the effects of size. In the first place these will vary according to whether territory or population is being used to measure size. The area of a country has the less pronounced effect on its centralization, though its effect on the form of government is apparently stronger. Nevertheless, it is hardly plausible to argue that territorial size is a necessary or sufficient condition underlying the adoption of federalism. The idea, for example, that in 1787 the federation of the then United States was 'dictated' because it was a large country misrepresents the case (Elazar, 1973). Other factors

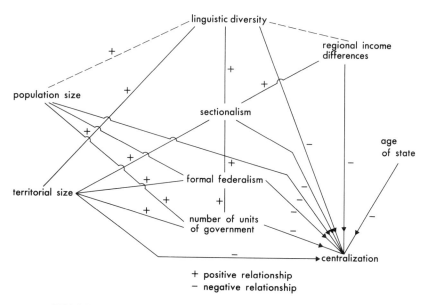

FIGURE 2.7   Factors in influencing the spatial distribution of power

were more important: federalism provided a means of achieving union while maintaining the regional (colonial) political identities; it also functioned as a mode by which popular government within a large republic could be secured.

The effects of territorial and population size, as they impinge on demands for decentralization, have been complementary. The steady reduction of distance friction through improvements in transport and methods of information exchange and circulation, which points logically to centralization and larger political units, has been paralleled historically in industrial nations by the growth of population, which has tended to act as a countervailing force through its influence on the subdivision of existing territorial units of government.

Cultural/economic diversities   It is argued that, through more localized policy-making, political decentralization can cater for a wider variety of policy demands (more expenditure on education in areas of greater demand, reduction in other services, and so on) than can centralized government. The more diverse the population, in terms of ethnic characteristics, the more likely it is that needs and tastes for the various public services will differ, leading in turn to pressure to decentralize government business. Conversely, in a more homogeneous population the preferences expressed in one area will tend to be similar to those of others, so that they can be met by a central authority.

Homogeneity can be measured in several ways. Diversity of linguistic, religious or racial composition can act as proxy variables to be related to the demand for decentralization: countries with more diverse populations will tend to be less centralized. Sectionalism is a second type of measure, and is more explicitly spatial in that it can be used to assess the degree to which sub-groups within the population living in a 'sizeable' area of the state identify 'self-consciously and distinctively' with it (Banks and Textor, 1963), frequently demanding some form of local autonomy. (In their classification of sectionalism Banks and Textor use the term 'sizeable' to mean regional.) Economic differences, particularly of wealth, are a third type of factor by which to measure homogeneity. Pommerehne (1977) used two indices to assess variations in economic wealth: household income inequality (Jain, 1974) and regional income *per capita* levels relative to the national average based on Williamson's (1965) analysis of regional economic variations. The underlying thesis is that variations of wealth will lead to different policy demands and hence local autonomy, which will be seen as a means to redress the economic irregularities between regions.

The strength of association between fiscal centralization and these measures of homogeneity varies. The studies by Oates (1972) and Pommerehne (1977) found the weakest correlation with variables measuring linguistic, religious and racial diversity, though this might be attributable in part to the nominal measurement of homogeneity. The variables refer to ethnic differences within countries as a whole, and do not relate directly to decentralization. The inclusion of variations between regions within the measurement of sectionalism may help explain its stronger association with fiscal centralization ratios. In many cases the sectionalism is rooted in ethnic differences (language, religion, etc.). The relationships between fiscal centralization and variations in economic wealth, on the other hand, are contradictory. Pommerehne (1977) demonstrated that, in spite of the argument that greater differences in household incomes (measured nationally) would be associated with greater decentralization, the reverse occurred (see table 2.4). He suggested that a possible explanation might be that centralized government is more relevant to programmes of income distribution. Greater regional variations in economic wealth, in contrast, are associated with greater decentralization; pronounced differences in regional prosperity can themselves contribute to sectionalist feelings.

TABLE 2.4   Correlates of fiscal centralization, ten industrial countries

CGE =	10.0	−	0.07P	−	0.01GNP	−	1.90S	+	344.3K	−	90.5RID
	(6.29)		(2.78)		(0.63)		(2.21)		(3.01)		(2.13)

$$N=10 \qquad R^2=0.667$$

CGE	Proportionate importance of central government consumption expenditure
P	Population (1968)
GNP	GNP per capita US $ (1968)
S	Sectionalism (S=1 where sectionalism is extreme rather than negligible; *vice-versa* S=0)
K	Kuznetz-index of household income inequality (0=perfect equality, 1=perfect inequality)
RID	Difference of regional income *per capita* relative to national average

The figures in brackets give the absolute value of *t* for the estimated coefficient.
Source: Adapted from Pommerehne (1977, 304)

Cultural and economic differences evidently strongly influence centralization, particularly in those cases where they are associated with specific areas of the state. The relevance of regional particularism as a divisive factor has not been overlooked by political scientists; as Blondel (1969, 55) argued, referring mainly to the need for central governments to decentralize their activities to regional seats of power, 'sectionalism related to geography has more profound political effects than any other form of sectionalism'.

Structure of government   Intuitively we would expect centralization to be related to the structure of government — whether countries are federal or not — and the number of sub-national governments that are established.

Using the three-fold division of countries discussed earlier, average fiscal centralization ratios for federal, compound and unitary states are 44 per cent, 47 per cent and 60 per cent respectively. In general, the existence of a federal constitution is associated with less fiscal centralization, particularly among industrial countries, though the high degree of decentralization in Sweden, which is otherwise a thoroughly unitary state, demonstrates the extent to which local government can be used to provide services. The number of sub-national governments is also positively related to decentralization (Viera, 1967), though this inevitably begs the question, which came first? Does the existence of over 79,000 local government units in the United States of itself dictate the extent of decentralization, or do the needs of devolution within a large and culturally diverse polity dictate such a number of units (Sherwood, 1969)?

Political culture   Though we have seen as a general relationship that decentralization is linked to economic development, there are substantial differences in the emphasis placed on local autonomy within different national political cultures. In this respect we can contrast the value allegedly placed on local autonomy within the United States as opposed to France. Nevertheless, cross-nationally the significance in quantitative terms of the effect of political culture is difficult to assess because of problems of measuring values of this kind. Within federal countries in which state–local relations differ, it is easier to isolate the importance of political culture. Elazar (1966) analysed the relationships between state and local governments in the United States in terms of the historical traditions favouring centralism or localism. Four main types were defined, the patterning of which followed regional lines particularly in Southern states, which have traditionally been associated with strong state governments. Elazar's typology, however, is contradicted by Stephens' (1974) argument that centralism was more strongly related to the population size of the state rather than to any cultural values.

Several kinds of factors have been found to be relevant in explaining differences of political centralization between (and within) countries. These include the size of the polity, its cultural heterogeneity in terms of ethnic or racial characteristics and the structure of government. Differences in political culture will also help to explain why some countries emphasize the advantages of local democracy and decentralization more than others.

Based on such variables, Clark (1974) has suggested a number of hypotheses linking national factors to local community autonomy, which he defines as the ability to take decisions affecting the community locally. The extent of such autonomy is a measure of the devolution from the political centre and its interaction with environmental variables measuring local physical resources, social and economic characteristics and the institutional structures. Figure 2.8 summarizes aspects of Clark's model; though much of this remains to be tested rigorously it provides a fertile set of hypotheses that help to explain local autonomy.

An obvious problem confronting empirical verification of Clark's model, and particularly any attempt at cross-national analysis, is the question of measurement. In a minority of cases — territorial size and the rate of out-migration, for example — measurement is relatively unambiguous and appropriate data are usually available. In others, notably the degree of social mobilization, measurement would be more complex, involving perhaps a composite index made up of variables measuring political participation, voting levels for national parties, etc. In some cases the factors are ambiguous, such as the number of separately distinguishable communities: the kinds of criteria used to identify them (for example, the relative closeness of regions based upon inter-regional trading flows, or the analysis of regional voting trends) will help pre-determine the types of community (if any) that are defined; furthermore, the areas defined by different criteria will be likely to differ.

Notwithstanding these methodological problems, the advantage of Clark's synthesis lies in the simplicity of the basic argument — that local autonomy is the outcome of two sets of factors, those influencing how much power is devolved from the centre and those that enhance the degree of local political power. These factors are not the only ones influencing local autonomy. Thus historical measurements, even if they are implicit within the ethnicity factor, could be added — for example, the mode of formation of the state (whether coercive, or voluntaristic), the duration of time over which state-building has taken place. Similarly, the dominant ideology, particularly if it is pluralist, will be important in fostering local autonomy; in pluralist systems, local political groups may command an 'automatic' legitimacy that is denied to the national government.

Another important feature of Clark's model is that it extends our argument that local autonomy is a more embracing concept than decentralization alone. Decentralization is defined within the set of factors influencing how much power is devolved from the centre. But it is the second set of factors — demographic, geographic, economic — that helps determine the political power of the localities. To B. C. Smith (1980) the importance of this distinction is that local political power may counteract the formal decentralization machinery or indeed, as in the case of France, that the localities may be able to influence decision-making processes so that what is usually cited as a highly centralist state acts in a more decentralist fashion than might be expected (Tarrow, 1977; Gourevitch, 1980).

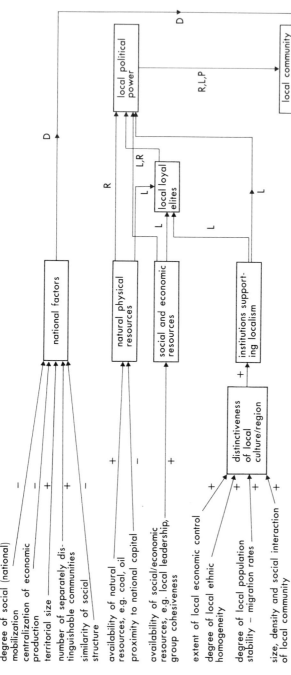

FIGURE 2.8   Factors underlying local community autonomy (adapted from Clark, 1974)

The recognition by geographers of the manner in which values and value systems underpin decision-making has added considerably to our understanding of spatial processes (Buttimer, 1974). As attributes that we prefer or would like to establish, values underwrite the social and political bases of society. This is equally true of the territorial distribution of power within the state: 'any preference for a certain scheme of areal division of power presupposes a decision on the ends for which power is to be exercised — a decision on the values power should serve and on the ways in which these values will be served' (Hoffman, 1959, 113).

The kinds of values determining how power is territorially distributed within the state can be sub-divided according to their level of generalization. The broadest, in the sense of being all-pervasive, are those that influence how the polity as a whole is organized and functions. Ylsivaker (1959) terms these 'basic values'. In his democratic, economically advanced state — the United States — these basic values were liberty, equality and welfare. From these, more specific 'instrumental values' can be developed as objectives to which the territorial distribution is directed: these would include values such as administrative efficiency, local autonomy, public accountability and territorial justice.

Basic political values, such as liberty and equality, are not easy to define, let alone to attain. The idea of equality can serve as a case in point. Intuitively, it is both a humane as well as a plausible objective of the political system. Furthermore, to the extent that equality and the demand for it have historically meant the right to be treated as an equal in political affairs, its interpretation is deceptively straightforward. However, in its application to the political system, a distinction must be made between equality relating to the demands made upon, and access to, the institutions of government and the equal sharing between citizens of the outputs of these processes. A question soon arises whether equal treatment is to be considered in terms of mathematical equality or in some proportional sense so that those 'in greater need', however this is defined, are dealt with preferentially (D. M. Smith, 1977). It is a dilemma that was first recognized by Aristotle and it remains as much a source of conflict between separate regions and localities within the state as between individuals and social groups within the polity. Both principles can be applied to different parts of the same political system: mathematical equality has been sought in the reapportionment of electoral districts to equalize the value of the vote, while programmes of fiscal redistribution are frequently engineered on a proportional basis so that individuals and areas defined as being in need receive more. These programmes, however, are aimed more at reducing interpersonal and territorial inequalities than establishing any absolute degree of equality, partly of necessity — in effect governments, in spite of their extensive interventionist role, have only been able to reduce inequalities — but also because not even the most ardent 'egalitarian envisages the obliteration of distinction among persons' (Lineberry, 1977, 28) — to this we might add, or among areas.

One of the other problems raised by an analysis of values underpinning the territorial distribution of power stems from their variety. Not only do the range and incidence of values employed differ between countries, but we can also trace differences within the same country at different stages in its political and economic development. Leemans (1970) has suggested that decentralization is used for a combination of objectives such as nation-building, local democracy, establishing the freedom of individual political communities, administrative efficiency and the social and economic development of the polity, recognizing that their importance varies (see figure 2.9). These objectives can also act as criteria by which it is possible to assess the implications of distributing power to sub-national governments.

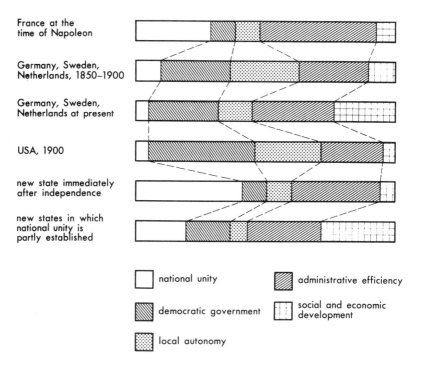

FIGURE 2.9   Objectives sought in the territorial distribution of power in various countries
(from Leemans, 1970, 28)

To the extent that the relative weighting given to such objectives varies between countries and within them (as within the ideologies represented by different parties within the state), their definition is closely related to the question of value preferences and ideological differences. One country might emphasize the advantages of local community autonomy premised on the notion of liberty, another the need to establish national uniformity in the administrative programmes of central government; the result is two different configurations of power, notably a more decentralized and a more centralized state respectively. To the political geographer the process of weighting, and frequently of trading-off, between objectives is important because of the possible variations in spatial outcomes. Local governments based on the needs of technical efficiency, for example on the internalizing of the spillover benefits of particular services, would probably result in a territorially larger set of political units than would be the case were greater direct citizen participation in local political processes to be the basic defining criterion.

Political objectives

State unity Territorial self-preservation is a basic goal underlying the political programmes of the state. Decentralization can be used as an instrument of state-building to compensate for factors that threaten its stability. To the newly established state with a relatively incoherent 'state-idea' (Hartshorne, 1950) and possibly threatened by centrifugal forces such as sectionalism, the imposition of a decentralized administrative structure by the central government can act as a powerful countervailing force. The division of France into departments in the late eighteenth century is the classic European example, based on the apparent need to destroy the traditionally strong provincial ties to avoid the possibility of the realm being subdivided into a multitude of little states under the form of a republic. More recent examples of the deliberate employment of decentralization as a forge for state/national identity are found in Third World countries, as in the recasting of intra-federal boundaries in Nigeria following the Biafran war. In newly independent states, as in African countries in which tribalism is a disuniting factor, local government can be used to amalgamate otherwise separate social groups.

Another way to maintain state unity is to devolve contentious issues to lower levels of government. This is especially relevant where conflict between opposing factions is endemic, as in ethnically divided states, or is likely to arise because of the nature of the issue, as in rezoning or a proposal to raise the rate at which local taxes are levied. In these cases devolution makes it less likely that the problem will become a national issue.

Even if the need to impose the territorial integrity of the state is less among the more established industrial countries (and this is open to question), decentralization is a necessary vehicle for reinforcing the unity of the state. It can act as the means by which central government policies are implemented throughout the state. The objective, if not necessarily the consequence, of policies and programmes being implemented nationally will be the reduction of disparities between localities in services provided by the state, which in turn will help to lessen any political conflict to which such spatial irregularities might give rise.

Though the decentralization of power to spatial localities can be used to enhance the state, the existence of alternative power bases to the political capital can itself be seen as a threat to the larger unit, a position that will be aggravated by their institutional recognition. In other words, political decentralization by its nature contradicts the unitary character of the state.

Local democracy   In much of Western Europe and North America the advantages of local government have been closely allied to its democratic nature: the local community can be governed by representatives elected locally. Local democracy is usually achieved through indirect methods with the election of representatives. In the New England township so admired by Jefferson and de Tocqueville and in parts of Switzerland, however, the idea of local democracy is extended to mean direct community decision-making. The community regulates its own affairs through collective voting and a system of popular administrative control through officials who are chosen from the electorate. Normally the township would have a population of less than 3,000, a size that facilitates direct democracy.

The size of the polity has frequently been causally linked with the attainment of democratic objectives, specifically the accessibility of the governmental processes and the extent to which individuals are able to participate in them. Classical political philosophers conventionally argued that size had a direct bearing on participation, though democracy in the Greek city-state was, by present standards, elitist.

Dahl and Tufte (1973) define democracy in the ideal polity as satisfying two criteria:

(1) citizen effectiveness — control of the decisions of government by the citizens.
(2) system capacity — the ability of the polity to respond effectively to the collective preferences of its citizens.

The evidence on the contribution by local and national governments to the first criterion is equivocal. In their survey comparing national political cultures, Almond and Verba (1963) suggested that local government was popularly considered to be more accessible, comprehensible and amenable than national government. Somewhat contradictorily, however, participation in local politics, measured for example by electoral turnouts, is often lower than in national politics. The second factor also pinpoints a limitation of local democracy. Local governments that lack the resources (financial, manpower or a sufficient territorial base) to meet the collective preferences of their voters offer a somewhat sham form of local autonomy. Suppose, for example, that pollution control of a major river is sought, a task that could be separately tackled by the individual jurisdictions along its course. Clearly it would take only one authority to undermine the programme by refusing to implement the pollution control measures. To ensure effectiveness, some regional agency would need to be established, even though this might conflict with the goals of local democracy.

The argument that local government, because it serves a more restricted population than a higher level of government, is likely to be more democratic — responsive to local needs, accessible to the greater proportion of the population — itself needs treating with caution. One argument in favour of centralization arises from the danger that a local government might become dominated by the interests of an oligarchy and fail to represent the community at large. Thus

> enthusiasm for community control, government close to the people and responsive grass roots institutions must be tempered by questions such as: Community control for what purposes? Government closer to whom? Responsive to what particular set of interests? State's rights, home rule and local autonomy have provided the rationale for racial segregation, the exclusion of the poor and the refusal of federal assistance to the undernourished. (Danielson, Hershey and Bayne, 1977, 10)

Administrative objectives

Decentralization is usually designed to meet certain administrative objectives. One of the more straightforward of these will be the need for central organizations, such as government departments, to establish offices throughout the national territory to effect the delivery of some service. Traditionally this need has been most apparent in such functions as the collection of revenues and taxes, law and order (police and justice systems) and internal communications, each of which is essential to the maintenance of the state. The list has, however, been extended to include personal and social services, education, health, welfare and facilitating services such as the provision of infrastructure accommodating local economic development.

Normally it is suggested that decentralizing authority to sub-national loci makes it more likely that policy outputs will more closely meet local needs, since the tendency (and danger) amongst national administrators, politicians and civil servants is to perceive the problems of the state uniformly

(Benson, 1961). Imposing solutions that are appropriate to the smaller unit — prohibition and the values of the Midwest small town, for example — over the wider national territory tends to be inefficient. However, the existence of local jurisdictions with policy-making powers can be at variance with services and programmes, such as transport, urban policies and education, that generate costs and benefits across local and regional boundaries and require national coordination.

Economic objectives

The fragmentation of the state into a network of sub-national jurisdictions impinges on the economic performance of governments. In their economic role, modern-day governments have three main responsibilities: the efficient allocation of resources, the establishment of an equitable distribution of income, and the ensuring of satisfactory levels of economic growth while maintaining overall stability (Oates, 1972). The last objective is least affected by decentralization: the activities of local and regional governments have little influence on such goals as full employment or price stability, nor probably should they where these questions of macro-economic policies are properly the concern of national governments.

Economists approach the issue of decentralization by looking at its advantages and disadvantages as it affects the efficiency and equity objectives of governments. Simplifying, this can be reduced to the question whether these economic objectives are better served within a decentralized system of government or not.

Efficiency considerations imply that decentralization is the preferred solution under certain conditions. One basic condition arises where the preferences for a public service differ among territorially defined groups. Oates (1972) has argued in his decentralization theorem that where there is a diversity of preferences for public services the existence of multiple governments is a more efficient solution than centralized decision-making. The theorem, however, assumes the absence of scale economies and of spillover effects across jurisdictional boundaries, the existence of either of which can outweigh the welfare benefits from decentralized decision-making, implying that such services should be made the responsibility of a higher level of government.

The existence of multiple governments can also enhance democracy by carrying decision-making by majority rule to a more local level. A hypothetical example will illustrate why this should be so. Suppose within an area that there are 100 citizens, 60 of whom favour policy P_1 and the remainder P_2. If the area was governed as a single jurisdiction (and assuming decisions were selected by majority rule on the basis of 'one man, one vote') then P_1 would be adopted, leaving a large minority, 40 per cent, dissatisfied. If the area was divided into two jurisdictions of 50 inhabitants and assuming that in Area 1 40 preferred P_1 and 10 preferred P_2, while in Area 2 the preferences were 20 and 30 respectively, then Area 1 would choose P_1 and Area 2 would choose P_2, leaving only 30 per cent dissatisfied.

Another way of expressing allocative efficiency is by looking at the spatial pattern of benefits that follow from the provision of public goods. These are goods whose consumption is equally available to all regardless of location or patterns of earlier consumption, though relatively few public goods are 'pure' in the sense of being uniformly available to all (such as defence programmes). Most public goods are 'impure' in that they are divisible among either groups of individuals or specific geographical areas, for example parks, fire protection. While the delivery of such goods is more efficient through a decentralized system of jurisdictions, the effect of decentralizing is to exacerbate the problem of externalities where the benefits of programmes spillover to adjacent jurisdictions. This results in the 'free rider' problem. Ideally the spatial structure of sub-national governments and the assignment of functions to them should seek to internalize the benefits (and costs) belonging to each good.

While allocative efficiency is served by local jurisdiction, distributive efficiency is better attained within larger units of government. Small jurisdictions are more likely to be homogeneous and have similar preferences for service mixes, while larger jurisdictions, because they will embrace both relatively affluent and poor areas, will facilitate redistribution. As it affects the redistribution of income a strong case exists for the centralization of decision-making: delegating such responsibilities would be partly self-defeating in that jurisdictions that elected to raise taxes and provide subsidies for low-income families would repel affluent sectors and attract poorer groups. Any notion of spatial redistribution is based upon some principle of territorial equity, the furtherance of which will best be achieved within the larger (often the national) territory. Nevertheless, as we shall see, redistribution between areas, just as between social groups, is a contentious issue.

CONCLUSIONS

This chapter has developed the theme of the territorial division of power in a number of ways. Most simply this is apparent in the *de jure* organization into sub-national governments, but these can be seen as indicative of different degrees of centralization. At an aggregate level it is possible to unravel statistical correlates of decentralization, though the conclusions that political geographers might want to draw from such analyses need to be heavily qualified, not least because of the problems of ecological fallacy, that is, the erroneous extrapolation of characteristics common to an area (high incomes, low levels of political participation, etc.) onto individuals living within that area. Subsequently the analysis outlined how the territorial division of power must be seen within the context of certain values and objectives.

Very broadly there are two contrasting models by which power is distributed, federalism and centralism. Centralist thought, particularly as it has been developed among French political philosophers, is unequivocal in arguing that the territorial areas of the state, to the extent that they are given functional responsibilities, should be subordinate to the central authority. To the Jacobin, France was considered an indivisible unit to the point that the deputy who advocated federating the country was accused of treason (Kesselman and Rosenthal, 1974, 19). Hence to Rousseau, such dispersal of power as was necessary should be merely administrative. In his plan for Corsica, local jurisdictions were not abolished but, to avoid any possible threat to internal stability, they were to be stripped of their historic rights, while in order to establish a measure of spatial uniformity similar status was to be bestowed on all localities.

The decentralist tradition in political philosophy has been based on a general antipathy to the concentration of power and the need to counteract excessive centralism by a system of 'territorial checks and balances'. As de Tocqueville in his classic work, *Democracy in America,* advocated, an intermediate level of authority (as in federal countries) would temper the excesses of absolute centralization. His argument also that 'few would support the state which was providing services which were of purely municipal interest' had its echo in Jefferson, one of the Founding Fathers of the American Constitution, who was anxious to preserve the rights of the locality: 'it is not by the consolidation, or concentration of powers, but their distribution, that good government is effected'. In the next two chapters we shall examine the spatial ramifications of these different types of state.

3

Territorial Integration and 'Disintegration' in the Unitary State

Although federal countries account for over half of the world's land area, a proportion that is greater if we restrict our attention to the states of the developed world, over three-quarters of all sovereign states are unitary. By including those countries defined in the previous chapter as compound unitary, the majority of industrial states can be broadly classified as centralist.

Geographically the unitary state is widely distributed, though it is strongly identified with particular parts of the world — among less developed countries with Africa, and among industrial states with Western Europe. In Africa, all but one of the newly independent countries have chosen unitary constitutions; Nigeria is alone in having adopted federalism to counterbalance regional–ethnic differences, even though these are a common enough feature of the Black African state. In Western Europe, only three countries have federal constitutions.

As far as the central ruling elites of these states are concerned, one of the reasons for the adoption of a unitary-style constitution has undoubtedly been the perceived need to establish the oneness of the state. The concentration of power rather than its distribution among regional loci is particularly conducive to the integration of the newly independent state, just as centralized economic decision-making will tend to favour efficiency in the distribution of resources, an argument that has special emphasis in the less developed country. Questions of territorial integration and political unity, however, are not confined to the newly independent countries. Though their incidence varies, these are issues that confront the majority of states. Unitary concepts, besides focusing power on a single rather than a multiple number of regional centres, will help provide the means by which the political centre can penetrate and integrate peripheral areas of the state.

The concept of the modern state involving a form of government that brought about the consolidation of a political territory from a strong core originated in Western Europe. In this chapter we shall discuss the factors underlying the integration of the West European state and also those that have led towards its 'partial disintegration' following the re-emergence of regional nationalism as a salient political force. Our focus is, then, on the evolution from the unitary to the compound unitary state.

Because such an analysis is time- and space-specific, it is important to point out some of the more obvious limitations. Historical, economic, political and geographical factors define unique conditions under which states evolve, so that any attempt at cross-national comparison is fraught with difficulties. Several themes distinguish the evolution of the West European state: the comparatively long time-span over which the processes of state- (and nation-) building have taken place, which included the period when society was transformed as a result of modernization; the establishment of state before nation; the process of territorial evolution through a historically long process of expansion (in contrast to states established in a single 'instantaneous' act of deliberate creation), though in including countries such as Belgium some exceptions must be admitted in this respect. Factors such as these distinguish Western Europe from elsewhere — from Eastern Europe where nation often preceded state, and from the Third World state imposed by a colonial power.

THE INTEGRATION OF THE STATE

Political integration is normally used to refer to the processes by which smaller communities are consolidated into territorially larger units of government. Local loyalties to local political institutions typically become secondary to the allegiance and support enjoyed by the larger unit. To Jacob and Teune, the vital construct underpinning political integration is the idea of community: people living within the integrated political unit share 'mutual ties of one kind or another which give the group a feeling of identity and self-awareness' (Jacob and Teune, 1964, 4). Political communities, and indeed processes of political integration, are relevant concepts at each successive step in the hierarchy of political units, from sub-national through to supra-national, though the integration of the state is arguably of most importance because the state is the dominant actor.

Where the idea of political integration is closely tied to the development of a cohesive political community then, as far as the state is concerned, this is bound up with the concept of the nation. What is termed the political integration of the state can be described alternatively, and more concisely, as national integration (or nation-state integration), by which is meant the achievement of a cohesive population, in cultural, economic and political terms, that is spatially coincident with the legal entity of the state.

National integration is important because it will help assure the survival of the state, but it would be wrong to assume that nationally integrated societies are conflict-free. Mass consensus is based on the acceptance of common national aspirations, or a common national outlook, which ultimately supersede the demands generated by the individual's membership of other groups, such as class. Because of this bedrock of mass loyalty to the nation — and ideally the nation-state — conflict, particularly between social classes, does not bring into question the territorial integrity of the state, though it can lead to the overthrow of regimes.

Partly because of its relevance throughout the spatial hierarchy of political units, the whole problem of integration has been extensively studied by political scientists (De Vree, 1972; Lindberg and Scheingold, 1971). One of the initial difficulties in its study arises from the ambiguity of the term, since political integration can be used to refer to both a process and an end-state (Merritt, 1976). As a process it involves the study of those factors that help explain how the unit becomes cohesive. These would include the growth of communal identity, the contribution made by social homogeneity and economic factors. The problem is deciding when integration has been achieved and in particular whether there is some (variously defined) critical level that, when reached, defines an integrated political unit.

There are two major schools of integration theory, transactionalism and neofunctionalism. Political geographers have shown greater interest in the former, largely because of its more explicitly spatial approach but also because of its greater use of quantitative measures to identify integration. Transactionalists seek to identify those factors that 'distinguish an organized and interdependent community from a random grouping of individuals, and what conditions are necessary to promote and maintain a sense of community among the population of a given region' (Hodges, 1978, 243). This necessary level of interdependence will be established through the network of mutual transactions that link the potentially integrated units. These transactions, or within the human geographer's terminology 'interactions', are measurable as flows, for example of mail or telephone traffic. In his important analysis of integration in East Africa, Soja (1968) used telephone traffic as a measure of transaction flow between the three countries of Kenya, Uganda and Tanganyika. His method assumed that integration was associated with reaching some critical level in the density of transactions — this was operationalized through the concept of salience, which indicated those telephone call flows that were 'greater than expected'. The level at which flows become salient, however, needs to be defined arbitrarily. Even so, where the central assumption of the theory is accepted, that the greater the density of mutually rewarding transactions the greater the likelihood of integration, the benefits of the approach to the political geographer stem from its recognition of territorial interaction as one of the bases for political cohesion.

However, this approach is probably more valuable to the political geographer studying integration between sovereign states rather than within them. Empirically there are more studies that examine supra-national integration than focus on national unification. In part we can account for this by data problems; for the time at which national integration in Western Europe was taking place, statistics covering the kinds of transaction flow potentially of value (inter-regional trade, for example) are at best sketchy. (Merritt's study of integration among the American seaboard colonies in the period leading up to the War of Independence is an exception; see chapter 4.) A more fundamental reason why integration theories are of less relevance when studying national integration within Western Europe rather than supra-national integration is that they emphasize the voluntaristic and peaceful elements of the process and condition of political integration. Both elements are more accurately ascribed to the emergence of the European Economic Com-munity than of its individual member countries, which are more 'appro-priately labelled and studied as cases of amalgamation by imperialism rather than . . . peaceful regional integration' (Puchala, 1974, 122). We shall be looking at the implications of this more fully in a later section.

State and nation

According to Strayer (1970), it was apparent as early as 1300 that the major political form would be the sovereign state. Because he included within his definition empires and city-states extant in Europe at the time, the appearance of the state as *the* institution is to be dated no earlier than the sixteenth century. After this time, following wars and the dismemberment of empires, Europe was progressively divided and re-divided into separate states whose distinguishing features were control over a specific territory, relative centralization of power, differentiation from other organizations such as the Church, and their functioning as the main repository of the means of coercion (Tilly, 1975).

At the outset it is important to distinguish between 'state' and 'nation', particularly as they are terms whose usage has become confused, a problem that the compound term 'nation-state' has made worse. The state is a legal and constitutional device through which political control over a defined territory is exercised. The nation, on the other hand, refers to an entity that has social and cultural, rather than legalistic, overtones. Definitions of the nation are legion, though a majority include the feeling of common association through the sharing of values, attitudes, memories and historical traditions and, very frequently, identification with a particu-lar territory.

The link between nation and state is provided by the aspirations of nationalism and its adherent the nationalist, the latter being someone who considers that the nation should be self-governing. Nationalist groups, therefore, strive for political self-control, an idea that was embodied within the principle of national self-determination used in the reconstruction of Europe after World War I (Cobban, 1945). It is through this link that the term 'nation-state' has won popular currency, though in the sense of one state being exclusively identifiable with one nation it is a term that could be accurately applied only to a small number of cases.

Nevertheless, nation-statism is a commonly sought goal; through social engineering and political mobilization the state attempts to 'standardize' the population to the point where it is sufficiently assimilated to be described as a nation-state. Nation-statism is of relatively recent origins: nationalism as a politically integrating ideology dates from the eighteenth century; prior to this date, integrative activity could be considered as mainly that of state-building.

Basing his argument on ideas borrowed from Talcott Parsons, Stein Rokkan (1975) developed a paradigm of political integration within a centre–periphery framework. Parsons (1966) had suggested that the processes of political development from the simple, subsistence, primordial community to the emergence of early political systems such as the city-states of Greece involved four crucial phases:

1. the establishment of a judiciary to manage and arbitrate on conflicts on a regularized basis;
2. the development of military power sufficient to impose physical control over a tributary population so that it would be able to obtain adequate food supply, manpower and other resources;
3. the emergence of novel, pervasive religious organizations; and
4. the development of technology and the emergence of extra-local trading.

Rokkan adapted this typology of economic, religious, military and judicial factors so that they became the channels linking the 'subject periphery' to the 'central establishment'. The centre was able to control its hinterland by virtue of its military superiority, which enabled it to exact necessary resources, and by a mix of the economic (trading), cultural–symbolic (religious) and legal links that brought the two types of unit, centre and periphery, into contact.

Evidently there is common ground between Rokkan's model (see figure 3.1) and the factors introduced in chapter 1 as representing crisis or problem areas typically encountered during the development of political systems. In Rokkan's model this involves four time phases: 'two centre-generated thrusts through the territory, the first military–economic, the second cultural; two phases of internal restructuring opening up opportunities for the periphery, the first symbolic–cultural, the second economic' (Rokkan, 1975, 570). In this section our concern is with the first two phases.

The first state-building (or penetration) phase involves the military

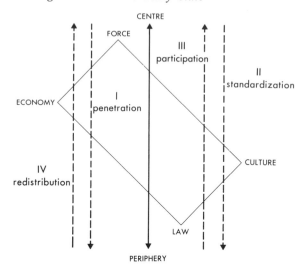

FIGURE 3.1   Centre-periphery interaction: the four
critical phases
(from Rokkan, 1975)

pacification of the territory and the build-up of a network of field administration services ensuring that the centre is able to meet the basic needs of government — the establishment of law and order, and the means to collect taxes. In Western Europe the process of penetration began in feudal times and was often associated with the division of the political territory into basic units of administration — the English county, Scottish sheriffdom, German *gau* and French *pays* are all roughly comparable in this respect — made responsible to some nominated representative of the monarchy. In Scotland the diffusion of the sheriffdom, largely completed by the end of the thirteenth century, marked the stages in the expansion of the 'effective national territory', the area over which the centre's remit held sway. These were established first in the Central Lowlands and the south-eastern area of the country, close to the political centre and to the English border, over which there was sporadic conflict, and latterly in more remote parts of the kingdom, in Galloway and the Highlands. The sheriff's duties — to act as representative of the Crown, to ensure the military efficiency of his area, to collect revenues and taxes and keep the fiscal records of his charge and to preside over the courts — demonstrate the process of state-building through the establishment of close links between the centre and locality. These functions were not dissimilar to those given to the *intendants* in France, officers appointed directly by the Crown to act as provincial representatives, a system that lasted until the seventeenth century.

It is in Rokkan's second stage that the process of mass social fusion is undertaken, giving the political unit a common identity. Because of the importance of nationalism as the source of a common national identity, this stage is best described as the nation-building phase. According to Rokkan's model, the phase is associated with centre-initiated policies aimed at cultural standardization, notably a common language and education system.

It was through the French Revolution that the ideal of the nation-state was first effectively proclaimed. Rousseau, in his *Social Contract,* laid the philosophical foundations for such a political community. Thus it was only through the establishment of unitary power within the state that man would be able to achieve freedom, equality and fraternity. Once the state had freed itself from its 'feudal shackles' — manifested through provincial localism and other practices that favoured local groups at the expense of the General Will — it would be in a position to act as an emancipatory force. Unity and centralization were to be the essential qualities by which the General Will could be realized. These ideas of Rousseau were to become part of the rhetoric of the Republican 'one people, one country, one government, one nation, one fatherland'. Nationalism provided the means by which loyalties to the old order, to the traditional *pays,* would become weakened and replaced by identity with the French *patrie.* The changes to be invoked by this — the development of a national consciousness associated with being French and a sense of patriotism towards the state — were not to be rapidly or easily made. A century after the Revolution, as E. Weber (1977) has argued in his careful analysis of the modernization of rural France, the country was moving towards national unity rather than having achieved it, and there were demonstrable contrasts between different regions of the state in the extent to which patriotic duty and national identity were part of the mass political culture.

National integration

The process of national integration, through which identities and loyalties become transferred from a pre-existing group such as the tribe or smaller ethnic division to a culturally different entity, is often associated with the more all-encompassing set of social processes known by the label 'modernization' (Rustow, 1967). By modernization we mean the broad set of societal changes that mark the passage from a 'traditional' to a 'modern' society. Characteristically it is associated with the development of industrialization, of urbanization and its attendant process of migration, with the growth of literacy rates and of other means of encouraging social communication, as well as with the emergence of new modes of transport that laid the basis for greater interaction over larger areas. The effect of modernization was to uproot the individual from a traditional subsistence economy, which resulted in a loosening of ties with the local area defined by the old order. The vacuum was to be filled by the development of ties with a different (usually larger) group represented by the nation. This was possible because of mobilization effects that made 'people available for new patterns of behaviour [putting them] in situations where they have new needs and new learning experiences' (Deutsch, 1979, 285).

Several key factors are commonly associated with the process of national integration. Deutsch (1953) identified eight recurrent factors that appeared to underlie the growth of nations:

1. Transition from subsistence to market economy.
2. The integrating influence of core areas representing regions in which the population is more mobilized and advanced.
3. Urbanization and the resulting mobilization of the population.
4. Development of basic communication networks allowing for migration, trading, etc.
5. Different concentration of skills, capital and social institutions between regions and classes around which nationalist aspirations could crystallize.
6. The recognition of the advantage of the nation as a means of mobilizing people into coherent groups capable of competing effectively for resources in the wider (global) arena.
7. The development of group awareness and the role of iconography (flags, anthem, etc.) as national mnemonics.
8. The role of politico-territorial socialization and of state coercion, e.g. the imposition of a common language.

The process of integration had in fact begun before the impact of modernization became apparent because of the early emergence of core areas, regions that because of certain historical, natural and economic advantages were able to spearhead the movement for integration.

Amongst political geographers, the growth and integration of political territories has been expressed through the core area concept. Whittlesey first articulated the idea, arguing that each state 'has crystallised about a nuclear core that fostered integration' (Whittlesey, 1939, 2), though the concept has its intellectual roots in Ratzel's laws of the organic evolution of states. The political influence and control of the core area in its classic form — as in France (Ile de France) and England (London) — were extended outwards so as to consolidate an expanding periphery. This process of territorial accretion can be traced historically and usually was as much if not more due to annexation through military conquest as it was to less violent origins such as consolidation through dynastic alliance or the voluntary union of territories.

The core area concept has not been without its critics, though it retains some validity (Muir, 1975). Whittlesey's claim as it might apply to the

European state system appears to oversimplify, if not over-state, the patterns of historical evolution. In their survey of 25 European states, Pounds and Ball (1964) concluded that the theory was applicable to some 15 countries, the remainder having either been established 'instantaneously' or emerged from cores that are now peripheral to the state or lying outside the present national boundary, as in Portugal. Those states that had emerged from an internal core area were considered to 'have a higher degree of unity and cohesion than the others' (Pounds and Ball, 1964, 40). Nevertheless, the existence of states that have developed from multiple or external core areas suggests that territorial integration is to be sought along a number of paths.

The importance of the core area, as also of the other developing urban complexes within the state, stems from the role urbanization plays in mobilizing the population and in exposing it to mass forms of communication. Other aspects of the modernization process — the spread of literacy and the development of mass media, the increase in trade and of personal travel — were to have a similar effect. To Deutsch, as a leading exponent of the transactionalist school, each of these aspects is of importance because of their contribution to the increase in general social communication that was the basis of national assimilation. That is, nationality is not an inborn characteristic but one that has to be learnt through the acquisition of habits and customs. The test of nationality is whether its members are able 'to communicate more effectively and over a wider range of subjects with members of one large group than with outsiders' (Deutsch, 1966, 97). This is not simply a question of speaking the same language, as the case of Switzerland shows: 'The Swiss may speak four different languages and still act as one people, for each of them has learned habits, preferences, memories . . . all of which together permit him to communicate more effectively with other Swiss than with the speakers of his own language who belong to other peoples' (Deutsch, 1966, 97).

National integration is a slow process, though it is one that in terms of Rokkan's model can be accelerated by the centre's policies of standardization. Among these we might include those expressly aimed at improving the 'communicative efficiency' of the population, notably the adoption of a common language and the influences that can be brought to bear on the politico-territorial socialization of successive generations through the education system. There is little doubt that a common language is a powerful agent of homogenization; attempts among new states, such as Indonesia, to win popular acceptance for a 'national language' bear witness to the strongly held assumption that linguistic diversity is an impediment to integration. Thus the existence of separate languages, and even of pronounced differences of dialect, will be at odds with the ideal of the unity of the state. In France, the demand for linguistic unity was one of the clarion calls of the Revolution for, as Robespierre put it, 'Dans une

Republique une et indivisible, la langue doit être une'. Schooling was to be the means of establishing French in the regions — and in 1863 about a quarter of the population spoke no French at all, while in more than half of the departments, particularly in Brittany, southern and eastern France, the population was mainly non French-speaking — as it was also the means of teaching children national and patriotic sentiments, beginning with the national pedagogy, 'The fatherland is not your village, your province, it is all of France. The fatherland is like a great family'. These policies were to bear fruit in much of France, though in those regions where there was (and still is) a clearly identifiable ethnic group, as in Brittany, their effect was to be rather more counterproductive.

THE RE-EMERGENCE OF PERIPHERAL NATIONALISM

One of the underlying assumptions of the modernization process was that it would lead to the homogenization of societies, founded on those common values and interests that acted to promote cosmopolitanism and to reduce parochial and localist influence within the state. In the long term it would result in the replacement of the primordial group as the object of terminal loyalties by a growing identification with the more all-embracing nation-state within which conflict would become expressed in economic rather than ethnic or territorial terms. As two noted political scientists have expressed it,

> The National Revolution forced ever-widening circles of the terri-
> torial population to choose sides in conflicts over values and cultural
> identities. The Industrial Revolution also triggered a variety of
> cultural counter-movements, but in the longer run tended to cut
> across the value communities within the nation and to force the
> enfranchised citizenry to choose sides in terms of their economic
> interests . . . (Lipset and Rokkan, 1967, 18)

Though the re-emergence of peripheral nationalism took the academic world, and particularly the sociologists and political scientists, by surprise, it would be wrong to suggest that, spatially, the homogenization effects of modernization would be universally apparent within the state. Under certain conditions it was recognized that regional differences may not be eliminated. Thus in Lipset and Rokkan's three-stage model of nation-building, which begins with the attempts by the centre to penetrate and standardize the periphery, the second and third stages are devoted to the establishment and cementing of political, social and economic links between and within each of the regions. Where these are developed inter-regionally, their effect will be to reduce regional particularism, but intraregionally, particularly where these links are superimposed on ethnic, linguistic, religious and/or economic differences, their influence can be to reinforce regional distinctiveness.

The term 'peripheral nationalism' requires brief explanation. Much as there has been confusion with the terms 'state' and 'nation', so have the nationalist movements as they have recently developed in areas such as Brittany, Catalonia and Scotland been variously described as examples of 'regionalism', 'sub-national loyalties' and 'ethnic pluralism'. Connor (1977) criticizes the use of such terms because of their failure to recognize the movements as being ethnic and nationalist, with the implication that they are not comparable to those movements seeking their own state apparatus that had led to the formation of countries such as Germany and Italy in the previous century. The use of the term 'regionalism' is to be especially deprecated not only because of its probable interpretation as a sectionalist movement, as found in the federal country, the salience of which will be reduced as modernization proceeds, but also because it assumes loyalty to a territorially larger unit of government.

Peripheral nationalism is to be associated with movements that have nationalist aspirations though equally in many cases it is to be linked to demands for greater regional autonomy rather than total secession and independence. We might view such movements as cases of 'regional nationalism', a term that combines the different kinds of autonomy that they generally incorporate. Furthermore, viewed from the centre, particularly where the central government's objectives are territorial integration and the assimilation of minorities, the nationalist movement is a regional phenomenon, to be accommodated by at most some measure of greater local autonomy. Nor as we have implied is it necessarily clear that such movements have mobilized mass support for independence, but rather for winning greater autonomy 'without sacrificing some of the benefits [of membership] of the larger system' (Enloe, 1974, 84). Figure 3.2 indicates the major cases of peripheral nationalism within Western Europe. Nationalism is politically salient when there are active political parties representing the ethno-territorial units and when the politics of the area is an active item on the national political agenda. Irredentist movements arise where a region is severed from an adjacent unit and reunification is actively sought by political activists.

Assessing national integration

The persistence of peripheral nationalism is evidence of the malintegration of the state (C. Williams, 1981). It implies that some regions are more fully integrated than are others, though this begs the question as to the kinds of criteria by which integration is to be assessed. Three major types of integrative factor are commonly recognized, measuring cultural, economic and political variables. Though capable of separate analysis, these are of greater significance to peripheral nationalism because of their inter-relationships: demands for greater regional autonomy stem from the interplay of cultural and/or economic variables in turn influencing the level of political integration.

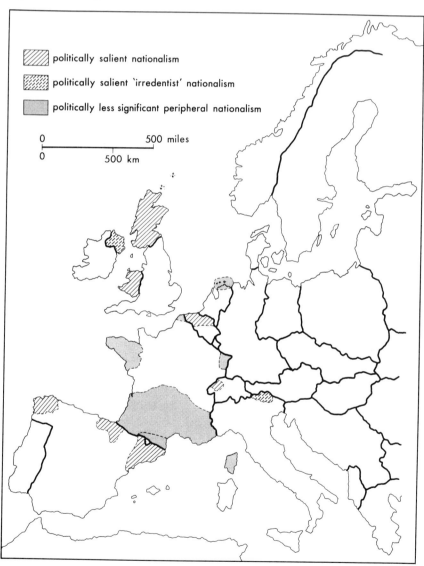

FIGURE 3.2   Peripheral nationalism in Western Europe
(adapted from Esman, 1977)

Cultural integration Since one of the tests of national integration is the extent to which a shared national identity is commonly subscribed to, culturally based differences that give rise to their own internal sets of loyalties are potentially divisive. Chief among these cultural factors are those associated with religion, or language or some other basis that helps support an ethnic group, membership of which gives the individual a value system that he will use to orientate himself to the wider national society. The impact of cultural divisions on political outlook is amply illustrated in Northern Ireland where 'national orientation' is closely correlated with religion. Hence of the three main identities, in which individual respondents 'thought of themselves' as either British, Irish or Ulster, Protestants were divided 39 per cent, 20 per cent and 32 per cent and Catholics 15 per cent, 76 per cent and 5 per cent respectively (R. Rose, 1971).

It is because of the salience of ethnicity that peripheral nationalism has been alternatively labelled ethno-nationalism. The accuracy of this can be examined by comparing ethnic diversity between countries and the demands for autonomy or secession (C. Williams, 1980). Kosinski (1970) devised an index of ethnic diversity within European countries on the basis of the size of the ethnic group(s) relative to the total population of the country. Taking only the non-federal countries of Western Europe (and excluding cases where guarantees of autonomy have been agreed through the federacy, as for the Swedish-speaking population of the Aaland Islands belonging to Finland), the average ethnic diversity score for states in which regional autonomy has been an issue is more than one-third greater than the score for those not so affected (table 3.1).

TABLE 3.1   Ethnic diversity and regional autonomy

	Average ethnic diversity score[1]	Countries
Regional autonomy an issue	66%	Belgium, Italy, France, Spain, UK
Regional autonomy unimportant or irrelevant	91%	Denmark, Finland, Holland, Iceland, Luxembourg, Norway, Sweden

[1] The smaller the percentage value, the more diverse is the population of the state.
Source: Adapted from data in Kosinski (1970)

The existence of separate ethnic groups within the state is not necessarily to be equated with ethno-nationalism. As a great many cases show, it is possible for the ethnic group to retain its identity, through its own internal system of loyalties, while simultaneously paying tribute to the state as the overriding authority. Ethnicity is not converted into nationalism until the group popularly demands it be a separate self-governing nation in its own right. It is with this qualification that table 3.2 should be read, recognizing that the figures for Scotland and Wales are indicative of the malintegration of the UK from the viewpoint of establishing a common national identity as a primary source of allegiance rather than an accurate predictor of ethno-nationalist potential.

TABLE 3.2   Territorial identities in the United Kingdom

Think of self firstly as:	Scotland (Glasgow) %	Wales %	Northern Ireland %
British	29	15	29
Scottish	67	1	—
Welsh	1	69	—
English	—	13	—
Ulster	*	*	21
Irish	*	*	43
Other	4	—	7

* Alternative not offered.
Source: Adapted from R. Rose (1970)

Economic integration   National economic integration is achieved once there are substantially comparable levels of social and economic development apparent between all the regions of the state. At one level it assumes that, as the developed economy brings in train regional specialization, each region interacts with others, is interdependent with them, though to varying degrees. But economic integration also assumes that each individual region enjoys roughly similar benefits from membership of the national economy, measurable through such indices as *per capita* income, the consumption of goods and services, mortality rates, the incidence of unemployment and the proportion employed in 'declining industries'. It is widely recognized that the benefits of economic development are not spread evenly. We shall discuss the implications of this later in the analysis of centre and periphery, but they have been linked to the development of nationalism (Orridge, 1981). *Per capita* income can suffice as an approximate measure of economic integration, which, as the case of Italy demonstrates (figure 3.3), can reveal large variation between the most and least prosperous regions. Italy is one of the more extreme cases of uneven development, though elsewhere in Europe it is not uncommon for personal incomes in affluent regions to be up to 40 per cent higher than those in poorer areas.

Even if we restrict our attention to levels of interaction, it is usually the case that some regions are more intensively integrated into the national economy than are others. Inter-regional freight traffic flows give a measure of this interaction. In the case of commercial road traffic in Britain, it can

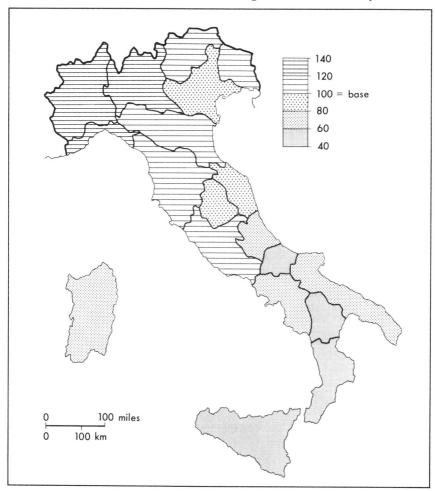

FIGURE 3.3 *Per capita* incomes in the Italian regions, 1975
(Italy=100)

be seen from table 3.3 that some regions are more connected with other regions. With the exception of the South East (whose statistic may be the result of the effects of size on economic diversification, which in turn influenced the amount of intra-regional traffic), those interacting less are located more peripherally.

Political integration   National political integration is linked with the extent to which social class is *the* basis of political conflict. Though other factors are cleavage-forming — notably religion, ethnic differences, regional

TABLE 3.3   Proportion of inter-regional to intra-regional freight traffic, Britain: 1967–68 (%)

East Midlands	49.4	Yorkshire and Humberside	27.0
East Anglia	39.0	Northern	18.9
West Midlands	32.8	South West	17.7
Wales	28.0	South East	15.6
North West	27.0	Scotland	6.0

Source: Calculated from data derived from Department of the Environment (1972)

interests, urban and rural groups around which political parties will emerge — in the integrated homogeneous polity these have been effectively superseded by conflicts stemming from the differences in the distribution of wealth between classes. For our purpose the significant point is that the defence of territorial interests, and hence of areal differences, will lessen and be replaced by class conflict. We can begin to test the truth of this by looking at two kinds of data measuring the opinions of individuals directly and their preferences in the aggregate through electoral statistics.

Within the politically integrated nation, differences of social class between individuals should overrule those of regional association. Budge and Urwin (1966) have tested the thesis of British political homogeneity, in part by asking electors within a Scottish (Glasgow) constituency whether they feel 'they have more in common' with those of a different class or the same class living elsewhere in Scotland or in England (table 3.4). The results were not unequivocal, though the authors claimed that national consciousness 'is just as widespread as class feeling among Glasgow electors' (Budge and Urwin, 1966, 119). The findings from the Craigton survey, which were confirmed in a follow-up study elsewhere in the city, belie the idea that Britain is politically homogeneous though the extent to which territorial identities override or equal those of class elsewhere is more problematic. There is some evidence to suggest that regional differences between north and south within England would be apparent for the same type of question; in arising between areas with a similar nationality, this is a more acid test of homogeneity.

Electoral data provide a more comprehensive picture through which to examine national political integration. Several types of question are pertinent: the measurement of regional variations in the support for national political parties, the relative contribution of class as a factor influencing voting choice and the existence and role of specifically regional parties.

In a comparative survey, Rose and Urwin (1970) used two measures to assess the territorial pattern of support for national political parties: the standard deviation of regional patterns of support for each party and a 'cumulative regional inequality index' computed as the difference, in

TABLE 3.4   Persons with whom Scottish electors feel they have most in common, Craigton (Glasgow)

	Second choice[1]	
Choice of persons	*N*	*%*
Scottish same class	4	2
Scottish different class	50	27
English same class	61	32
English different class	4	2
No preference/D.K.	67	37

[1] First choice not tabulated because of its domination by 'Scottish same class'.
Source: Adapted from Budge and Urwin (1966)

percentage terms, in a party's support and all voting preferences in the area. Two elections were analysed, one near to 1945 and the other to 1970. Table 3.5 summarizes the results for some of the countries analysed by Rose and Urwin. One drawback of the survey is that, because the sizes of the regions used in the analysis vary so greatly, it is not possible to draw meaningful conclusions comparing the experience of countries. Within individual countries the change recorded is slight — possibly because the analysis is looking at the latter part of a process spread over a much longer time-span — though where changes are apparent this is more often associated with the reduced importance of regional variations.

Though the underlying trend apparent in Rose and Urwin's analysis was towards the nationalization of voting support, it is not necessarily a simple, unilinear progression. A succession of national elections in which the territorial factor steadily diminishes can be followed by one in which it takes on renewed importance. The results of the 1979 general election in Britain, in which the swing to the Conservative party was substantially higher in 'Southern Britain' (figure 3.4), re-emphasized the split between north and south. Of the 339 seats gained by the Conservatives, no fewer than 261 belonged to the southern half of England (the standard regions of the South East, East Anglia, South West, the East and West Midlands) together with Wales; in a comparable result in 1955, in which the party gained 334 seats in all, some 223 were in this area.

In effect the 1979 election gave renewed emphasis to a pattern that, as Hechter (1975) has shown, has been a more or less consistent feature of British elections since the latter part of the nineteenth century. Hechter looked at eight elections between 1885 and 1966 and regressed the Conservative vote (within each county) against seven variables measuring the level of industrialization. (The Conservative party vote was analysed because of that party's traditional stance against regional autonomy and its strong association with the core area of South East England.) The persistently anti-Conservative areas were concentrated in the nationalist

TABLE 3.5 Regional differences in party voting (%)

		Mean standard deviation in party vote	Mean cumulative regional inequality index
Anglo-America:			
Australia	1946	6.7	0.09
	1972	4.4	0.16
Canada	1945	11.6	0.36
	1972	9.4	0.27
New Zealand	1946	4.5	0.04
	1972	5.7	0.07
UK	1945	7.7	0.09
	1970	5.7	0.43
USA	1946	20.3	0.05
	1972	10.4	0.05
Scandinavia:			
Denmark	1945	6.4	0.20
	1971	4.3	0.12
Finland	1945	6.2	0.22
	1970	5.8	0.24
Norway	1945	9.0	0.24
	1969	8.7	0.21
Sweden	1944	5.6	0.15
	1970	4.3	0.12
Continental Europe:			
Belgium	1946	8.8	0.14
	1971	7.3	0.25
France	1946	6.9	0.13
	1973	5.5	0.10
Italy	1946	6.1	0.28
	1972	5.1	0.12

Source: Adapted from Rose and Urwin (1975)

homelands and in a number of peripheral regions within England, an overall distribution (with the major exception of Wales) that bears close correspondence to the 1979 election.

The existence of regional political parties provides the most overt evidence of national political malintegration. Such parties are by definition tied to a territory embracing only part of the state, their objectives being generally to mobilize support across class lines and to win concessions, including autonomy or the right to secede, from the state. Electorally their importance varies; of the parties listed in table 3.6, the Slesvig party in Denmark is of relatively minor significance, while in Belgium the first two parties listed have traditionally gained the lion's share of the total representation, which has underlain the pattern of chronic instability that has characterized the national coalition governments.

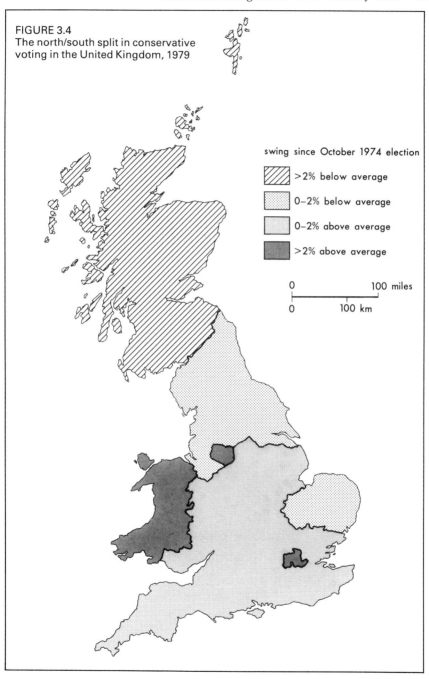

FIGURE 3.4
The north/south split in conservative
voting in the United Kingdom, 1979

swing since October 1974 election

>2% below average

0–2% below average

0–2% above average

>2% above average

0   100 miles

0   100 km

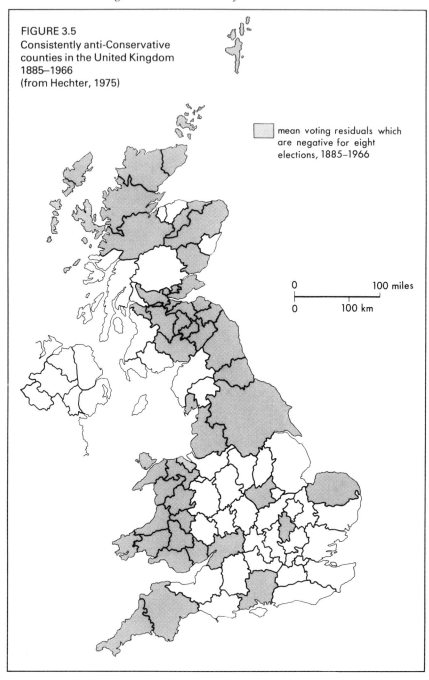

FIGURE 3.5
Consistently anti-Conservative
counties in the United Kingdom
1885–1966
(from Hechter, 1975)

mean voting residuals which
are negative for eight
elections, 1885–1966

0   100 miles

0   100 km

TABLE 3.6   Electorally active regional political parties in non-federal West European
states, 1980

State	Parties
Belgium	Volksunie (Flemish), Rassemblement Wallon, Front Democratique des Francophones
Denmark	Slesvig party
Finland	Svenska Folkpartiet
Italy	Union Valdotaine, Sudtiroler Volkspartei
Spain	Partido Nacionalista Vasco (Basque), Galician nationalists, Catalan nationalists
United Kingdom	Scottish Nationalist Party, Plaid Cymru (Wales), Irish nationalist parties (Northern Ireland)

Defining and identifying centre and periphery

The distinction between a centre (or core) and a periphery has been a
device widely employed in the social sciences to analyse the relationships
between two types of unit. To the political geographer the model's
importance is in its use to examine the relationships between sovereign
states and between constituent areas making up the state. More specifically
from the viewpoint of national integration and disintegration, the model
can help in explaining peripheral reaction to political domination. This
involves two related aspects: the economic and the cultural domination of
the periphery by the centre. We shall discuss the former in this section,
leaving the question of cultural domination to the next section.

The articulation of the centre–periphery model is not easy, requiring as
it does an exposition of the nature of the relationships and the linking of
these to a spatial framework (McKenzie, 1977). It is possible to define
centre and periphery in aspatial terms, the centre being equated with
particular social groups that constitute, or are close to, decision-making
elites. Galtung (1971) introduces space more explicitly in defining the
periphery as an area geographically distanced from the centre where
administrative, cultural or economic power resides. In other words, the
centre is a decision-making nucleus separated from the periphery, which is
(or thinks of itself as) remote from the decision-makers. One of the
defining features of the relationship is the idea of the domination of the
periphery; another is the concept of dependence upon the centre.

Relations of dominance and dependence are not restricted to their
political forms, but include social and economic dimensions. Galtung's
model is global, representing an interlocking set of inter- and intra-national
sub-systems of centre and periphery that form an integrated network of
dominance and dependence across and within national borders. The
imperialist relations between centre and periphery, basically those of

exploitation, are broken down into five types — economic, military, political, cultural and communicational — each denoting different modes of unequal exchange between centre and periphery.

Naustdalslid (1977) examines economic imperialism, the basic mode, using measures similar to those of Galtung but with the specific objective of defining centre and periphery at the intra-national level, based on Norway. Eight variables are analysed, measuring four dimensions:

1. Development — gross regional product *per capita* and the percentage employment in non-primary sectors.
2. Regional wellbeing — average *per capita* income and the levels of private consumption of goods and services.
3. The 'vertical interaction structure' — a measure of the unequal exchange characteristic of a colonial relationship, the periphery exporting raw materials and/or goods that are in a semi-processed state while importing processed goods. Measurement of this factor is difficult and was attempted through the index of economic asymmetry relating to the inter-regional pattern of import and export of goods classified according to sector and degree of processing. The rate of out-migration was also incorporated as a measure of verticality.
4. The 'feudal interaction structure' — the extent to which interactions between territorial areas are mediated through the centre and consequently can be controlled by it. This was measured by the degree of industrial concentration (the location of the country's 500 largest firms) and of industrial specialization. The more diversified the unit, the more it occupies a central location.

The analysis confirms the importance of the Oslo region as the national centre, which, together with secondary foci associated with the major urban centres (Bergen, Trondheim and Stavanger), economically dominates a periphery that is represented most visibly in northern Norway as well as the 'exclave' county of Sogn og Fjordane (see figure 3.6).

Regional economic disparities are a universally acknowledged feature of the process of development. They are probably more pronounced within the earlier stages of industrialization when for several reasons — the localization of key resources, the advantages of scale economies, and the restricted amount of surplus income available for investment — development is usually associated with a few, specific localities. According to Myrdal (1957), development subsequently spreads to other areas from the leading region, which nevertheless is able to retain its status because of backwash effects; where spread effects are strong enough in the other regions, growth will be sufficient to lead towards greater regional economic convergence. This was empirically tested by Williamson (1965), though only one country (the United States) had sufficient historical data to provide an adequate basis for testing. The evidence from the USA did

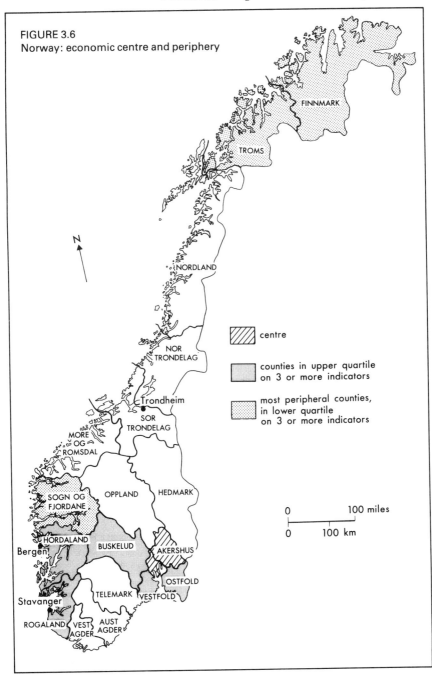

FIGURE 3.6
Norway: economic centre and periphery

provide some support for the convergence thesis, though regional disparities do remain and, as we shall see in the next chapter, are a salient feature
of the politics of the federation. Overall, regional scientists assume that,
even if regional economic equilibrium is an attainable goal, this is only
likely with the active intervention of the state and over the long term.

Long-term convergence is an important feature from our viewpoint in
that it would reduce the significance of centre and periphery as economically disparate entities. There is a counter-argument, however, that a
system of regional stratification, as encapsulated in the core–periphery
distinction, is an inevitable and lasting outcome of industrial capitalism and
its interaction with the class system. In general terms this could be
expressed as the result of 'a social class structure — which cuts across
regions — consisting of particular kinds of relations between people, their
organizations, and institutions [which] create regional disparities in wealth
and movements of people' (Cuneo, 1978, 132). The interaction between
the class structure and the capitalist mode of production, which results in
the regional concentration of large corporate businesses, forms the crucial
first stage in the process. This will mean that the head offices of the large
corporations will be concentrated in the centre, which consequently will
contain a disproportionate share of the 'capitalist class' — those owning
or effectively controlling the means of production. Because 'big business' is
able to offer higher wages, income disparities between regions result and
will be popularly incorporated into perceptions of relative wealth and
power, in turn stimulating inter-provincial migration (see figure 3.7).

This represents only a brief sketch of Cuneo's argument, though it
suggests a number of 'indicators' by which we can begin to identify centre
and periphery. These would include data on the proportionate importance
of large-scale industry within the region, *per capita* incomes, social class
structure, inter-regional migration rates and the perception of power
disparities between regions. In Canada (see chapter 4), such data
suggested three types of area — centre (Ontario), periphery (Atlantic
provinces, Saskatchewan and Manitoba) and semi-periphery (British
Columbia, Alberta, Quebec), the latter being an intermediate type of unit
that is more similar in make-up to the core than to the periphery. Applied
to the United Kingdom, the model would favour a similar three-fold
division. Regions such as Scotland and the North of England, and, in a
number of respects, South West England, are peripheral in character,
while the English Midlands is more semi-peripheral. The South East of
England (London and the Home Counties) constitutes the core. It is in that
region where *per capita* incomes are highest and where economic control is
located. The large number of company headquarters and the skewed social
class structure of the region (the South East has a disproportionate number
of households in the professional and managerial classes) are indicative
of this. Within the present century the region has acted as a major

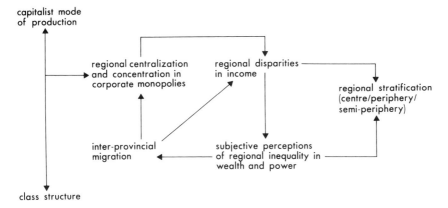

FIGURE 3.7   A class model of regionalism
(adapted from Cuneo, 1978)

magnet for in-migration. As table 3.7 shows, there is some association
between these economic disparities and popular attitudes to the centralization of power. As with several of the other measures, there is a clear
gradational effect with distance from the core, though it is only in Scotland
that a majority feel that government is over-centralized.

TABLE 3.7   Opinions on the centralization of government in London[1]

	London/ SE	Midlands	North	South West[2]	Cornwall[3]	Wales	Scotland
Content	72	65	52	57	N.A.	52	26
Too centralized	21	29	45	37	58	38	65
Don't know	7	6	5	6	N.A.	7	9

[1] Question: 'Some people think that government is much too centralized in London.
Others are quite content with things as they are. What do you think?' From Butler and
Stokes (1974).
[2] South West includes Cornwall.
[3] Cornwall question: 'Do you think government is too centralized in London?' From
British Election Survey quoted in Rallings and Lee (1977).

Internal colonialism

Our analysis of centre and periphery has been couched mainly in economic
terms. Because demands for regional autonomy have arisen in the main
from ethnic minority groups within the state, what is lacking is the
inclusion of the specifically cultural dimension. The internal colonial
model, particularly as it has been developed by Hechter (1975), is an

attempt to explain resurgent ethnic minority nationalism by specifically arguing that this is a reactive mechanism to cultural and economic domination by a core group. In contrast, then, with diffusionist explanations of integration, which were discussed earlier in the chapter, the internal colonial model actually predicts the occurrence of peripheral nationalism.

The basic argument of the model is that a cultural system of stratification overlies the more characteristic economic configuration of classes. Cultural domination arises because, in the process of modernization, certain areas and groups, as the result of some advantage, become more advanced and are able to use this to establish their economic and political superiority. Efforts by the core group to maintain their status will lead them to subordinate minority groups within a cultural division of labour. The outcome will be apparent not only in the overall economic structure of the peripheral ethnic areas but also, more specifically, in the occupations of the minority group members, as indeed in their general wellbeing. In other words, the economic differences between centre and periphery can be causally linked to the cultural differences between core and periphery groups (Hechter, 1975).

Hechter's own examination of the model was drawn from the experience of the British Isles, in which the English ruling class acts as the central ruling elite subordinating the peripheral nations of Wales, Ireland and Scotland. If the colonial analogy is to have any currency, processes similar to those apparent within the standard colonial relationship should obtain in these 'internal' cases. These will include economic exploitation to fit the needs of the metropolitan core, exploitation of periphery workers and chronic patterns of out-migration from the colony (G. Williams, 1978). Industrial development in the periphery, where it is allowed to develop, will basically serve the needs of the core regions; in this sense dependence is likely to be characterized by greater economic specialization in the periphery, whereas the core will enjoy a diversified economic base. As a theory concerned with the exploitation of the periphery by a core region, its relevance varies with different parts of the British Isles. It is probably most applicable to Ireland, which, apart from the industrial enclave around the Lagan valley, remained economically backward and largely non-industrialized, besides being subjected to a series of measures emphasizing the cultural superiority of the core group. Chief among these were the Penal Laws and the attempt to prohibit the use of the Irish language, a policy that also, however, applied to Wales. Their effect was to reduce the popular usage of the minority languages, though it might be more precise to argue that they accelerated a process that would have occurred as a result of the influence of modernization. Applied to the cases of Wales and Scotland the evidence is somewhat contradictory. In Scotland the industrial economy suffers from a number of structural weaknesses, having a disproportionate share of declining industries, though, as Brown (1972) showed, its economy is less specialized than are a number of the economies of English regions. Furthermore, the economic malaise suffered in Scotland (and Wales) is shared by some of the English regions.

It may be that the internal colonial model is more applicable in some countries than in others. Reece (1979) has presented an impressive list of factors supporting the model's application in the case of Brittany. This includes:

1. the cultural domination of the Bretons by the French following the annexation of the area in 1532 but particularly after the Revolution. Cultural superiority is a pervasive force, furthermore; it is evidenced not only in the language policy but also in stereotype images Frenchmen have of the Breton.
2. coincidence of ethnic and class stratification, with the effect that Bretons are relatively unrepresented within the top executive and public service posts. Similarly, Bretons 'forced' to migrate to the metropolis occupy distinct residential zones and are found more often in low-status occupations.
3. the use of regional planning by the centre as a sop to the region. Thus public monies are more often devoted to less labour-intensive projects such as tourism, military bases and nuclear power stations.
4. the lack of a network of urban centres serving the interior of the region ('Breton cities . . . serve as way-stations for the movement of primary products . . . to metropolitan France' — Reece, 1979, 284) and the lack of a railway network properly serving the region. That is, the two arms of the rail network facilitate inter-regional traffic, and especially traffic with the metropolis, more than they do communication within the region itself.
5. the traditional under-representation of the region at ministerial level in the national government.

By comparison with the English, the French have been traditionally less tolerant of regional, and ethnic, diversity so that the colonial analogy may be more apposite in France. The overriding importance attached to the state as an indivisible entity led Hayward (1973) to describe it as a 'state-nation' rather than a nation-state. According to Arnaud (1979), in the state-nation it is the *French* nation that has become the focus, leading inevitably to the oppression of national minority non-conformist groups, such as the 13 million Occitanians in the southern part of the country.

As a means of explaining peripheral nationalism, the internal colonial model has been subject to considerable criticism (Page, 1978; Kolinsky, 1978; Lovering, 1978a). Among the problems of the model we can single out the following:

1. The meaning of the concept 'cultural division of labour' is left somewhat loose so that it is only at the expense of spatial generalization that the colony can be identified. As Day (1980) suggests in the case of Wales, Hechter's arguments would be more appropriate for rural 'Welsh' Wales than they are for the industrial and mining areas of the south.

2. Hechter's core group is defined simply by England in its relations successively with Scotland, Wales and Ireland. This conceals the variations apparent within England; for example, the economic disabilities of the periphery are also shared by parts of the core, notably Northern England.

3. Lovering (1978b) criticizes the model for the ambiguity with which the term exploitation is used — that is, who is exploiting whom? (In this sense the analysis has anthropomorphized the political territory, in that it conceals the dominant and dependent groups.)

While these criticisms are directed at the analytic rigour of internal colonialism, radical critics of the model would not dispute that the reasons for peripheral nationalism are rooted in the uneven development of industrial societies and in the systems of class relations and patterns of dominance with these. A. D. Smith (1981), however, criticizes the importance attached to economic advantage and disadvantage in the model, which are seen to follow inevitably from the ethnic group's occupation of a particular space within the national territory: 'such a "territorial reductionism" fails to do justice to that other crucial variable, history, with all its cultural attributes' (Smith, 1981, 35).

These criticisms by no means exhaust the problems identified with the internal colonial model: we have not, for example, specifically mentioned the question of Spain, where Basque and Catalan nationalism is unexplained by the analysis, and only partly explained by a subsequent modification by Hechter and Levi (1979). Nevertheless, the emotiveness of the colonial analogy, however true in reality, has mobilizing potential among peripheral nations. Thus, 'when social differences in the periphery are clearly associated with cultural differences the disadvantaged group will . . . react by asserting its own culture is equal to, or superior to that of the dominant core. Once this occurs it is easy for the disadvantaged group to think of itself as a nation . . .' (G. Williams, 1978, 63).

Relative deprivation

Images of reality — that is, a belief that central control has been relatively disadvantageous to the region's prosperity — rather than objectively defined reality, underlie the feelings people have of relative deprivation which, in turn, help explain the demands for greater local autonomy. The concept of relative deprivation itself is not without ambiguity: Is relative deprivation to be gauged in economic, political, cultural or status terms? How is it to be assessed given the difficulty of objective definition? Evidence from the Kilbrandon Commission (Commission on the Constitution, 1973a, b) suggests that peripheral areas within the UK do feel themselves to be deprived economically, though more in some regions than in others (see table 3.8).

TABLE 3.8   Subjective and objective measures of regional inequalities

Region	*% feeling that region was well off financially[1]*	*Relative GDP/cap. (% of UK figure)*	*Beneficial government expenditures minus tax receipts (£/cap.)[2]*	*Central government expenditures on local services/cap. (% of English total)[3]*
South East	76	113	−39	96
West Midlands	67	109	−22	93
Yorkshire and Humberside	55	99	+13	100
North West	48	98	+5	107
East Midlands	62	98	+14	92
South West	25	88	+25	95
East Anglia	34	87	+37	96
North	19	85	+31	133
Wales	24	88	+45	130
Scotland	22	86	+32	133

[1]   Question: 'Compared to other parts of Britain would you describe your region as well off financially?'
[2]   Data for 1964.
[3]   Data for 1968–69.
Source: Commission on the Constitution (1973a, b)

Because the feeling of being relatively deprived is a subjective assessment, the perceived economic relations are important even though they may in fact be erroneous. Home Rulers will claim that membership of the larger political union is inequitable in that there is a mismatch between revenues raised from the region and the amount returned from the central exchequer. Such was the basis of a long-standing debate between the Scottish nationalists and the UK government, the argument that, when put at its simplest, Scotland was subsidizing England. The evidence indicates that the reverse is true: Scotland, together with a number of other regions, is effectively subsidized by the more affluent regions. Furthermore, *per capita* expenditure on social and educational services and physical infrastructure is in nearly every case higher in Scotland than in England. Nevertheless, because of the obvious differences in regional economic prosperity, especially in unemployment, it was easy for the nationalists to present a convincing argument, particularly with the emergence of North Sea oil as an electoral issue in the 1970s. Thus in an electoral pamphlet the nationalist party argued: 'England expects Scottish oil to help pay for the third London airport and new city of Maplin (£2,000 million), the Channel Tunnel (£800 million) . . . These projects damage the Scottish economy by concentrating even more jobs and prosperity in the south of England.'

Whatever the truth of the situation, the argument was a persuasive one in electoral terms — in the October election of 1974 the nationalist party gained its highest ever number of seats in Parliament. The expectation of economic gain is a powerful stimulant to separatism, though, equally, the fear that secession could lead to a decline in living standards reduces the demands for separatism. In the Kilbrandon Commission survey (UK), only 10 per cent wanted devolution when this meant that the 'region would be worse off than now' compared to a figure of 55 per cent were economic conditions not to deteriorate.

Though it is necessary to approach the concept of relative deprivation with a certain amount of caution, the importance of the idea stems from the possibility it harbours for generating conflict. Gurr (1970) has developed a general model of conflict in which he argues that relative deprivation leads to frustration, which in turn fuels discontent and results in violence; in extreme cases this could lead to demands for territorial secession. This is only likely where the feeling of relative deprivation is widely felt among a territorially distinct population. But one of the problems for the political elites in the peripheral regions will be to mobilize broad support across individual sub-regions as well as across class divisions. Just as there will be interpersonal differences in relative deprivation, so it is likely that deprivation is more keenly felt in certain areas than in others. These territorial differences, combined with different perceptions of what devolution will mean economically for the locality, generate cleavages within the periphery, as we shall see in the case of Scotland.

Alternative configurations

One of the striking features of the map of peripheral nationalist move-ments in Western Europe is their variation in political salience. (For a historically based explanation of these differences see Orridge and Williams, 1982.) France contrasts with Spain, where peripheral national-ism has been a major factor in the politics of the state in the post-Franco period, while the United Kingdom occupies a 'median' position, in terms both of the importance of the periphery within the overall politics of the state and of the responses of the state to it. These differences between countries are in some cases replicated within them: in Spain the three main peripheral nationalisms are in the Basque, Catalan and Galician regions, but it is in the first two that the political movements have been the more active and significant to the state. Indeed, because of the continuing violence in the Basque region it is in that area that the problem is most acute.

Part of the explanation for these differences can be attributed to spatial variations in the distribution of political and economic power within the state. Gourevitch (1979; 1980) has argued that whether peripheral nationalism becomes politically salient depends on the degree of congruence between the areas most important for the political leadership of the state and for its economic development.

> Where both political leadership and economic dynamism take place in the same region . . . peripheral nationalism is weak . . . but where [they] take place in different regions, one of which has ethnic potential (acting as the homeland for an ethnically distinct population), the latter region is likely to develop strong, politically relevant nationalism. (Gourevitch, 1979, 306)

Such a development is more likely where the 'original economic or political core' stops providing political leadership or fuelling economic growth to the extent that it had, or where the ethnic core's economic base has been given a fillip because of the development of new resources.

Gourevitch's analysis represents a major extension of the core area model. As Pounds and Ball (1964) suggest, territorial unity is to be linked to the idea of a strong core providing, in Gourevitch's terms, both political and economic leadership. France is the most clear-cut example; none of the regions with which economic dynamism has been shared, notably the North and Lyons areas, had ethnic potential. The major region with ethnic potential, Brittany, has been consistently peripheral both politically and economically and therefore lacks a sufficient power base (see Clark's model, figure 2.8). This offers a stark comparison with the case of Spain where the Basque and Catalan regions were the first to industrialize and remain among the more economically dynamic areas of the state, while Castile has acted as the political core.

These spatial patterns of political and economic leadership can change and it is as a result of these variations that peripheral nationalism can re-emerge as a significant force. The relationships between Scotland and England provide an example. During the nineteenth century and for much of the first half of the present century, England supplied both political and economic leadership; because Scotland too enjoyed a measure of the economic prosperity, nationalist feeling was at a low ebb. After 1945, however, England was seen to decline as a major industrial and imperial power, which eroded its powers of leadership. Its economic decline meant that it was in that much weaker a position to tackle the problems of the Scottish economy, which by the inter-war period had begun to show signs of serious structural deficiencies. This change in England's relative status coincided with the discovery of North Sea oil (in the late 1960s), which altered the economic balance between the two countries.

As political power, or the demand for it, tends to follow from economic power, shifts in the relative economic status of the core and periphery will bring in their train shifts in the political balance of the two types of unit. Changes of regional economic status are not uncommon in industrial societies and are brought about by a combination of factors — the depletion of resources underlying the growth of regions that were early to undergo industrialization, the loss of demand for the products of such regions, and the growing attractiveness of other areas for newer types of industry spurred on, perhaps, by the development of new resources. In Belgium, the growth since 1945 of Flemish nationalism fits the general model. The economic decline of Wallonia and the industrial growth in Flanders could be defined in Friedmann's (1966) typology as 'downward' and 'upward transitional areas' respectively. The downward transitional area is characteristic of older, established regions, with declining economies, high rates of unemployment, obsolete industrial plant; the area has to adjust to these problems by reducing the intensity of economic activity. The upward transitional area, by contrast, is a zone of rapid economic growth attracting large flows of capital. These descriptions broadly relate to Belgium since 1945, though it is because the upward transitional area has ethnic potential that the political balance between the two linguistic groups has been altered, leading to demands for the 'federalization' of the country.

ACTION AND REACTION IN CENTRE–PERIPHERY POLITICS

According to the systems approach, a political system adapts to changes in its operating environment because the price of failing to adapt will be an erosion of the system's stability. One method of examining the sequence of events linking centre and periphery is within the action–reaction framework suggested by the systems model. That is, changes within the environment — the voicing of peripheral discontent — stimulate reaction by the centre that, depending upon its response, will to a greater or lesser extent placate the periphery.

Periphery options: exit, voice and loyalty

Though some exceptions have been noted, our analysis has suggested that peripheral nationalism is more likely in areas that are less economically advanced or, in Friedmann's terms, are downward transitional areas. If it is a characteristic of such areas that they suffer from chronic unemployment (or underemployment) and experience in other ways a measurably lower standard of living than other regions, then one of the typical responses has been out-migration. This is not the only response, however, that is available to the periphery.

The exit, voice and loyalty model of Hirschmann (1970) provides an instructive framework within which to examine the interaction of centre and periphery. Hirschmann's model sought to examine the behavioural responses of consumers to the decline of organizations supplying goods and services. A decline in quality could provoke one of two actions: either the consumer could employ the 'exit' option, transferring his custom elsewhere, or he could 'voice' his discontent, hoping that the quality of the product might improve at some future date. Loyalty operates as an intervening variable: presumably because of their favourable past experience with the product and/or because of inertia, consumers have a certain loyalty to the organization, which, however, they may well use as a bargaining tool to gain concessions.

Firn (1978) has adapted the exit–voice model to the example of Scotland. Though Hirschmann has applied his model to the state, its application to an issue such as devolution is more complex than examining the responses to the decline of a single commercial organization. Governments are responsible for a whole bundle of services (including organizations such as bus companies or a single-product industry) some of which are tangible, while others, no less important, provide the citizen with moral or cultural support. Applying the model also assumes that it is possible to identify the level(s) of government responsible for the decline in quality; though in practice it should be difficult to make an accurate identification, because of the overlapping and sharing of responsibilities between national and sub-national governments, in popular currency the 'offending' organization is the UK government.

Traditionally the response of the Scots has been out-migration — the exit option. The response of the central government has been to treat the problem as one of regional economic management, offering a package of incentives to encourage industry to establish itself in such areas. The apparent inability of the central government to solve the problems of the Scottish economy helps to explain the switch in behaviour to the voicing of discontent transmitted through electoral support for the nationalist party. Such voting is to be associated, however, less with the demand for territorial separatism than with dissatisfaction with the two major parties, Labour and Conservative, both of which are clearly identifiable as 'centre' parties. Though the nationalist vote does not indicate any strong or irreversible slide towards secession (the 1979 general election saw a reduction in the number of nationalist-held constituencies from 11 to two), it represents a strong voice of peripheral discontent to which the centre needs to respond.

Centre responses

There are several strategies by which the central government can meet peripheral demands for regional autonomy (Lerner, 1966). Providing no threat is posed to the centre's existence, it can ignore the periphery and emphasize the essential unity of the state. Alternatively, recognizing the cultural and other differences between itself and the periphery, the centre can actively promote, or at least tolerate, such differences. This method would encourage 'territorial pluralism', and the one condition limiting application of this second alternative would again be that the status of the centre should not be threatened. If it were, 'dissidence reduction' would be a relevant option to ensure the territorial integrity of the larger unit. Physical coercion can harbour within it the seeds of further violence; at the very least it will raise the question of the legitimacy of the centre's authority in the periphery.

What responses the centre makes will depend upon the nature of the periphery's demands. If these are separatist the conflict is a zero-sum game. If, on the other hand, the demands are for something short of total separation, a gain for one party does not necessarily dictate a loss for the other and bargaining is possible. Recognition of the peripheral demands for what they are — which might vary from a loose territorial pressure group through to a movement demanding greater autonomy and finally to a separatist movement — is important in terms of the tactical leeway left to the centre while maintaining the existing territorial framework of the state. Rudolph (1977) has argued that the responses of central governments will also reflect the magnitude of the threat posed to the centre by peripheral protest. As figure 3.8 shows, the threat factor can vary from a minor political embarrassment through to the instability of the state. The centre's response is measured by the degree to which the movements are given institutional recognition, varying from cases where there is effectively none to the federal plans in Belgium.

The threat to the state can be violent or non-violent in character. In a number of countries peripheral nationalists have conducted campaigns of civil violence, though few have been successful to the point of establishing an insurgent state within the periphery. Yet in extreme cases, notably in the Basque region and in Ireland in the period leading up to and including the civil war in the early 1920s, these campaigns can pose a serious threat to the centre quite apart from the economic disruption imposed upon the disaffected region.

In the majority of cases, however, opposition is transmitted through legislative channels; the most visible are those defined by the electoral

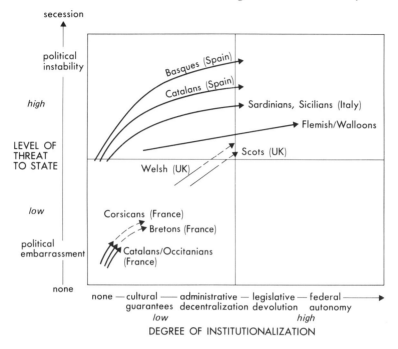

FIGURE 3.8   Centre responses to peripheral nationalism in Western Europe
(adapted from Rudolph, 1977)

system. Apart from the regional parties themselves, the electoral system can be used in other ways to register peripheral protest. Because voting in elections is an implicit recognition of the legitimacy of the state, abstaining can become a means for registering opposition. This was the case in the Spanish referendum of 1978 (ratifying the new constitution, which included proposals for regional autonomy) in which several groups in the Basque and Galician regions campaigned for local abstention. Overall within Spain the abstention rate was 32 per cent; in the Basque and Galician regions this rose to 51 per cent.

In Britain, the switch to the voicing of discontent in the peripheral nations was transmitted through support for the nationalist parties. Though this was more a protest vote than a vote for nationalism, the nationalist party gains posed an electoral threat, particularly to the Labour party. This was because the party needed the Scottish vote before it could gain office; only in the landslide election of 1945 had the party won sufficient constituencies in England to secure a majority in Parliament. Despite their otherwise strong ideological preferences for centralization (for reasons of economic management and redistribution), it was successive Labour administrations that furthered devolution, first by setting up the Commission on the Constitution, which reported in 1973, and subsequently by the introduction of the Scotland and Wales devolution bills.

The Conservative party, though for different reasons, it also a centralist party. As Hirschmann suggests, the consumer is able to bargain by using loyalty as a weapon; in this way the Scottish electorate were able to win concessions from the centre. Also, as Johnston (1979) has amply demonstrated, politicians are pragmatic — vote-buying is a common and accepted tactic in British politics as it is elsewhere. Thus, particularly following the electoral successes of the SNP in February 1974, 'the pork barrel was rolled out for Scotland prior to the October 1974 elections [both] parties competing vigorously to offer additional and tangible economic benefits' (Esman, 1977, 274). While Labour offered to establish new industries and disperse government offices to Scotland, the Conservatives promised other advantages.

Proposals and outcomes: the case of Britain

The idea of giving regional autonomy to Scotland and Wales, and possibly to the separate regions within England, was based on a number of arguments. The proposals for the two peripheral nations were aimed at combating the centrifugal forces reflected in the growing electoral support enjoyed by the nationalist parties. However, as in the other West European states, the case for regional autonomy did not rest on the ethnic factor alone. The arguments commonly used to support and oppose the idea of regional devolution are set out below (Craven, 1975). They included arguments that have already been discussed as general principles underlying the area and power debate, while as a question of spatial reform — the use of the city region model to define appropriate units — we shall come back to the problem in the final chapter.

Arguments favouring devolution:

1. Democracy — too much centralization had led to remoteness (see table 3.7 above). One factor favouring the region is that loyalties exist at this level and another is its growing use by a number of *ad hoc,* undemocratic administrative bodies (water, gas, electricity boards, etc.)
2. Inappropriateness of inflexible national standards determining how public services should be provided.
3. The need for more integrated ('corporate'), horizontal decision-making within regions across central government departments rather than vertically by them (see chapter 7).
4. As a palliative to secessionist pressures.

Arguments against devolution:

1. Devolution would be a possible brake on the otherwise long-established trend towards greater equality. Regional oligarchies would probably vary in their commitment to egalitarian programmes and, anyway, their ability to implement necessary programmes would vary according to their resource base.
2. Fiscal redistribution from rich to poor regions would be more difficult and the resulting inequalities may be a source of continuing political conflict (see chapter 4 for discussion of experience in federal countries).
3. Devolution could be antithetical to the protection of minority rights, for example of rural interests within a highly urbanized region.
4. Greater difficulties in coordinating administrative policies across regional boundaries.
5. Devolution gives peripheral nationalists a lever by which separatism becomes possible.

The implication of these arguments is that regional autonomy is a reform that can be applied throughout the state and not only in those areas from which ethnic conflict has arisen. However, because the latter areas give rise to 'special' conditions, one outcome of which is their greater 'threat potential' to the centre, there is some rationale to singling them out. Thus in Italy, in spite of the fact that the 1948 constitution admitted the principle of regional autonomy, it was only implemented then among the four ethnically distinct regions. Friuli-Venezia Giulia was added to the list in 1963, and the remaining 15 'ordinary regions' did not get autonomy until 1970.

A similar split in the centre's treatment of ethnically and non-ethnically different parts of the periphery characterized the proposals for devolution in Britain. It was a split that became apparent with the Commission on the Constitution, the Majority Report recommending that devolution be restricted to Scotland and Wales while the Minority Report advocated autonomy for all regions (1973c). The subsequent restriction of devolution to Scotland and Wales brought reaction from some of the English regions, which considered that autonomous decision-making powers over regional economic questions would give the regions with developed responsibilities unfair advantages. This was particularly the case in the North of England, an area with similar economic problems to those of Scotland (Guthrie and McLean, 1978). The problem, as a local government leader from Tyneside expressed it, was that the 'transfer of power to a very strong Scottish assembly will lead to a serious economic imbalance between the North East and other regions favourable to Scotland at the expense of ourselves' (Tyne and Wear C.C., 1977, 4). Northern protest was not directed at securing an assembly of their own, but with a Scottish assembly able to offer greater economic incentives to industrialists, the lack of such regional powers would be a real disadvantage.

It was partly because of the desire to avoid such territorial conflicts that federalism was eschewed as a possible model by the Constitutional Commission. Were each of the nations of England, Wales and Scotland to act as separate federal units, together with Northern Ireland, the federation would suffer from a chronic imbalance — England, it was argued, with more than 80 per cent of the federation's population would inevitably dominate the national assembly. Even were England to be subdivided into a number of federal units, the Commission argued that the south eastern unit would be able to dominate the federation. (This is an argument to which we shall return in our discussion on federal countries.) This assumes, however, that issues with which the federal assembly deals have clear territorial implications that are identifiable as gains or losses to particular units within the federation; this is the case in issues like the allocation of federal spending programmes, but there are other issues that are not spatial. Also, certain key areas (welfare, infrastructural services, etc.) have by definition been given to the component units and to that extent removed from the influence of other regions' voting powers in the federal assemblies.

The picture is complicated further in Britain by the differences in devolution proposed for Scotland and Wales, which would have given more extensive powers to Scotland. The detail of the differences need not concern us; the important point is that the centre will vary its responses according to the differences between the ethnic peripheral regions. These differences arise mainly from variations in assimilation within the overarching nation-state, and from the 'threat factor' posed by the peripheral nationalism. The less assimilated the region, the stronger is likely to be its territorial identity or nationalist feeling. Such an area, particularly if it has electoral importance, is a stronger candidate for devolution. (In Spain, devolution has already been established in the Basque, Catalan and Galician regions and is being extended, haltingly, to other areas, firstly Andalucia — one of the more economically deprived parts of the state.) For various historical and geographical reasons, Scotland has retained a stronger identity than has Wales: it has its own legal and educational systems, it is somewhat further from the core area of England, besides which, because of the gerrymander by which the peripheral nations are given disproportionate representation within the Westminster Parliament, Scotland carries the greater weight electorally.

These differences between Scotland and Wales were emphasized by the voting patterns in the devolution referenda. While the basic outcome was the sweeping rejection of devolution — in no single Scottish region or Welsh county did the proportion favouring the proposal exceed 40 per cent of the registered electorate, a figure that had it been attained nationally

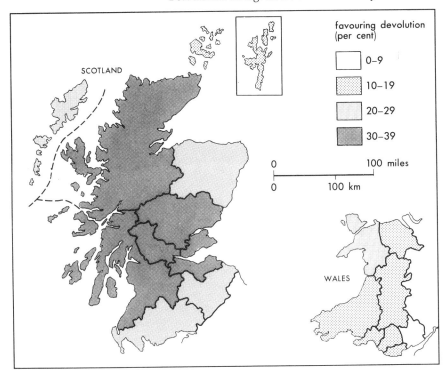

FIGURE 3.9   The devolution referenda in the United Kingdom, 1979

would have satisfied the legislative requirements set before autonomy could be implemented — opinion in favour of it was greater in Scotland, and it is clear from figure 3.9 that there are differences in attitudes. In Wales, whose nationalism is more cultural than economic, the pattern of responses correlates to some extent with the 'more Welsh' areas — Welsh-speaking, Nonconformist and essentially non-urban. Support for devolution was lowest in the industrial, traditional mining and heavily urbanized areas of the south-eastern portion of the country. In Scotland, by contrast, the urban-industrial Central Belt was more emphatic in favouring devolution, while the area showing least enthusiasm for the proposal was the Orkney and Shetland islands. The latter argued that, because of their remoteness and other special conditions, they should be given a 'devolved' assembly, possibly along the same lines as the Faroe Islands had enjoyed since 1948. Within Scotland, therefore, there are centre–periphery strains; for the regions considering themselves peripheral (those outside the Central Lowlands and particularly in the island groups), devolution was seen to be to their potential disadvantage because of the domination of the assembly by the interests of the populous areas.

CONCLUSIONS

The processes underlying the trend from unitary to compound unitary state, marking the integration and 'partial disintegration' of the state, are complex and it has been possible in this chapter to outline only some of the key themes underlying the interaction of the state with its regions — political integration and the assimilation of different groups within the nation-state, the concept of political core and periphery and its inter-relationships with regional economic disparities. Though the number of countries introduced was small, in one major respect they share a feature characterizing the majority of sovereign states: multi-ethnicity. For the newer states, the first lesson stemming from the experience of the West European state is that ethno-territorialism is not something that inevitably loses salience the more modernized society becomes.

Our survey suggests that the extent to which peripheral pressures have led to the disintegration of the state is limited. Indeed were each of the peripheral movements secessionist — and that, as it has been seen, is something that needs to be examined carefully — the most striking thing about them, compared to their nineteenth-century counterparts, has been their lack of success. Quite apart from the coercive means that the centre has at its disposal, there are perhaps economic reasons why peripheral regions do not seek independence but, rather, regional autonomy under the protective umbrella of the larger jurisdiction.

As the experience of the UK since 1979 illustrates, in contrast to the rest of the decade, regional autonomy is an issue that can be both a non-political as well as a major political issue. The underlying causes of demands for autonomy — regional ethnic pressures on the one hand and a suite of administrative reasons stemming from over-centralization and the advantages of the region, on the other hand — are likely to persist, but they are stronger in countries such as Spain, Italy and Belgium where the trend towards the adoption of quasi-federal practices has been the more pronounced. This reflects the importance of territorially based schisms within national political life. In the next chapter we shall look at these more closely in the federal countries proper.

4

Federalism: Regional Diversity within National Union

Federalism occupies a special place in the territorial organization of political life, partly because of its explicitly spatial configuration but more generally because of the recognition it gives to the several levels of legitimate authority and allegiance. The Dutch political philosopher, Althusius, in his book *Politica* (1602), captured its essential spatial characteristic when he defined a federal union as built upon a number of smaller unions at successively higher levels in the territorial hierarchy of communities. Thus the hierarchy of unions extended from the village and the town to the province, kingdom and empire. As this suggests, the term federalism can be employed as a relevant concept to governments at various levels. It can apply, although loosely, to cases of political organization in which there are multi-level jurisdictions, as in metropolitan centres, while it also has relevance to understanding supra-national organizations. Historically, its major applications have been in the internal ordering of states through constitutional means. The United States, Canada and Australia form the major English-speaking federations among the industrial countries; together with Switzerland, they are also termed the 'classic federations'. The two other federations in Western Europe — Austria and West Germany — are more recent creations.

In a phrase much quoted amongst political geographers, federalism has been described as the 'most geographically expressive form of all political systems' (Robinson, 1961, 1). Its geographical significance is rooted in its recognition of the constituent parts of the national territory; being conferred with permanent status by the constitution ensures their overall place within the political processes of the state. To the geographer, the existence at sub-national level of sovereign governments is of significance in its direct imprint on the economic landscape (W. S. Logan, 1968). More immediately important to the political geographer, federalism offers an institutional mode that balances the centrifugal and the centripetal forces within the state that Hartshorne (1950) has emphasized; in other words, federalism can address itself to a central problem confronted by all states — how 'to bind together more or less separate and diverse areas into an effective whole' (Hartshorne, 1950, 105). Thus, to the Founding Fathers of America, a federal constitution provided the means for forging national unity while retaining the degree of decentralization (or non-centralization) consistent with their ideas of territorial democracy and the plural state.

DEFINING FEDERALISM

Federalism, as was suggested in chapter 2, is a difficult term to define. Part of the difficulty stems from the differences between countries in the way in which federalism operates. In general, a minimal definition will include recognition of two levels of government that constitutionally are considered equals; this being so a number of countries, notably those in the Third World and in the socialist bloc, with federal constitutions but that otherwise are autocratically governed are described as not 'truly federal'. By implication, democracy is a necessary condition for federalism to operate.

The variations in the implementation of federalism are reflected by the variety of definitions that have been suggested by political scientists (Davis, 1978). One noted authority on the subject, after reviewing a number of books on the subject, concluded that federalism is a myth and that it has no practical significance for the way government operates in those countries that claim to be federal (Riker, 1969). At an earlier date the same author had defined federalism as where '(1) two levels of government rule the same land and people, (2) each level has at least one area of action in which it is autonomous and (3) there is some guarantee of the autonomy of each government in its own sphere' (Riker, 1964, 11).

The advantage of the legal approach to studying federalism is the broad comparative framework that it develops. The classical approach to analysing federalism has been through its institutional structure. The chief architect of this approach, K. C. Wheare (1963), defined the federal principle as 'the method of dividing powers so that the general and regional governments are, within a sphere, coordinate and independent'. The precise definition of federalism, however, will determine which governments can be termed federal, and in this respect the differences between Wheare and Riker are striking. Wheare admitted only three federations — the United States, Australia and Switzerland. He also studied Canada, but did not consider its enabling legislation, the British North America Act of 1867, to be by itself a federal constitution because the provinces lacked co-equal status with the federal government. Riker, on the other hand, was able to draw his case studies more liberally to include Third World and socialist countries.

Interest in federalism among political geographers was stimulated by Livingston's (1952) more socio-spatial approach to the subject. He uses the term to refer to countries where the diverse cultural/ethnic groups comprising the total population are territorially segregated. To Livingston federalism is a response to the 'stimuli' of the federal quality of society. The kinds of diversity to which Livingston was referring included those based on differences of language, religion, historical and cultural traditions, but he did not discount the existence of strong sub-national identities with which each of these factors could be associated. Once groups distinguished by such criteria attain sufficient size their separate representation within a federation becomes feasible, though Livingston was careful to emphasize that the actual boundaries of the constituent units need not coincide precisely with the distribution of the different social groups.

In Livingston's framework, such social diversities, besides being reflected in the constitution, are also transmitted through various 'instrumentalities', a term used to include the political habits and attitudes of the country, for example in the provincial make-up of the Canadian cabinet. Indeed, it is by examining 'the pattern of these instrumentalities and not by checking its constitution against an *a priori* list of the characteristics of a federal constitution' (Livingston, 1952, 7) that the federal character of a country should be assessed. Insofar as Livingston's approach to federalism is more a function of societies than it is of constitutions, it is clear that the countries incorporating federal qualities will be more numerous than the constitutional federations. Most of the countries defined in chapter 2 as compound unitary states (such as the UK and Italy) have federal qualities in the sense meant by Livingston. Federalism is therefore being used as a relative concept. In spite of the advantages of Livingston's analysis, particularly the emphasis on sociological factors, the problem inherent in his interpretation is where to draw the boundary line between countries that are more/less federal (Davis, 1978).

In different ways both the legal and sociological approaches — though not the only methods by which federalism can be assessed (Davis, 1978) — provide useful insights. It would be helpful, however, at this stage to be reminded of the major characteristics of federalism. Duchacek (1970) has provided ten yardsticks that can be used to compare federalisms, based largely on the US model. Questions 1–4 distinguish the federal from the confederal association, the latter being a looser form of union in which authority is delegated by the member states, which are themselves freely able to secede from the compact. Questions 5–10 can be used to distinguish federal from unitary states.

1. Has the central authority exclusive control over diplomacy and defence as appropriate to a state in its relations with other states?
2. Is the federal union constitutionally immune to dissolution by secession?

3. Is the exercise of authority by the central power independent of the approval and resources of the individual constituent units?
4. Who has ultimate control over amendments to the constitution?
5. Are the component units immune to dissolution?
6. Is the collective sharing in federal rule-making adequately secured by equal representation of unequal units in a bicameral system?
7. Are there two independent sets of courts, one interpreting federal laws and the other state laws?
8. Is there a judicial authority in the central authority but above the central authority and the constituent units determining their respective rights?
9. Have the constituent units retained all the powers that the constitution has not given to the central authority? Are these retained powers substantial or marginal?
10. Is the territorial division of authority clear and unambiguous?

Federalism as territorial pluralism: some questions

Though federalism is a difficult type of political institution or process of government to define, its essence is that it facilitates the voicing of separate regional interests within an overarching political union. Put another way, federalism is an exercise in territorial pluralism. Hence, in the classic federations, the territorial separation of powers was to be the means of ensuring that sub-national interests would not be subordinated to the national will, of 'preventing the concentration of power in a few hands'.

Following from this basic argument, we can explore several implications. Some follow from the set of questions that Duchacek poses as essential to defining federalism. For example, what machinery exists to ensure that the interests of the states or provinces are represented nationally, and, given that the separate units differ in terms of their size, economic wealth and other factors underpinning their 'power potential', what safeguards are there to counteract the possible domination of the federation by the larger units? Because of its deliberate non-centralization, federalism attempts to avert the territorially structured division between a politically dominant core and a dominated periphery, which we discussed in the previous chapter; in theory, the separate states and the federal government are equal partners in the federal compact. How realistic is this, particularly when we add to the political map the spatially uneven configuration of economic growth and decline? If, for example, the federal state is (or has been) clearly divisible into an economic core and periphery that are more or less coterminous with the political map, what implications does this have for the political operation of the state and its stability?

Secondly, we need to explore how federalism copes with ethnic pluralism, a question that is all the more pertinent in the light of the previous chapter. Because of its territorial nature, federalism is of potential value to the problem of multi-ethnicity where the ethnic groups are territorially segregated; where, in other words, they can be given regional autonomy. Limiting ourselves to regional-level ethno-territorialism within the industrial federations effectively restricts analysis to Switzerland and Canada, though both of these help in assessing two basic questions: To what extent does federalism counteract the potential of ethnic conflict as a destabilizing factor undermining the state? By granting regional autonomy to an ethnic minority, can federalism be an effective instrument to counterbalance the ethnically inspired demands for separatism that are a feature of the more centralized states?

A different range of questions is raised by the interrelationships between the regional and the federal governments. Because of the voluntary origin of the classic federation, the 'spirit of the federal compact' is something over which state or provincial governments will be especially vigilant. As the experience of the federations has been one of overall centralization, with the federal government assuming a greater role, regional governments will be sensitive to sovereignty infringements, that is, to attempts by the national government to control matters that the states rightfully consider as within their own sphere of competence. This implies that there is a discrete division between federal and state governments in their functional responsibilities, which is in fact far from the truth — as a means of governing, federalism has become associated with the need for increasing cooperation between the levels of government. Nevertheless, there will be certain issues that the regional governments will protect the more zealously because incursions by the federal government will be seen as a threat to their own power base. We shall examine the problem in the light of one issue, the problem of territorial stability. The 'indestructibility' of the intra-federal boundaries is essential to the maintenance of the federal spirit, but at the same time presents its own problems for the state. We might argue that, as territorial entities the states may be inappropriate for administrative needs, but any pressures for boundary change invariably meet constitutional obstacles that effectively block change.

Initially, a different question will be tackled. Federalism, it is sometimes argued, is a mode of government more appropriate for a state in the early stages of its formation than it is later. The argument assumes that unification from voluntaristic beginnings is a gradual process and that, at least initially, federalism is of value specifically because it allows for the expression of regional loyalties. In the mature federation, particularly if it is industrialized, vertical loyalties (for example, class) will tend to assume greater importance; together with the growing sense of national identity and gradual trend towards centralization within the federal authority, these undermine the position of the component states. Before looking at some aspects of this question, we shall briefly review the ways in which federalism evolves and the reasons commonly considered as having contributed to the act of federalizing.

THE EVOLUTION OF FEDERALISM

The constitutional underpinning of federalism does not mean that it is a rigid form (or process) of government. Certain facets, it is true, are assured relative indestructibility, including normally the areal configuration of states and provinces. Nevertheless, insofar as it can be described as a process of government (Friedrich, 1968), federalism typically evolves as a set of working relationships between the national and sub-national governments. This means it is possible to trace changes in the relative importance over time of the different levels of government; a common trend has been the increasing centralization of federal regimes. In attempting to outline the evolution of federalism, however, it is evident that even among the small number of industrial federations the development has been along different paths. Vile (1977) 'overcomes' the problem by outlining a general model of federal development based on the US model, while recognizing that differences exist between federations. This is particularly the case for Canada: since Confederation in 1867, the provinces have become relatively stronger at the expense of federal government and national unity, which is a reversal of Vile's model.

The overall progression identified by Vile marks the process from the time at which the federal bargain is first struck through a number of stages in which the national government becomes increasingly assertive (see figure 4.1).

FIGURE 4.1   Stages of federal evolution (dates refer to the USA)
(from Vile, 1977)

To succeed, the federation will normally have to overcome critical periods in its early development when national and sub-national loyalties are seen as competitive rather than complementary. The nature of the conflict is neatly encapsulated in General Lee's dictum 'Am I a Virginian or an American'. At the extreme, such conflicts may be resolved only through civil war, which in the case of the United States proved a watershed in the cementing of national unity. (In Australia during the first decade of federation several states threatened secession, notably Western Australia, while the Swiss federation of 1848 was established immediately following the Sonderbund War.) The final stage, termed the 'unitary–federal' state, occupies an intermediate position between federalism and the decentralized (compound) unitary state. Characterized by strong national and weaker regional governments, the unitary–federal state has become the major policy-decider while implementation (with considerable discretion) is left to the lower levels of government. Though uncertain whether the United States has moved into this phase, Vile suggests that each of the Western European federations exhibits, to varying degrees, this stage of federal evolution.

A different approach to understanding how federation evolves has been suggested by Sawer (1969). He divides the process into three stages — coordinate, cooperative and organic — emphasizing that for individual federations the progression does not represent an inevitable sequence and, indeed, might even be partly reversed. Under a coordinate distribution of powers, a clear distinction is made between the functions and responsibilities of federal and state governments. At this stage the functional sphere of state governments is generally substantial. This phase will be more characteristic of the earlier state of federation because it ensures an important position for the constituent units and lessens the possibilities for the federal government to impose the national will. However, the conventional belief that federalism in the nineteenth century in the US operated dually — national and state governments acting independently — has been challenged by Elazar (1962), who argues that the relationships between the two levels of government were cooperative rather than coordinate.

Regardless of when cooperative federalism, which involves the functional interlocking of the different levels of government, first developed, it is clear that it was given a considerable boost by the growth of nationwide social and economic planning. Many such programmes, through their spillover effects, ignore state boundaries and logically demand coordination by a territorially more embracing jurisdiction. In the minds of some, this trend brought into question the very value of an areal division of government conceived in an earlier period. Increasing federal involvement and the development of inter-state bodies were a natural outgrowth. In the United States the New Deal (after 1932) marked the beginning of major federal welfare programmes; though they appeared centralist, they actually served to underline the interdependent nature of federal, state and local governments. Cooperative federalism has come increasingly to mean the processes by which federal revenues are shared among the regions and localities and by which national programmes are engineered within a federal–state–local framework. Grodzin's marble-cake analogy graphically describes the complex relationships that have evolved:

The American form of government is often, but erroneously, symbolized by a three-layer cake — federal, state, local government. A far more accurate image is the rainbow or marble cake, characterized by an inseparable mingling of differently colored ingredients, the colors appearing in vertical and diagonal strands and unexpected whirls. As colors are mixed in the marble cake, so functions are mixed in the American federal system. (Grodzins, 1966, 265)

Sawer's final type, organic or administrative federalism, is only properly identified in West European federations, whose operation differs in several respects from that of North America and Australia. The legislative powers of the *Länder*/cantons are much more limited than those of the state or province; in Austria, the extreme case of organic federalism, all laws of the member *Land* are subject to a power of general veto by the national government in those cases where they are considered to 'endanger the federal interest'. In other respects the component units are assured greater significance, particularly in their implementation of federal legislation. The Swiss canton has modest legislative powers (mainly education, police, cultural matters) but 'a wide administrative competence, and it is this which continues to give the cantons a real base, with localist sentiments and constitutional guarantees acting as supports' (G. Smith, 1972, 266).

The reasons for federation

One of the key questions underlying federalism and one to which considerable research has been directed is why certain countries have adopted federal constitutions. Federalism is of especial significance precisely because it has proved to be the only means, other than through imposition by an absolutist ruler or government, by which common political institutions have come to be shared by areas that would otherwise remain separate. Its importance, then, is that it is 'the main alternative to empire as a technique for aggregating larger areas under one government' (Riker, 1964, 53).

Dicey's statement in 1885 that federalism originates where separate political communities desire union but not unity incorporates the idea of regional diversity within a commonly agreed, overarching political arrangement. Beyond this, political scientists differ in their opinions about what factors have contributed to federal origins. Table 4.1 summarizes the main factors according to four political scientists. Riker's understanding of federal origins is behavioural — in that it involves complementing interaction between political elites representing the two levels of authority — and essentially militaristic — the gains to one in territorial control and therefore military and defensive superiority being matched by greater security for the other from external aggression. The other formulations are

TABLE 4.1   Factors necessary for the establishment of a federal union

W. H. Riker	K. W. Deutsch	K. C. Wheare	R. L. Watts
Federalism is a bargain between national leaders and officials of constituent governments and is determined by two main conditions:	Essential conditions underlying emergence of an 'amalgamated-security community' of which federalism is a type:	Factors necessary for union:	Federalism is a 'balance' between conflicting forces for unity and diversity.
1. 'National' leaders wishing to expand territorial control offer concessions to rulers of the constituent units.	1. Mutual compatibility of main values.	1. Sense of military insecurity and common defence.	Unifying factors:
	2. Distinctive ways of life.	2. Desire for independence (particularly from a colonial power) for which union is necessary.	1. Desire for political independence.
2. Units willing to give up some independence because of military threat/desire for greater protection.	3. Expectation of stronger economic ties and gains.	3. Possible economic gains.	2. Expectation of economic gain.
	4. Gains in political/ administrative capabilities of some or all of participating units.	4. Previous political association.	3. Need for administrative efficiency.
		5. Geographical contiguity.	4. Military/diplomatic gains.
	5. Superior economic growth of some or all participating units.	6. Similarity of political institutions.	5. 'A community of outlook' founded on religion, language, race or culture.
	6. Strong communications between territories and different strata.	7. Leadership at the right time.	6. Contiguity.
			7. Previous political association.
	7. A broadening of the political elite.	Factors encouraging regional autonomy:	8. Similarity of institutions.
			9. Political leadership.
	8. Mobility of persons, at minimum among the politically relevant strata.	1. Previous history as a separate political unit.	10. Successful history of federal association.
		2. Differences of economic structure.	
	9. Multiplicity of methods and actual communications and transactions.	3. Geographically determined isolation.	Factors encouraging regional autonomy:
			1. Territorial 'social diversities'.
			2. Regional economic interests.
			3. Administrative convenience.
			4. Conflicting external relations.
			5. Ethnic/cultural diversities.
			6. Geographical dispersion.
			7. Historical identity.
			8. Dissimilarity of political institutions.
			9. Regional political leadership.

Source: Riker (1964); Deutsch *et al.* (1957); Wheare (1963); Watts (1966)

more directly historical and empirical in approach. Deutsch's list of nine essential conditions is based on an examination of ten historical examples of integration and disintegration, varying from England in the medieval period to the dismemberment of the Austro-Hungarian empire in the present century. Wheare's necessary factors are those found to underlie the federal origins of the United States, Switzerland, Australia and Canada. Watts' list is based on an examination of federal experiments among Commonwealth countries.

In a major analysis Dikshit (1975) has attempted a cross-national study and synthesis of the factors underlying federal origin. His list of unifying and divisive factors is an extension of Wheare's, except that he enumerates all possible rather than only the essential items. Yet he concludes that it is 'not only diversity, but regionally-grouped diversity within unity [that] is the essence of a centralised federation' (Dikshit, 1975, 233).

Dikshit's analysis stresses the way in which federalism allows territorial diversity to coexist within a larger political and economic unit. Other students have given considerably more emphasis to the role of economic factors in bringing about federal union. Although most writers have acknowledged the importance of economic motives — the advantages federation would bring in terms of larger markets, the removal of tarriff barriers and suchlike — in the case of scholars such as Wheare and Deutsch these economic factors parallel, if not are subordinate to, political impulses. Marxists, on the other hand, would argue that these economic motives are paramount in explaining federation and, indeed, that the advantages it would bring were recognizably in the interests of the dominant classes.

Beard's study, *An Economic Interpretation of the Constitution of the United States* (1965), is one of the most important to argue for the dominance of the economic motive. Beard claims that merchant capitalists, in particular, sought the adoption of a federal constitution because a strong central government would be able to protect their interests inasmuch as it could repress the then prevalent agrarian radicalism, protect their commerce and prevent the printing of paper money. Post-revolutionary war politics to Beard were largely the conflict between the urban, merchant capitalist class and the farmers. As Fifer (1976) has shown, the rural vote for federalism was markedly lower, and the adoption of the federal constitution was witness to the interests of the dominant urban, capitalist classes.

While a number of studies have investigated the origins of federalism on a comparative basis, none has to date done so within a Marxist perspective. Individual studies partly fill the gap: for example, Ryerson (1969) emphasized the role of the rising industrialists of Central Canada in explaining the emergence of federal, or in their terms Confederation, proposals. Subsequent studies have confirmed that a variety of industrial and commercial interests underlay the progress towards Confederation.

The search for rules to explain the origins of the federal state has produced a voluminous literature. It may be that there is no single universally important factor; in other words, where in one federation the security factor is dominant, in another the economic motive is paramount. The field remains a fertile one for the political geographer.

CENTRALIZATION

One of the general trends underlying federal evolution is the gradually increased importance of the national government. The 'traditional' view of federalism as it affected the distribution of legislative authority (in the constitutions of the United States and Australia for example) enumerated those limited powers over which the central government had exclusive control and those that were administered concurrently by both levels of government; control of the remaining fields was left to state governments. Giving the states the residual powers emphasized their autonomy while also reflecting that the beginnings of federation had been dependent on the willingness of the individual states to form a union. Nevertheless, in questions of finance and regulation, such as inter-state trading, the trend has been towards centralization, while concurrent responsibility between national and state governments has emerged in a larger number of other fields. It is this cooperative working that makes any assessment of the relative functional importance of the levels of government difficult. Riker (1964) devised a crude index of the temporal changes in an analysis of the federal and state contributions to 17 budgetary items (defence, education, social welfare, etc.) in the US based on an ordinal scale (1=exclusive federal responsibility; 5=exclusive state responsibility). Average scores in 1790, 1850, 1910 and 1964 of 4.1, 4.0, 3.5 and 2.8 suggest an overall trend towards centralization, though comparatively few functions have become the exclusive realm of the national government.

Centralization within federal countries (as also in unitary states) is closely linked with the processes of economic development and modernization. The trend is stimulated by the growth of fiscal centralization: central governments become increasingly important as the source of funds associated with services originally financed and administered locally. Two major factors associated with the process of development — the growth of inter-regional mobility and improved methods of communication — influence the extension of the spatial limits within which the costs and benefits of public services operate. Increases in mobility will spread the benefits gained from education (for example) so that decisions made by regional/local jurisdictions on educational provision will affect the whole of society (Weisbrod, 1964). Improved communication will mean, for instance, that residents in economically poorer areas will learn of and expect similar kinds of public services to those in more affluent regions. Inevitably this implies redistribution, which is best achieved through a central agency.

'Nationalization' processes

Another process suggested by federal evolution is the emergence of a corporate national identity alongside that associated with the component units of the federation. In the stable federation the two identities co-exist in a complementary, rather than competitive, fashion. Empirical data to support this are patchy, however. On the basis of a content analysis of colonial newspapers in the period 1735–1774 (using a count of the items centred on inter- and intra-colonial news as surrogates for 'American' and localist identities respectively), Merritt (1976) argues that during the 40 years prior to the War of Independence inter-colonial links became more important. During the period 1735–44 three-eighths of news space was devoted to local items; by 1765–74 this had decreased to less than one-quarter, while a similar proportion was allocated to events in other colonies.

While the successful federation will overcome any internal crises raised by conflicting identities, the growth of national sentiment tends to override identity with the smaller unit. In the complex case of Switzerland, the *primary* type of unit with which identities are linked is spatial (either Switzerland or the canton), rather than linguistic (see figure 4.2). It is also clear that national identity has become more pronounced among the younger age groups. Public attitudes towards federation in the United States also tend to suggest that identities with the intermediate tier, states, are weaker than with the nation or with the locality (Ylsivaker, 1959; see figure 1.2, p. 17).

The Swiss data also demonstrate that primary identity with Switzerland rather than the canton is positively associated with the frequency of travel by German-speaking Swiss to the French-speaking cantons and vice versa. In other words, greater inter-regional travel encourages the formation of identities with the larger social (and territorial) group (Kerr, 1974). This illustrates the more general argument in chapter 3 that in industrialized societies, with their high levels of spatial interaction, the state becomes integrated politically as well as economically. This argument is of especial significance for federal states in that ultimately it brings into question the need for such a form of government; federalism, in other words, may be a more suitable solution at an early stage in the development of states when the economic and political differences between the component units are more apparent. It was, for example, the apparent lack of regional differences between the constituent states that led Riker (1964) to question the continued relevance of federalism in Australia.

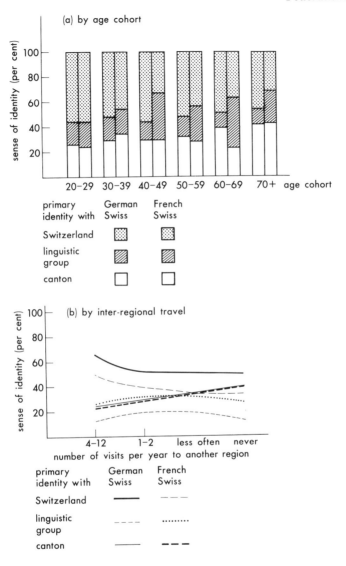

FIGURE 4.2   Sense of primary identity in Switzerland
(data adapted by Kerr, 1974)

As has been argued previously, one of the alleged effects of modernization has been the decline of territorially based differences within the polity
and their replacement by functional cleavages (Durkheim, 1964; Parsons,
1966). Modernization in this sense is linked to the growth of political

centralization and 'national standardization'. Through the growth of more intense interaction, represented by inter-regional trading, migration and communication of ideas, peripheral parts of the state are integrated so that sectional or otherwise competing economies, politics and cultures are replaced by a single, all-pervasive economy, policy and culture (Schwartz, 1974).

The development of national voting patterns, a feature common to federal as well as non-federal countries, is closely linked with the emergence of the politically integrated state. From one perspective political scientists have sought to show the gradual shift in emphasis from territorial differences acting as the principal societal cleavage to those based on functional–economic, particularly class, variations. But regional (or territorial) variation in voting patterns might also be eroded through advances in private and mass communication. The emergence of a national broadcasting service, of a press that is not so exclusively tied to the individual state or group of states, and of national political parties, for example, will encourage the interchange of ideas over the national territory and the discussion of national issues even though these may be altered according to the particular conditions of the sub-national constituency.

What evidence there is among federal countries tends to support the 'nationalization' thesis. Looking at the Democratic presidential vote in the United States, Cox (n.d.) demonstrates the decline in differences of support between states and the emergence of a national voting pattern. In table 4.2 each row measures the average vote over five presidential elections by states and counties; during the period analysed, the differences between states declined to less than 40 per cent of their earlier level.

TABLE 4.2   The nationalization of the Democratic US presidential vote, 1920–64

Elections	Standard deviations US (states)
1920–36	14.7
1924–40	14.0
1928–44	12.2
1932–48	9.5
1936–52	8.4
1940–56	7.3
1944–60	5.7
1948–64	5.3

Source: Adapted from Cox (n.d.)

Stokes (1967; 1969) extended the discussion by looking at the changing relative importance of national, state and constituency factors in American elections. His argument is that, with the growth of national parties, competition for support will be nation-wide. Where the swing in the party vote from one election to another is similar regardless of constituency, then nation-wide factors are the most apparent. Conversely, if the magnitude of the swing varies between constituencies and/or states, then sub-national factors are more significant in determining the pattern of support. His data demonstrate the decline of the constituency due to 'the increasing mismatch of constituency and media audience [having] lessened the visibility of congressional contests and, with it, the magnitude of forces distinctive to the constituency' (Stokes, 1967, 197).

Voting is part of the larger concept of political culture — the set of attitudes and beliefs that influence how the political system operates. The existence of major sub-national governments within federal countries makes it possible to trace differences of political culture. In a detailed analysis of the United States, Elazar (1972) distinguishes three major cultures, which he considers have been determined by the major migration currents through which the American continent has been settled: (1) the moralistic culture, stressing society over the individual and associated with high levels of political participation: (2) the individualistic culture, emphasizing private rights and the gains from political participation for the improvement of one's own position, and (3) the traditionalist culture, strongly paternal and associated with low levels of participation and minimal government intervention. Though the patterning of cultures does not correspond exactly with the states, which tend to be dominated by one or a combination of cultural types (see figure 4.3), regional patterns are apparent: the traditional culture is dominant among Southern states, while moralistic states are most developed in the Upper Midwest and, as an outlier, Oregon.

Most studies of political cultures in America have suggested that regional differences are still apparent. Glenn and Simmons (1967), examining differences in attitudes towards social, political and moral issues between younger and older Americans, concluded that regional opinions (comparing Southern and non-Southern states) have become more polarized. Using factor analytic techniques, Savage (1973) has examined the stability of state political cultures since the nineteenth century. Two sets of variables measuring political action (basically the speed of adoption of political measures such as 'fair housing' legislation, gasoline tax, the acceptance of provisions for unemployment insurance, etc.) and profile characteristics (urbanization, literacy, the number of telephones, malapportionment, electoral turnout, etc.) were used to classify states into three types (table 4.3) covering three time-periods, the mid-nineteenth century, early twentieth century and 1930–70. According to the intensity of membership, states were further classified as being within the core, domain or sphere of the cultural type (figure 4.4). What Savage's model suggests is

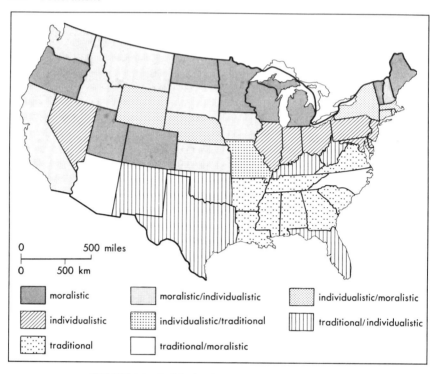

FIGURE 4.3   Political cultures in the United States
(from Elazar, 1972)

that, over time, the three broad political cultural types have maintained their identity and that this has been strongest in the core states and least so in the 'sphere' where there is the greatest intermingling of the cultural characteristics.

TABLE 4.3   Major cultural region types and their characteristics

| Characteristic | Type of cultural region | | |
	Northwestern	Industrial	Southern
Democratic association	Populist/grass-roots/localist	Competitive	Paternal
Citizen orientation	Participant/moralistic	Participant/individualistic	Low participation/traditionalistic
Economy	Agrarian–service	Industrial–financial	Agrarian–industrial
Settlement pattern	Urban centres/sparse hinterlands	Metropolitan	Small town/rural

Source: Adapted from Savage (1973, 94)

So far our discussion of the nationalization of federal countries, and the consequent extent of 'delocalization', has been based on the experience of the United States. However, the existing as well as the evolving relationships between the national and sub-national spheres differ between federal countries because of the characteristics unique to each country. In table 4.4 the relative magnitude of national, regional (state) and local components in explaining constituency variations in party voting — based upon Stokes' methodology — illustrates the differences within the English-speaking federations. Voting in Australia is the most nationalized — indeed, national influences are more apparent in Australia than in Britain (Stokes, 1967) — while in Canada regional and local effects are more significant. However, we should approach the implication of these findings with caution.

As Riker (1964) and others have argued of Australia, federalism, to the extent that it is predicated on regional diversity, barely seems justified. Looking at voting preferences, however, the states are still salient even though the regional factor is nowhere near as important as the functional —

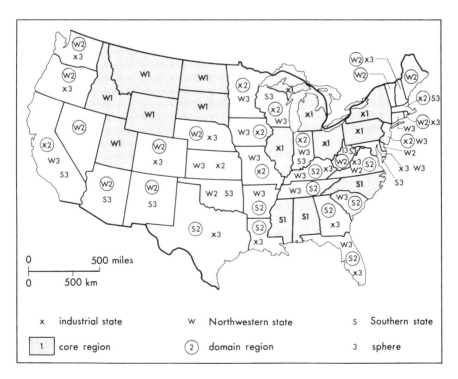

FIGURE 4.4   Patterns of multilinear cultural evolution in the United States (48 states)
(adapted from data in Savage, 1973)

TABLE 4.4   National, regional and local variance components: Australia, Canada and the United States

	Australia (1966–72)	Canada (1953–58)	United States (1952–60)
National	0.66	0.16	0.32
Regional	0.11	0.50	0.19
Local	0.23	0.34	0.49

Source: Adapted from Kemp (1978)

economic cleavage (Holmes and Sharman, 1977). States do show clear preferences for political parties: between 1946 and 1975 New South Wales, South Australia and Tasmania consistently gave above-average support for the Labour party while Queensland has favoured the Country party. Further, inter- as well as intra-state variations are generally apparent when individual issues are voted upon, as in constitutional referenda. Kemp (1978) analysed the 'nexus' referendum of 1967 by which it was proposed to amend the constitution so that the membership of the (lower) House of Representatives could be increased without correspondingly increasing the size of the Senate. Such a change would be to the advantage of the more populous states, and to a limited degree voting for and against the amendment correlated with state size. Voting preferences showed state-wide influences leading to the conclusion that

> the boundaries of the states have not merely legal, administrative and political reality; by some mechanism the arbitrary state boundary comes to assume considerable significance in mass political decisions on national questions, so that the response of electors in a remote rural seat may be more like that of their co-citizens in a capital city hundreds of miles away than of their neighbours in a contiguous constituency in the next state. (Kemp, 1978, 245)

In this respect state boundaries act in a 'wall-like' manner, a conclusion supported by studies of other elements of the political culture (Holmes and Sharman, 1977; A. R. Stevens, 1974).

Canada is an interesting case in terms of the nationalization thesis not only because, in contrast to the 'general' model, regional influences remain important but also because the provincial influence has increased since Confederation, frequently at the expense of the federal or national standpoint. As table 4.4 shows, sub-national factors far outweigh national ones in explaining changes in voting preferences. Regional politics, in the form of conflict between central Canada and the peripheral provinces and in Quebec, are among the dominating features of Canadian federalism as we shall see later in the chapter. Differences of region are more important than those of class in helping to explain variations in party voting (Blake, 1967). This in turn helps to support the hypothesis that strong nationally organized parties, which Canada lacks, underlie the nationalization of political attitudes. This absence can be attributed partly to the cultural/ linguistic and regional economic cleavages that divide the state and partly to its size, which has an attenuating effect on internal communication. This is not to deny, however, that class-based conflicts within the federation are not apparent; if less 'concrete' aspects of political culture than voting are assessed, such as attitudes towards the political system (whether participation is favoured and considered efficacious) and ideological positions, then class differences are more apparent.

To summarize, federal countries vary in the extent to which they have become nationally homogeneous and consequently 'deregionalized'. Electorally, regional differences in party support, although in most federations less important than earlier, do persist. Differences of political culture also appear to have been maintained, so that, as A. R. Stevens (1974) has demonstrated, state boundaries do reflect real changes in political culture. Federalism, through its spatial segmentation of political processes, encourages the maintenance of territorial differences. However, the salience of regional differences varies between federations, being less in Australia than in North America and more important in the Anglo-American than the European federations.

THE CONSTITUENT REGIONS

In the classical federations political union was established through the consent of constituent units. Even at their establishment the evidence indicates that some areas were more anxious to federate than others. Support for the idea of federalism in the United States between 1787 and 1790 was greatest in the urbanized portions of the colonies and least in the more peripheral, rural parts (Fifer, 1976). Similarly in Australia and Canada, the larger, industrialized states and provinces were more in favour of federation than the more peripheral, smaller, predominantly agrarian units. In each case, federalism has had to accommodate regional diversities, which we shall discuss under two major headings. We shall first examine the implications of differences in population size and economic wealth, and then the relationships between federalism and ethnicity.

Regional disparities and the federal balance

The way in which the national territory is subdivided into component states and provinces can have a direct bearing on the working of the federation.

Though the units of a federation are considered 'equal before the constitution', inequalities in size, population and economic wealth undermine their equality in political terms. In part, federalism exists because of such territorially based diversities; were the units more similar (in terms of socio-economic composition, political institutions, etc.), its very use may be unwarranted. Should the differences between the units be too marked, however, the stability of the federation may be threatened.

The significance of the variations in structural composition between the units lies in their influence on the balance of the federal system. Tarlton (1965) has used the terms 'symmetrical' and 'asymmetrical' to describe the extent to which units have problems and interests that are common nationally. In the perfectly symmetrical federal system, each unit would be of equal territorial and demographic size and have similar social, economic and political characteristics. The emphasis on equality is related to the idea that each unit would exercise similar power nationally. In the asymmetrical federation, on the other hand, units would be unique, differing from other units and the federal system at large.

Not unexpectedly, most federations lie between the two extremes. Initial advantages (of resource localization, location, etc.) together with subsequent processes of spatially uneven patterns of economic development make the perfectly symmetrical division unlikely. Moreover, in conditions of total asymmetry it is unlikely there would be a sufficiently strong state idea to establish a federal union. The more pronounced the asymmetry, the higher the levels of conflict within the federation; in Canada, with its multi-ethnic and bilingual provinces, territorial differences and conflicts are more in evidence than in Australia where the divergences between states are less marked. Differences in the incidence of symmetry are also 'measurable' within federations. Tarlton contrasts the symmetry of the states of California and Mississippi as they relate to the United States as a whole. As the social, economic and ideological features of the Deep South state differ more markedly from the national norm than is true for California, federal–state conflict would be more likely in Mississippi. The more asymmetrical state threatens the federation's stability by its greater likelihood of vertical conflict with the central government.

Differences in population size and economic wealth between the component units are common to all federations. Of the three federations of North America and Australia, Australia has the smallest difference between the least and most populous units, New South Wales and Tasmania. In the United States and Canada, the smaller units (Alaska and Prince Edward Island) are less than 2 per cent of the size of the largest (New York and Ontario). Patterns of economic wealth, measured by *per capita* income, do not differ as substantially as for population (see figure 4.5). Nevertheless in 1976, *per capita* income in Mississippi, the poorest state, was less than 60 per cent of that of the most affluent, Alaska. In

Canada, a similar gap separates Newfoundland and Ontario. In Australia differences are less marked, *per capita* incomes in Tasmania being 80 per cent of those of the affluent mainland states. Relationships between the factors are complex: Alaska and Tasmania are both relatively small, but are at opposite extremes in terms of *per capita* wealth.

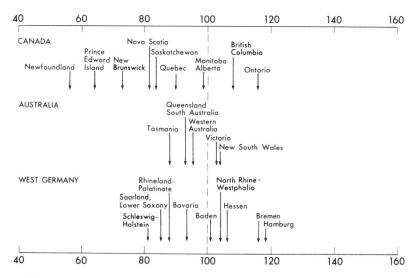

FIGURE 4.5 *Per capita* income disparities: Canada, Australia and West Germany (compiled from official publications)

The importance of such differences is in their link with perceived power disparities within the federation. J. S. Mill outlined the problem when he suggested that 'there should not be any one state so much more powerful than the rest as to be capable of vying in strength with many of them combined' or, expressed alternatively, any state so small that its interests are persistently over-ridden by those of larger units. Given a system of equal voting power (one man, one vote), larger units may be able to ensure policy-making in their own interests. Secessionist moves in the relatively small states of Western Australia and Tasmania earlier in the present century can be traced to such a perceived sense of weakness within the newly formed federation. Yet, as Wheare recognized,

> It is this divergence [in size] which leads the poorer or less populous states to desire a federal rather than unitary government for in it they see a safeguard for their independence. The agricultural states with their smaller populations find in the federal form of union their safeguard against the wealth and population of the East and especially New York . . . (Wheare, 1963, 50)

Several factors modify the influence of size as it impinges on the power relationships within a federation. Inequalities will tend to be more pronounced (or 'visible') in those federal unions made up of a smaller number of units. The division of the United States into 50 states has meant that national policies have not been so self-evidently dictated by one or a small number of larger states, in contrast to the position in Canada where federalism 'has allowed Central Canada to use the federal government to force Maritimers and Westerners into a mould cast in Ontario' (Bercuson, 1977, 4). The formation of coalitions of the smaller units, as the associations between the Maritime and Prairie provinces have shown, can be used as a counterbalance.

To offset the differences in size of the component units representation within the national legislature is frequently based on population *and* area. Most federations have a bicameral legislature and many have adopted the American system in which representation in the Lower House is based on population, while that in the Upper House is based on area. Representation by area ensures that otherwise unequal units have equal voting power. Equal representation is achieved by a variety of practices: in America and Australia, the states are treated as exact equals; in Canada, Ontario, Quebec and the Maritime and Western provinces collectively have 24 seats each.

The underlying reason for the equal representation by area clause within federal constitutions was the need to safeguard the interests of the component units of the federation. Such a safeguard is ranked highly by the units. It was because Newfoundland was not to be given any further representation in the Senate than that already given to Nova Scotia, New Brunswick and Prince Edward Island that it rejected membership of the union in the 1860s. Nevertheless in Australia and Canada, in contrast to the United States, the Senate has been a weak champion of state/provincial interests, partly because of the parliamentary system of government and, in Canada's case, partly because the Upper House is appointed. Particularly in Canada, which is the more asymmetrical of the two federations, the inability of the Senate effectively to protect the interests of the smaller, peripheral provinces in the national arena has contributed to the federal–provincial conflict.

In the parliamentary federation, the cabinet is the major policy-making body and in Canada some redress to the individual Maritime and Western provinces is offered by their assured representation on it. However, as table 4.5 shows, this is more related to population than divided equally by area so that the two central provinces — Quebec and Ontario — hold an absolute majority of places. Several provinces, notably in the Maritimes but also Quebec, have had a proportionately greater share of ministerial representation, while representatives from Western provinces have been relatively fewer. The discrepancies are due to inter-provincial variations in support for the major political parties. Western political protest, directed against the federal government, has led to support of minor parties that have failed to gain office. Western provinces, therefore, are at a double disadvantage within the federal government: as relatively small units they can be out-voted by central Canadian interests, and by supporting minority parties they have tended to alienate themselves further from national politics. The development of Canadian regionalism underlines the importance both of balancing territorial interests and of safeguarding the interests of the smaller units through an effective federal instrument of government that gives each component unit equal representation.

TABLE 4.5   Territorial distribution of cabinet ministers in Canada (by province)

Province	% of national population (1971)	% of ministers[1]
Newfoundland	2.4	4.6
Prince Edward Island	0.5	2.4
Nova Scotia	3.7	8.4
New Brunswick	3.0	7.6
Quebec	27.9	30.4
Ontario	35.7	29.2
Manitoba	4.6	5.2
Saskatchewan	4.3	3.7
Alberta	7.5	4.2
British Columbia	10.1	4.3

[1] Percentages corrected to account for different lengths of time provinces have been in Confederation.
Source: Adapted from Van Loon and Whittington (1976, 317)

Variations in economic wealth also influence the relationships between the states and provinces and in extreme cases have threatened national unity. Relatively poor states will seek to improve their financial base, the promise of which may (as in the case of the Canadian Maritime provinces) have influenced their decision to join the political union. For the richer states the economic advantages of extending the federation will be in the expansion of the domestic market, though insofar as they are expected to subsidize the poorer units the wealthier areas may claim that the demands being made on them to underwrite the federation are disproportionate. The effects of differences in wealth therefore duplicate or reinforce the problems caused by size disparities. Based on a simple federation comprising only two units, May (1969) has suggested the following scenarios:

1. given a large, wealthy unit and a small, poor unit, the former is likely to dominate the federation.
2. given a large, poor unit and a small, rich unit, the latter will either acquiesce to the demands of the larger state, and through fiscal transfers improve its financial base, or attempt to secede.

There have been too few federations with only two units to test May's hypotheses, though the secession of Bangladesh from Pakistan provides some support. However, in the more typical arrangement of multiple units the relationships become more complex. The smaller/poorer units can form coalitions so as to counteract the voting power of the large units. Simeon (1972) has demonstrated, furthermore, that in Canada relative poverty could be a useful weapon to the poorer provinces in the sense of giving them a 'moral claim' among their peers; in the distribution of federal funds, negotiated between the provincial and federal governments in Ottawa, Maritime provinces were given first priority because of their obvious need.

Fiscal redistribution, involving the transfer of income from richer to poorer units to help the latter to meet minimum national standards of public service provision, is a feature common to most federations. The methods by which redistribution is achieved, however, vary considerably (May, 1969). In Australia, demands by the three 'claimant' states of Western Australia, Tasmania and South Australia for financial assistance stimulated the establishment of the Commonwealth Grants Commission, which reallocates resources horizontally between units. The effect of such redistribution has been to more than compensate for the financial disparities, in that expenditure *per capita* on basic services in the claimant states is higher than in New South Wales and Queensland (table 4.6). In the United States, redistribution is achieved through General Revenue Sharing and is determined by an equalizing formula aimed at establishing an equitable allocation among the states. In West Germany, the Basic Law stipulates that within the state there be a 'unity of living standards' between *Länder*. There are four ways to ensure that regional differences in fiscal potential are reduced: (1) by vertical transfers between Bonn and the *Länder*; (2) by horizontal transfers between rich and poorer units; (3) by the sharing of common tax revenues; and (4) by special grants paid by the national government (Conradt, 1978). In Switzerland, redistribution is based on the division of cantons into three financial classes — strong, average and weak. The poor cantons, by forming coalitions with those of

TABLE 4.6 State expenditure on social services, Australia, 1973–75 ($/cap.)

	New South Wales	Victoria	Queens- land	S. Aust.	W. Aust.	Tasmania	Australia
Education	112	125	100	130	120	138	117
Health	69	62	62	76	103	77	70
Law and Order	22	19	24	22	26	30	22

Source: AGPS, Grants Commission, 42nd Report, 1975, Table E4

average strength, have been able to out-vote the richer cantons in the federal chambers, thus forcing redistribution (Frey, 1977).

Fiscal redistribution within federal countries is similar to that within unitary states, but an important difference is that the transactions can be a more sensitive political issue, partly because they take place between sovereign co-equal units. In most federations the issue of fiscal redistribution provides a continuing source of conflict (Smiley, 1974), dividing the units into 'haves' and 'have-nots'.

Federalism and spatial conflict

Because of the form of political association represented by federation it can be argued that in federal countries, in contrast to the situation of the more centralized unitary state, there should be no apparent division of the territory into centre and periphery, at least in political terms. In reality, because of the differences between the component units in size and economic wealth, their equality is undermined, and the associated political disparities can become part of the popular perception of the federation. In Australia and Canada — in both of which disparities are more apparent because of the relatively small number of states/provinces — survey evidence has demonstrated that New South Wales and Victoria, Ontario and Quebec are commonly identified as representing the core units of the federation (Schwarz, 1974; Holmes and Sharman, 1977). This is most marked in Canada where repeated public opinion surveys have shown that the two central provinces are popularly considered to have more power than the other provinces. The economic structure of the other industrial federations is less clearly associated with a single dominant highly industrialized, metropolitan core. To the extent that Canadian regional economic structure has been discussed in core–periphery terms, we can contrast it with the position in the United States where at successive historical periods major industrial–metropolitan foci have emerged to challenge existing ones giving a polycentric rather than monocephalic urban–industrial structure.

Should one state (or several adjacent ones) come to be too closely associated with national policies, in their formulation and/or their benefits, and because of its greater population be able to dominate the federal government, the spirit of the federation will have been eroded. Thus issues of national concern are treated with circumspection by the component units anxious to preserve their own territorial self-interests and to meet their own political priorities, while simultaneously preventing other units from becoming over-advantaged. We can identify two broad types of issue, those requiring a 'one-off' decision and those of a more continuing nature, particularly economic questions, over which federal–state and inter-state policies and preferences conflict.

Federal capitals   The choice of site for the federal capital is an example of the first type of issue. A preferred site, besides being accessible, or one that would afford physical development, would avoid over-association with any of the component units. Existing major urban centres, therefore, were avoided. Consequently, in marked contrast to centralized states, the national capital in federal countries is not the primate city or even, in some federal countries (West Germany, Switzerland), among the first five centres of the urban hierarchy. (Vienna is the exception, though as a former imperial capital it is a special case.)

Typically, the choice of site represents a political compromise. Washington and Canberra were developed on 'neutral ground' (Dikshit, 1975) disassociated from either the existing states or larger urban centres. Canberra was selected from a short-list of possible locations that all met the basic requirements as agreed between the states shortly after federation, that a national capital be established within New South Wales at a distance of at least 100 miles from Sydney (Linge, 1975). Other federal capitals, though not developed on virgin sites, also demonstrate the principle of compromise. The selection of Ottawa, which had been the capital of the province of Canada before Confederation, was a compromise between the larger centres of Quebec and Toronto, which had already been selected as provincial capitals.

Controversy can also develop over the governing of the capital city. Normally its administration is made a federal concern: its establishment within a federal district ensures its separate status from any component unit though denying its citizens the channels for local democracy normal elsewhere in the state. Ottawa demonstrates the problems arising where the governing authority of the national capital is a constituent unit of the federation (Rowat, 1977). The problem is compounded by the 'two nations' controversy — as a mainly English-speaking city, governed by the English-speaking province of Ontario, to the people of Quebec it is an alien capital in an alien territory.

The European federal capitals differ in several respects from those of the Anglo-American federations. Bonn was chosen as a compromise between the existing urban centres (which, however, if they were not peripherally located were badly damaged at the end of the war), though its choice appears also to have been influenced personally by Adenauer and by the fact that the area was electorally important for the majority Christian Democratic party. Yet, as is also true for Berne, Bonn is administered by the *Land*/canton in which it is located. Potential conflict is averted by their 'low-key' status as capitals: Bonn is considered only a 'provisional' capital, while federal establishments (parliament, courts, government departments) in Switzerland are shared between Berne, Lausanne and Zurich. Vienna provides a further variant in being a separate *Land*. Because of the *Land*'s pronounced urban composition, matched by its strong support for socialist parties, there has been a history of conflict between the capital and the more conservative rural provinces.

Economic conflict   Economic issues generate a more continuing source of problems, bringing either neighbouring states into conflict or the units against the federal government within the national political arena (Johnston, 1980). Issues of regional economic planning, the location of industry, and transport are the kinds of fields in which the states will have important, but not exclusive, responsibilities. These will be shared by federal, state and local governments, each of which operates according to its perceptions and goals. As far as federal government is concerned one of the problems in establishing and coordinating national economic policies stems from the distribution of power to sub-national governments (Reischauer, 1977).

Direct conflict between states with common borders arises mainly from economic rivalry. Several types of conflict can be recognized; the most common is where each constituent state strives to increase and expand its own economic base, using tax and other incentives to attract commerce and industry. Conflict can also result from the different views held by neighbouring states about how a shared resource can best be used. Where rivers have been used for infra-federal boundaries, their economic use demands cooperation between the riparian states. The history of conflict over the River Murray, shared by New South Wales, Victoria and South Australia, mirrored the traditional rivalries between the states; the first two have traditionally seen the river's potential in irrigation and conservation terms, while South Australia, anxious to channel trade through the state, has seen the river as an internal highway (Wright, 1978).

While conflicts of this nature can (and do) take place between local governments within unitary states, they tend to be especially acute in federal countries. National governments become necessary as umpires matching the territorial interests of individual states with those of the wider supra-state area. Thus it was only after the intervention of the federal government over the Murray Waters issue that the riparian states began to cooperate. States will place their own economic interests uppermost and, as public goods theorists have suggested, a regional jurisdiction cannot be expected to put itself into a disadvantageous position by slowing down its economic growth, particularly if it has no guarantee of other units doing likewise (Olson, 1965). Where, as in Australia, states have the powers to control economic activity so as to reduce metropolitan over-concentration, the effect of unilateral action by one state would merely be the directing of investment to a neighbouring, competing unit (Lonsdale, 1972).

The result of rivalries between the states and/or between major cities of each unit is to make the effective coordination of national urban policies more difficult (Bourne, 1975). In West Germany, beginning in the 1950s, each *Land* devised separate policies to attract industry by subsidies and infrastructural improvements, a system that developed into competitive bidding between the units. 'Even though uniformly lower subsidies would have been advantageous for all länder, competition meant that each . . . had to participate in the outbidding game if it did not want to lose all chances of attracting new industries into its depressed areas' (Scharpf *et al.,* 1978, 91). Regional industrial policy has since 1969 become a joint federal/*Länder* responsibility, each decision on how subsidies are allocated requiring the consent of the federal government and a majority of the *Länder.* Scharpf *et al.* (1978) show that, as a result of this development, consensus has been reached on how competition between subsidies can be avoided but, because of the positive benefits falling to each *Land,* not on the spatial areas and funds over which the subsidy programmes operate.

In other issues, conflict arises from the different economic preferences of the constituent units and of the federal government, for example over the management of natural resources. L. Pratt (1977) demonstrates how successive Albertan governments have sought to ensure control over the province's natural resources and their benefits. This has led the province into direct conflict with the federal government, most recently over oil. The sharp rise in oil prices in the 1970s has made the province affluent (Alberta produces over 80 per cent of Canada's oil), particularly following the imposition of increased royalties and taxes by the provincial government. The federal government, anxious to redistribute some of the natural resource benefits, imposed an 'export' tax on oil so as to subsidize Eastern consumers as well as other measures, a move that alienated both the provincial government and the Albertan business elite.

Alberta's aggressive defence of its jurisdictional rights against the encroachments of the federal government is symptomatic of wider regional politico-economic cleavages that historically have divided Canada. Though uneven patterns of development are characteristic of all industrial federations, in Canada the federal parliament had been less successful at balancing economic interests between the component units comprising the federation. This problem has been equated by the 'disadvantaged' provinces with the disproportionate influence of Central Canada within the federal government.

Viewed from the Western or Maritime provinces, federal economic policies have appeared to encourage the growth of a core industrial area surrounded by primary-producing hinterland provinces. Tariffs protecting Central Canadian industries have ensured that their products will find markets in the peripheral provinces, which are denied their more 'natural' trading partnerships with adjacent areas in the United States. The historical conflict over railway freight rates illustrates the different perceptions of the Central and Western provinces. To the former, the building of the Canadian Pacific Railway was essential to link east with west and as a symbol of national unity. But the higher running costs in the

Western provinces, given the vast distances and sparseness of population, led to the policy of 'fair discrimination' by which rates were up to three times higher than in Central Canada. Prairie economic interests demanded the construction of railways linking the Canadian Pacific with the United States. Though eventually established, they were resisted by Ontario because of the probable economic and national repercussions.

The conflict between the economic interests of Western and Central Canada has frequently been reflected in the electoral behaviour of the Prairie provinces. D. Smith (1977) has described the Prairie electors as historically registering a kind of floating protest vote. In the national elections of 1921, an electoral watershed, the Progressive party took 38 of the 43 seats in the Prairie provinces marking an agrarian protest against regrowing urban domination both of the Canadian economy and of its national politics. In subsequent elections the Prairie vote has consistently rejected the Liberal party (which has won most national elections) because of its associations with Central Canada, preferring minority parties. This, however, denies the Prairie MP a place in federal governments.

The regional split between Western and Central Canada was re-emphasized in the national elections of early 1980, when the Liberals, who regained power in the federal parliament, failed to gain any seat west of Manitoba, while the Progressive Conservatives gained most of their support from the West (table 4.7).

It was against this background of regional polarization that constitutional reform was attempted in the early 1980s. Though not a new issue, the federal government under the leadership of Pierre Trudeau sought to repatriate the constitution, i.e. remove any influence Westminster had under the British North America Act of 1867 over the amendment of the constitution by bringing the constitution 'home'. Previous attempts to repatriate the constitution, as in the 1920s and 1930s, had quickly floundered on such thorny issues as the right of veto. If the amendment of the constitution were to be decided internally then, as in most other federations, the procedure would depend on a majority of the provinces or states favouring the change. However, given that in Canada two provinces accounted for approximately two-thirds of the population at the time, it was hardly likely that they would accept anything other than the power of veto. Restricting the power of veto to the two populous provinces inevitably stigmatized the others as lower in status.

In the most recent attempts at repatriation the issue of constitutional reform incorporated a far wider set of issues. These concerned powers over the direction of the economy, the methods by which the revenues from resources should be shared, control over offshore resources and, a proposal favoured by the federal government, the issuing of a Charter of Rights. These issues pitted the provinces against the federal government, sometimes singly over particular issues (for example, Newfoundland's fight

TABLE 4.7   The 1980 Canadian general election

	Liberal party	Progressive Conservative party	New Democratic party	Totals
Maritime provinces	19	13	0	32
Newfoundland	5	2	0	7
Nova Scotia	5	6	0	11
New Brunswick	7	3	0	10
Prince Edward Island	2	2	0	4
Quebec	74	1	0	75
Ontario	52	38	5	95
Prairie provinces	2	33	14	49
Manitoba	2	5	7	14
Saskatchewan	0	7	7	14
Alberta	0	21	0	21
British Columbia	0	16	12	28
The North	0	2	1	3
Yukon Territories	0	1	0	1
Northwest Territories	0	1	1	2
Totals	147	103	32	282

Source: Keesing's Contemporary Archives, 6 June 1980, 30290

against federal control of offshore resources) and sometimes more generally (as in the widespread provincial opposition to repatriation). The priorities given to the issues varied between the provinces and the federal government; ultimately a compromise allowed repatriation to proceed, while the provincial governments were to win concessions in the other fields.

Ethnicity and national unity in federal countries

Differences in ethnic composition have been prominent among the centrifugal forces operating in opposition to the integration and stability of sovereign states. (The term ethnic has been defined earlier to include social divisions based on language, religion and national or racial origin.) Differences of national origin, in particular, operating through the growth of nationalism have acted as one of the prime forces underlying the territorial determination of sovereign states and their secession from pre-existing polities. Beginning in the nineteenth century and reaching its zenith in Europe in the period after World War 1, national self-determination was employed, if not always accurately in a spatial sense, as the basis for the partitioning of states. However, only a fraction of the world's states are mono-ethnic and in that sense truly 'nation-states'. Connor (1972) identified 13 countries as mono-ethnic — the two Germanies, Norway, Iceland, Denmark, Netherlands, Luxembourg, Ireland, Portugal, Lesotho, North and South Korea and Japan — though the inclusion of some of these countries, the Netherlands and Denmark for example, is problematic. Insofar as ethnic divisions pose a real (or potential) threat to the state, the importance of federalism, as was suggested in chapter 2, is linked to the argument that it provides a means of accommodating the problems arising from ethnic diversity, at least in those cases where the ethnic groupings are sufficiently large and spatially concentrated. By guaranteeing local autonomy, particularly over those questions that are considered important to the maintenance of ethnic identity, the potential for conflict within the national political arena is reduced. Particularly where the ethnic group(s) form a minority such decentralization can allay perceptions of domination by the majority, besides affording access to the political system.

The paradox is that while most sovereign states are multi-ethnic only a few have adopted federal constitutions (Duchacek, 1977). One reason is that the ethnic groups are either too small or too dispersed to warrant local autonomy. Despite its multi-ethnic composition, federalism in the United States has not generally been associated with ethnic territorial segmentation, partly because federation pre-dated the growth of the nation's demographic diversity and partly because the spatial mixing of ethnic groups has reduced the feasibility of any state or group of states being dominated by one or a few groups. Chicano, Negro and Indian groups provide exceptions, though in each case suggestions for their being granted statehood (as for Negroes and Indians earlier in the present century) have not been realized. Since the idea for a Black state was mooted in the South, the Black numerical dominance has been eroded by out-migration to northern cities (where Black demands have turned to urban ghetto community control), leaving them in a minority in each state of the South. Similarly in Australia, there is only a weak connection territorially between federalism and ethnicity: Aboriginal claims to statehood have been ignored, though not entirely — they would participate in the possible future establishment of Capricornia — while recent immigrant groups, from Southern Europe particularly, are too small and intermingled.

Among the other industrial-world federations the pattern of internal boundaries is partly conditioned by ethnic differences, but in none of them is there a perfect spatial match between the political and ethnic divisions. The Swiss cantons partially match linguistic variations, though their number, 26, bears no relation to the number of languages. Similarly in

Canada, the French-speaking group is largely concentrated in a single unit, Quebec, while for geographical, economic and historical reasons the Anglophone majority is divided into nine provinces.

Most multi-ethnic states are marked by ethnic conflict, though to varying degrees. Other political institutions besides federalism (which in any case may be inappropriate) exist for accommodating ethnic demands — such as elections based on proportional representation and/or various methods of positive discrimination (Enloe, 1973). It is, however, federalism that is generally seen as the preferred method: in each of three contemporary cases of major inter-communal strife stemming from ethnic differences — Cyprus, Lebanon and Ireland — federalism has been offered as a possible solution. Thus the Sinn Fein party has proposed a united, federal Ireland based on the four historic provinces of Leinster, Munster, Connaught and Ulster, in which the latter (which would include the three predominantly Catholic counties of Donegal, Cavan, Monaghan, significantly excluded at the time of partition) would be given 'substantial' local autonomy.

Such proposals assume that, given that the conditions of size and spatial concentration are met, federalism can assure (minority) ethnic rights, on the one hand, and national coherence, on the other. We shall discuss two major ethno-territorial industrial federations, Switzerland and Canada, in the light of these assumptions. Clearly, a sample of two is too small to allow any general conclusions, but because they are such disparate cases it is possible to analyse the relationships between federalism and ethnicity under different spatial conditions.

Switzerland   According to Napoleon, Switzerland could exist only as a federal entity; experience with the short-lived experiment (1798–1803) in centralist government, inspired by revolutionary ideals, had taught this lesson. The country's association with federalism had begun 500 years earlier, though between 1291 (when the three communities of Uri, Unterwalden and Schwyz formed the 'perpetual league' for the purposes of common defence) and the end of the eighteenth century the country was linked by a loose confederation. It was not until 1848 that centralized federalism emerged with a constitution based largely, but not exclusively, on that of the United States. One of the important differences was the rejection of the American style of executive government in favour of a small collegiate body, the Federal Council, on which representation from the more important cantons and major linguistic groups was to be assured.

Swiss society is divided chiefly by geography, language and religion. The French political geographer, André Siegfried, suggested that the mountainous nature of the country had lent itself to a federal form of government. While it is difficult to substantiate such direct links between the physical environment and particular forms of government, it remains true that within Swiss society the strong local identities at sub-cantonal level closely correlate with physiographic characteristics. Federalism has also reinforced the spatial divisions within the state where much of the administration of day-to-day government is controlled within the cantons. Linguistically the federal constitution recognizes four languages — German, French, Italian and Romansch — though the latter two are spoken by only 10–11 per cent of the population. German is the majority language (69 per cent) though the French-speaking population (19 per cent) forms a significant minority. Swiss Alamann majorities account for two-thirds of all cantons and three of the country's five cities with populations of more than 100,000 (1971). In terms of religious affiliations, Protestants outnumber Roman Catholics approximately 60:40 and, unlike the patterning of languages, the cantons are divided more equally between those with a majority of either religion. German- and French-speaking majorities account for eight-and-a-half and three of the Protestant cantons, and seven-and-a-half and three of the Catholic cantons respectively. The remaining Catholic canton, Ticino, is Italian-speaking and is alone in being effectively unilingual.

The spatial mismatch between the linguistic and religious boundaries is underlined by the configuration of cantons: while the linguistic boundaries cut across the governmental divisions, religious boundaries are more aligned to them (see figure 4.6). It is this factor of cross-cutting cleavages that students of Swiss federalism have suggested helps to explain the basic stability of the federation. An early definition of the cross-cutting hypothesis argued that 'A society . . . which is ridden by a dozen oppositions running along lines running in every direction may be actually in less danger of being torn with violence . . . than one split along just one line'. Thus where individuals are members of more than one formal or informal group their attitudes will be moderated as a result of the cross currents stemming from multiple membership.

In spite of these claims the precise contribution of the cross-cutting character of the cantonal division to the stability of the federation is difficult to assess. Lijphart (1977) has shown that the cantons are marked by less cross-cutting than is true for the nation as a whole. Further, there is a pronounced tendency towards linguistic homogeneity in the cantonal network: 17 cantons, concentrated in Northern and Central Switzerland, are more than 90 per cent German-speaking. Added to this, the federal structure of power places issues that are sensitive linguistically and religiously at cantonal level so that group conflict is resolved sub-nationally. Through its spatial segmentation federalism also serves to moderate political conflict so that cleavages that are significant in cantonal terms are less so nationally. Protestants in the mainly Catholic canton of Fribourg, for example, form a distinct group, zealously overseeing such issues as religious education, though nationally they identify more with the canton than with their religious affiliation largely because of the absence of religious questions in the national arena.

Though Switzerland is noteworthy for its lack of internal conflict between ethnic groups, particularly in view of its considerable diversity, conflict has not been entirely absent. The Sonderbund War of 1847, precipitated by the secession from the confederation of the Catholic cantons of Lucerne, Uri, Schwyz, Unterwalden, Zug, Fribourg and Valais because of religious grievances, illustrated the need to safeguard minority rights in the constitution. Equally the 1848 constitution was careful to avert any similar threats to the federation, expressly forbidding 'all separate alliances and treaties of a political character' (Article 7).

The tendency for the cantons to be dominantly German- or French-speaking, apart from Romansch-speaking Grisons and Italian-speaking

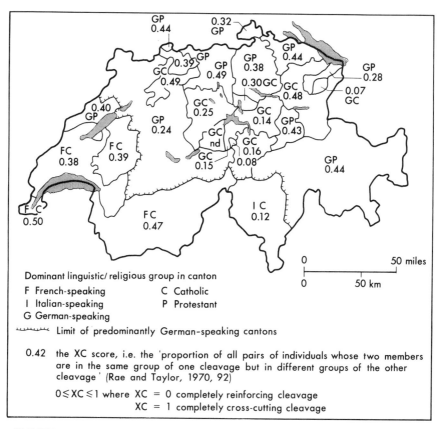

FIGURE 4.6   Linguistic and religious fragmentation and cross-cutting cleavages in
Switzerland
(xc scores data from Lijphart, 1977)

Ticino, has had its influence on federal politics. The Ligue Vaudoise, an anti-centralist movement established among the French-speaking cantons of Western Switzerland, though not a formal (constitutional) alliance, was established to oppose the increasing centralization of the Federal Council after 1945. During the war, centralizing forces had been powerful and in the post-war years the Federal Council deliberately sought to consolidate its enhanced position. A national referendum, instigated by the Ligue, halted the progress of centralization, though the results (Swiss Alamann 48.3 per cent, Romand 64.5 per cent, all cantons 50–70 per cent in favour of reducing central powers) revealed the schisms between the linguistic groups. A loss in cantonal power was seen as a greater potential threat to the minority group. Further, as Kerr (1974) argues, 'the hypothesis is that the stronger the centralisation . . . in a linguistically divided society, the greater the chances are that these divisions will find expression in a heightened sense of linguistic identity and in strong anti-centralist feelings', an argument that could be applied equally to Canada.

The Jura problem, partially resolved in 1979, is the major exception to the absence of recent inter-ethnic violence in Switzerland. The problem arose from the secessionist demands of the French-speaking minority within the the Bernese canton, which had been expanded to include the French Jura following a treaty of 1815. Religion further divides the canton: while the German-speaking population (84 per cent in 1971) is mainly Protestant, the French-speaking area is divided between the two religious groups. Solutions to the problem were sought along various lines, the cantonal government in Berne attempting to meet it consociationally — that is, by mutual agreement among elite members of the two linguistic groups — though subsequently, following outbreaks of violence, Berne agreed to the holding of local referendums that the Jurassiens demanded. Several referendums on the issue have been held in the part of the canton claimed; only in the 19th referendum did a majority of voters agree to the need for a new canton and then only in the three northernmost Catholic districts.

It is in the complex interrelationships between the ethnic divisions that the Jura secessionist movement is of interest. Lijphart has suggested that it is because the French-speaking Catholic population of the Jura is a minority on both ethnic characteristics, cantonally and nationally, that the sense of relative deprivation within the dominantly Protestant German canton was accentuated. Support for this was suggested by the outcome of the 1972 referendum: in the southern districts of the Jura, whose population is Protestant, there was no absolute majority demanding secession, whereas there was in the French-speaking area as a whole. The preferences of these southern areas were tested in a further local referendum in 1974, the eventual outcome of which has been their retention within the Bernese canton (see figure 4.7).

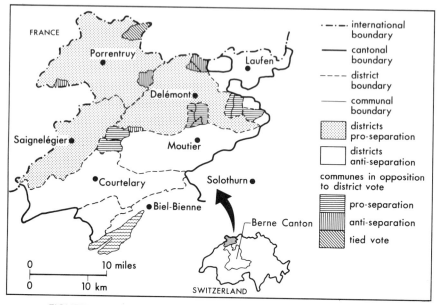

FIGURE 4.7   Separatist voting in the 1974 referendum in the Jura
(from Steinberg, 1976)

The Jura problem helps underline the value placed on cantonal government. The area was peripheral to the core area of the Bernese canton and secessionists claimed that local self-government was necessary to meet their particular ethnic and economic demands. Economic factors added to their sense of relative deprivation; it was argued that the cantonal government had not done enough for local industries.

In general the Swiss example shows that federalism can play a fundamental role in the management of ethnic diversity. Fundamentally the network of cantons achieves a spatial segmentation of the ethnic cleavages; while establishing a cross-cutting pattern, it is equally notable for the emergence of governmental areas dominated by one of the linguistic groups, thereby reducing some of the potential contact between ethnic types. The number of cantons in relation to the ethnic divisions has also been important. Had there been four cantons based on the linguistic areas, the picture of federal stability would have been different. Finally, the pattern of decentralization ensures that the cantons have competence over sensitive issues.

Canada   This country demonstrates a different facet of the relationships that can develop in ethno-territorial federations. From the viewpoint of the spatial structure of the federation, the origins of the Quebec crisis appear clear-cut, stemming from the coincidence between the provincial boundaries and the French–English cleavage. In 1971, 26 per cent of the Canadian population was French-speaking, forming a substantial minority. Some 84 per cent of the French-speaking population of Canada, however, was concentrated in Quebec province, and within the province (outside Montreal city) the francophone population exceeds 90 per cent. Though there has been some migration to other non-contiguous provinces —which federalists consider important for the 'Canadianization' of the French-speaking population — and while Francophone minorities spill over into the adjacent provinces of Ontario and New Brunswick, the match between the linguistic and provincial boundaries remains a dominant factor. Through possession of a distinct territory by a population with differing ethnic characteristics from its neighbours, both essential features of the nation-state, Quebeckers have been able to retain and develop their own nationalism as distinct from the wider Canadian nationality.

Though the language factor has acted as a division (recognized by such federal policies as that of bilingualism), it is not the only cleavage separating the French and English populations. French Canadians are predominantly Roman Catholic, though the majority religion nationally is Protestantism. While this split is also reflected in the provincial boundaries, though not so emphatically as in the case of language, the political significance of the religious differences is in the role that the Church has played in Quebec's cultural development. During Canada's early history, religious differences formed more evident cleavages than did the linguistic split.

Economic differences overlay and reinforce the cleavages formed by language and religion. Historically Quebec has lagged behind Ontario and the Prairies, though since 1945 its economy has undergone rapid industrialization. Added to the inter-provincial differences, there are economic inequalities between the French- and English-speaking populations within the province. The existence of an English-speaking economic elite can be traced to the British conquest. Various indicators demonstrate the favoured position of the English-speaking minority: in 1971, 17 per cent of the male labour force of British Isles ethnic origin were in high-income occupations (defined as more than $10,000 per annum) compared to only 7 per cent of French origin. The Report of the Commission on Bilingualism and Biculturalism (1968) exposed the connections between economic stratification and language more explicitly. In Montreal, of the 83 per cent English-speaking in the higher-income brackets, only one in five could be expected to know French. Other than in employment within the provincial bureaucracy (from which middle-class support for separatism developed in the 1960s), the opportunities for higher-income, white-collar occupations for the majority, without learning and using English, were limited. Since 1961, however, a policy of 'repatriation' of executive jobs in industry has reduced the gap between the two groups.

These differences within the province of Quebec have been of equal, if not greater, importance in helping explain Quebec nationalism as have its inter-regional relations within the Confederation at large. This suggests a modification of the core–periphery internal colonial model, which emphasizes the part played by inter-regional relationships. Hence, while within the Canadian context Quebec, together with Ontario, acts as the core, Quebec is peripheral to Ontario. In centre–periphery terms, particularly in the patterns of economic domination, the Western and Maritime provinces are more clearly peripheral to Central Canada than is Quebec to Ontario. Finally, within Quebec there is a cultural division of labour, though McRoberts (1979) doubts whether this is to be associated with any deliberate strategy of economic domination by the Anglophone minority. Rather, the differences 'seem more closely linked to structural conditions arising from the replacement of France by Great Britain, and later the United States, as the economic "metropole"' (McRoberts, 1979, 314).

Quebec nationalism as it has developed since 1960 differs from its predecessor. Traditionally it sought to protect the linguistic and religious values of French Canada over which the Confederation Act of 1867 provided some safeguards. The drive for cultural preservation remains strong, but contemporary nationalist thinking, endorsed by the Parti Québecois (PQ), contends that greater provincial control of the economy is essential to preserve cultural identity. During the 1960s — the period of Quebec's 'Quiet Revolution' — growing antagonism to the federal government and foreign, especially American, investment emerged as issues galvanizing an increasingly politicized working class and an emergent Francophone middle class. The first electoral successes of the nationalist party in the provincial elections of 1970 were among the working-class constituencies of East Montreal. In the subsequent elections of 1973 and 1976 the party expanded its social and territorial bases, capturing 71 of the 108 seats (Saywell, 1977).

Federalism has helped maintain and enhance the cultural and political distinctiveness of Quebec. Demands for local autonomy by the Francophone population at the time of Confederation were met in the British North American Act insofar as the province was to be allowed to use French as the official language in the provincial legislature and in the courts, and in delegating control of the education system. In national affairs French and English speakers have been represented proportionally in the federal cabinet, though the minority group has been relatively under-represented in the federal bureaucracy (Van Loon and Whittington, 1976). The establishment of local autonomy laid the foundations for the province's 'special status', by which Ottawa transferred powers over health and welfare to Quebec and allocated sufficient revenue for their operation.

The Quebec issue is of interest because it has developed within a federal country. Dikshit (1975) argues that its origins are due largely to the lack of cross-cutting cleavages. The roots of the problem, as we have suggested, are cultural, social and economic differences between the two groups. Consequently, a strong 'national idea' in Canada, from which would develop a unified state-idea, has failed to materialize. Federalism, through its territorial diffusion of power, has enabled Quebec to build a political power base that makes its demands heard within national governments, particularly because (in contrast to the Western provinces) of its electoral association with the Liberal party. Also, though the Quebec problem is considered as one of secession, economic and geographical realities strongly suggest some kind of continued association with Canada. Rene Levesque, the PQ leader has suggested a 'New Canadian Union', a loose, confederal association based on ideas similar to the European Economic Community. In the 1980 referendum, however, Quebec elected to stay within the Confederation, though the federal government agreed to a remodelling of the constitution (see p. 125 above).

(see p. 125 above)

THE TERRITORIAL STABILITY OF FEDERALISM

The constitutional basis for reform

One of the hallmarks of federalism is its territorial stability, which is attributable to what Duchacek (1970) describes as the relative indestructibility of the states and provinces. Most federal constitutions do include provisions allowing for the establishment of new states (Bowie and Friedrich, 1954), though in the industrial federations these are more likely to result from the admission of former federal territories to statehood than from the subdivision of existing units. As a result intra-federal boundaries ossify and can bear more relation to historical than contemporary patterns. One of the traits of federal evolution, as we have suggested, is that the costs and benefits of administrative programmes increasingly transcend state boundaries. Equally, insofar as the boundaries in countries such as the United States and Canada were established prior to the large-scale metropolitanization of the population, they have become increasingly contradictory. Over 30 Standard Metropolitan Statistical Areas (SMSAs) in the United States were inter-state in 1971, including five of the country's most populous metropolitan areas. Local traffic therefore becomes inter-state commerce, while the controlling of the physical development of such areas becomes a matter of coordination between states.

The reason for the stability of intra-federal boundaries is the guarantee of integrity given to the signatory units of the federation, so that any alteration to boundaries requires their sanction. S.124 of the Australian constitution states: 'A New State may be formed by separation from a State but only with the consent of the Parliament thereof'. In the United States, both the existence and territory of a state (and the right to its equal representation with other states in the Senate) can be changed only with the consent of the state. In Switzerland, as the Jurassien problem illustrates, the question of territorial boundaries is decided by local and national referendums, which democratizes the decision-making process. The post-war reunification of Basle Town and Basle Country cantons, originally split in 1833 following claims by the rural population of urban domination, was necessitated administratively by the spread of the urban area. However, the fusion of the two half-cantons took several years following local referendums and, because both were signatories to the 1848 constitution and any change to the latter is a national concern, a state-wide referendum.

Because political association in the classic federations resulted from agreements between existing states, the component units enjoy relative permanence. Were it otherwise, and especially if the central government is able to recast boundaries unilaterally, the autonomy of the regional units could be 'seriously undermined' (Watts, 1966).

Among the industrial federations a partial exception to the rule is West Germany. The constitutional territorial safeguards accorded to the *Länder* are outwardly less exclusive, the federal government being empowered itself to initiate the process of territorial reform. The difference can be traced to the special origins of federalism in post-war West Germany. Federation had been imposed by the allied powers, largely as a result of pressure from the United States reacting to the over-centralization of the Third Reich. The boundaries of the *Länder* were determined more by the division of the country into Allied Occupation Zones than by history or cultural factors, with the exception of the two northern city-states and Bavaria. Boundary revision was anticipated because of the superimposed nature of the *Länder*, particularly as the division was strongly asymmetrical. Even though the dominance of North Rhine–Westphalia was less emphatic than that of Prussia had been in earlier German federations (Brecht, 1945), over which there had also been proposals for territorial reform, one *Land* in the post-war federation accounted for a quarter of the national population and nearly 30 per cent of the GNP in 1973.

Although a number of changes to the *Länder* have been made, the prospect for comprehensive reform has receded as the network of units has become increasingly entrenched. The unifying of Baden–Württemberg, which had been split between the French and United States zones, followed a referendum in 1951 relatively soon after the establishment of the federation. Other referendums, as in the one held in Rhineland–Pfalz in 1975 where the electorate rejected the area's transfer to the neighbouring *Länder* of Hesse and North Rhine–Westphalia, have maintained the *status quo*. Proposals for national reform (see figure 4.8) have also met resistance from the established *Länder*; particularly within the decades immediately after 1945, given the possibility of German reunification,

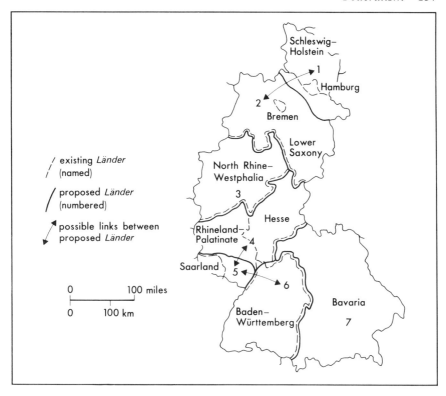

FIGURE 4.8 Alternative federal patterns in West Germany

there seemed less point in redrawing the internal divisions of West Germany. Renewed demand for reform in the 1960s, however, led to the establishment of a commission in 1973 which recommended a national division into five or six more equally sized *Länder*. As Mellor (1978, 187) argues, 'The longer delay is allowed, the more difficult any voluntary or acceptable change in boundaries will become, especially as the procedure for change is so complex'.

The kinds of criteria that have been used as the basis for the territorial reform of the component units of federal countries are broadly similar to those applied to local government reform (Leemans, 1970). In the West German constitution, Article 29 states that any changes in boundaries must have 'due regard to regional ties, historical and cultural connections, economic expediency and social structure'. In an opinion poll in Canada, seeking the preferred division of the national territory into provinces, two criteria — economic complementarity and the special problems of metropolitan areas — were most in evidence (Schwartz, 1974). The Maritime and Prairie provinces were combined into single units, Montreal and Toronto were made into city-states, leaving a reduced Quebec and Ontario, while British Columbia would remain.

Some political geographers have been active in suggesting the criteria for reform and in devising alternative federal divisions. Brunn's (1974) division of the United States into 16 city–hinterland states is predicated initially on the need for the structure to be urban-orientated. The metropolitan-based functional region reappears in a number of reform schemes; besides its spatial and economic rationale, the political reasoning for the solution stems from what a number of studies of American federalism have seen as the failure of the states (partly by design, because of rural over-representation, and partly by their fiscal inability) to deal effectively with urban problems. In his scheme, Brunn suggested other criteria for reform: for example, the smaller number of states would ease the administrative coordination of federal and state programmes, while also contributing to the reduction of variations in the provision of welfare, education and health services, their economic complementarity and similarities of political culture and ideology.

Programmes for the comprehensive reform of state boundaries lack political credibility, however, relying as they do on the willingness of the states to commit territorial suicide. As Grodzins (1966) recognized, while the boundaries of the states may be 'some of the worst inanities of the American federal system', they are 'fixed in the national constitution and defy alteration for a foreseeable time'.

Sources of challenge to the territorial structure

The territorial stability of federal countries is challenged from several directions. Duchacek (1975) lists four main internal threats:

1. the development of functional interests that transcend political boundaries;
2. the persistence of ethnic identities challenging either the configuration of specific boundaries (e.g. the Jura problem) or the state itself (e.g. Quebec);
3. regional challenges, e.g. the development of supra-state organizations in the United States;
4. the development of megacities, which 'engulf' states and frequently cross state boundaries, and whose economic problems have been soluble only by national governments.

Regardless of whether change actually occurs, three types of possible territorial outcome can be identified arising from such conflicts. The existing units may be altered politically, either through subdivision or amalgamation, leaving the federation with a greater or smaller number of states. The former type of movement has been more common, reflecting those cases in which the states conceal minority populations demanding greater autonomy. (There are similarities here with regional autonomy movements in unitary states.) The third territorial response is most common — new jurisdictions covering administrative coordination between states or formed by their subdivision, but in neither case leading to the political dismemberment of the units. The case of Australia will serve as an example of the pressures for territorial change and the forces for stability (Paddison, 1982).

In Australia there has been a tradition of debate, if somewhat spasmodic, over the possible ways in which the country could (and should) be partitioned virtually since the founding and territorial delimitation of the mother colony, New South Wales (Ellis, 1933). While the boundaries of the colonies (later to become the states) solidified, demands both from 'below' (locally) and 'above' (the federal government as well as its predecessor, the imperial parliament) have sought the repartition of the country. Local demands in the form of new state agitation have highlighted the problems of division in which the states are considered too large. The issue has also been incorporated into the political platforms of the national parties, most notably that of the federal Labour party. At its most radical, in 1920 the Labour party proposed a unitary system of government in which the country would be divided into 31 'provinces' with delegated responsibilities. New state agitators, on the other hand, have sought redivision within a federal framework.

The pattern of division and subdivision of Australia during the nineteenth century, prior to federation in 1901, helps explain the emergence of new state movements (see figure 4.9). The boundaries of the colonies for the most part were drawn arbitrarily on geometric lines, and pre-dated the settling of the internal areas of the continent. The colony of New South Wales was initially defined to cover the entire eastern half of the continent, and it was only after protracted petitioning of the imperial government in London that settlers in the Port Phillip and Moreton Bay areas were able to establish the self-governing colonies of Victoria and Queensland. Following the establishment of the six states, achieved by 1862, no further subdivision of the country has been made, with the exception of the short-lived Central Australian State. This is in spite of agitation for further partition, particularly in the eastern states.

Several common themes have underpinned the separatist movements in pre- and post-federation Australia (Whebell, 1973). Most originated from a nucleus with a location peripheral to the colony's (state's) capital. Remoteness from the state capital is of itself seen as a disadvantage, the more so because in each colony/state the political centre had become also the chief economic focus. The disabilities caused by remoteness and the political and economic centralization within Sydney were the principal

FIGURE 4.9   New state movements in Australia since the mid nineteenth century

arguments leading to the subdivision in the 1850s of New South Wales into the three eastern mainland states. Subsequently, similar arguments were used for the subdivision of Queensland, the largest state. As a colony, the Queensland parliament had narrowly failed to vote for its own dismemberment into three political units, while during the debates leading up to federation it had mooted the idea of putting boundaries into the melting-pot.

Since federation, new state agitation has been most active and come closest to reaching its objective in New South Wales, particularly in the northern part of the state where the New England Movement, in a local referendum in 1967, just failed to secure the majority necessary for subdivision (Woolmington, 1966). The separatist vote was higher in the more peripheral districts, while it was because of the inclusion of the Hunter Valley, with its more urban and industrial population and hence closer associations with the metropolitan centre of New South Wales, that an overall majority was not gained. Differences in urbanization and industrialization within the area of the proposed state were significant, for the conflict between the protest movement and the state government was couched in urban vs. rural terms: in spite of a rural gerrymander in the

New South Wales parliament, metropolitan interests were seen to prevail, retarding the economic development of rural, peripheral areas within the state.

The failure of the new state movements to achieve their objective is attributable to several factors. During the pre-federation period, and after 1862, the prescribed boundaries of each colony 'hardened', political and business elites in the capital cities ensuring that there was no further subdivision. The federal constitution consolidated the territorial position of the states by making the question of their division a state, and not a federal matter. Attempts by New England protestors in the 1920s to draw the national government more directly into the issue brought a positive response from Canberra; an all-party committee recommended that the federal government itself 'should have clear power to bring new states into being after a referendum of the people and without the consent of the state legislature'. State governments, however, were able to resist such incursions into their territorial sovereignty. Nevertheless, the state government in New South Wales has been influenced by the political pressures exerted by the New England agitators, and has moved towards a regionalized and more decentralized system of administration.

Several of the problems of federalism as a territorially divided form of government have emerged recently as national issues in Australia. This has followed from the experience of the short-lived Labour government of 1972–75. For ideological reasons the party is more committed to centralization. Whitlam, the Labour party leader, had been a consistent advocate of more centralization:

> If we were devising a new structure of representative government for our continent, we would have neither so few state governments . . . We would not have a federal system of overlapping parliaments and . . . we would have a House of Representatives for nation-wide and international matters, an assembly for each of our dozen largest cities and a few score regional assemblies for the areas of rural production and resource development outside those cities. (Whitlam, 1969, 122)

As a major part of its election programme of 1972, the party was committed to national reforms aimed at improvements in education, health and welfare, and the provision of public utilities. One immediate problem was the question of the appropriate territorial institution through which the federal funds could be channelled. The states were considered too few and internally too heterogeneous to act as meaningful areas through which federal programmes could be delivered (Wettenhall and Power, 1974). At the same time, with over 900 separate authorities, local governments were too numerous to contemplate coordination. Furthermore, their restricted areas, particularly the metropolitan areas, would lead to substantial spillover problems. As a compromise, regional bodies were to be voluntarily formed, covering areas devised by amalgamating local authorities (M. I. Logan *et al.*, 1975). Federal grants were to be used as an incentive to local authorities to amalgamate.

The use of regions and the regional programmes themselves led to conflict between national, state and local governments (Paddison, 1977). The amalgamation of local governments into larger units, albeit on only an administrative plane, threatened a possible loss of status. The states too were hostile, including those with Labour governments. The use of 'local governments' in the regional programmes was viewed as an infringement of state rights. Most of the state had their own regional forms of administration and the federal government's schemes were seen as an attempt to bypass the states.

Underlying the regional policies was the belief that the states were an obstacle to needed national reforms. Equalizing the 'quality of life among the regions of Australia', an explicit goal of the Labour government, necessitated greater centralization, because the states were considered 'too small and weak' to deal with national issues. Yet in hindsight the programmes would have gained a greater measure of success had they involved the states more directly: with their cooperation, decentralization on an intra-state basis would have met fewer obstacles.

FEDERAL VERSUS NON-FEDERAL STATES: SOME CONCLUSIONS

In chapter 2 it was argued that power is distributed territorially to meet particular ends — political, administrative and economic. In this final section we might usefully draw together some of the threads of our discussion on federal and non-federal states.

The territorial integrity of the state is among the most fundamental of the political goals. However, it is one on which federal and non-federal countries cannot be directly compared because of the different premises on which they are based. In the classic federation, establishment of the more embracing jurisdiction followed the voluntary association of the component states or provinces. In unitary states, power is devolved from the centre parsimoniously: the need to safeguard the overriding national interest is the kind of reason used to explain centralization, but in reality central governments are reluctant to shed power to the regions. In contrast to the federal states, political integration in a number of the West European countries analysed involved the use of coercion, the union being established through annexation by a 'core group' rather than by the voluntary accession of co-equal territorial partners. Nevertheless, the persistence of ethno-territorial groups in the unitary states has forced the consideration of quasi-federal practices and, in some countries, their adoption.

Decentralization is frequently associated with 'better' government. Though lacking in precision, the sorts of factors implied by the term are whether in comparison to national governments the decentralized body is more accessible, more sympathetic and quicker to respond to local needs. In practice, the evaluation of decentralization is more complex than such a simple checklist suggests: because of their proximity, regional governments may be more responsive to local needs, but, as the history of racial discrimination in Southern US states shows, they may also be more responsive to particular groups. Another qualification is that the extent to which the regional unit enjoys financial independence will affect the degree to which the regional government will be able to respond to local needs and tailor its policies accordingly. The contribution of regional autonomy in Northern Ireland to industrial development and regional planning, areas that remained exclusively under provincial control until the termination of devolution in 1970, rather than shared with the London government, demonstrated the advantages of decentralization. Even the Northern Ireland Labour party, though politically opposed to the ruling Unionist government, argued that devolution had enabled the province to meet its regional economic problems better than other regions of the UK facing similar industrial decline; in terms of such indices as job creation there is some evidence to support the claim (Moore and Rhodes, 1978).

Giving each region greater autonomy over such fields as regional and industrial development, however, complicates the process of national spatial planning, besides encouraging inter-regional competition for the attraction of industry. The advantage of the higher (spatially more embracing) jurisdiction is its ability to coordinate economic and other activities across regional boundaries. It can also ensure that the fiscal and other disparities between regions, which are inherent in the 'asymmetries' produced by the division of the national territory into regions and by the operation of the development process producing a spatially uneven distribution of economic wealth, do not become so great as to threaten its own stability.

One of the apparent 'costs' of federal systems of government is the greater variation in how essential public services are provided. This reflects the greater number of decision points in the federal system, and insofar as the variations match local needs is only meeting what is commonly considered to be an objective of the territorial distribution of power. Comparing educational expenditures in four federal and four unitary systems, Cameron and Hofferbert (1974) confirmed that intra-national variation was greater in the more decentralized type (table 4.8). They were also able to show that in federal countries the distribution of total educational expenditures compounded regional disparities in real income. Conversely, in the unitary systems the broad impact of educational expenditures 'is, in distributional terms, to equalise the within-nation

TABLE 4.8   Intra-national variations in educational expenditures per pupil (1965–66)

	Coefficient of relative variation
Unitary systems:	
England (45 counties)	7.4
Netherlands (11 provinces)	5.2
Norway (20 fylker)	11.9
Sweden (25 län)	16.9
Federal systems:	
Canada (10 provinces)	29.0
Germany (10 *Länder*)	15.6
Switzerland (25 cantons)	26.8
United States (50 states)	20.3

Source: Cameron and Hofferbert (1974)

disparities' (Cameron and Hofferbert, 1974, 246). In other words, redistribution from the wealthiest to the poorer, non-industrial, frequently peripheral areas is more effective in unitary systems.

Whether equity is an important objective to which the political system should be oriented depends on the value preferences of different societies. In the United States the political advantages associated with decentralization tend to weigh against the achievement of greater equity in how public services are delivered. In the unitary state, by contrast, greater emphasis on uniform standards tends to reduce spatial disparities in public service provision. Though we must approach the data with some caution, the Devolution Attitudes Survey in the UK, part of the research evidence collected by the Commission on the Constitution (1973a), found that, if decentralization meant a worsening of either the regional economy or the standard at which public services were provided, public opinion was more in favour of a territorial *status quo*. Such differences between the UK and US help support Livingston's idea of a federal culture, in which there is a more profound commitment to decentralization (and to its possible 'costs').

5

Local Services and the Fragmented State

In the two previous chapters we were mainly concerned with the implications of a spatial division of power at the central and regional level. The political region was emphasized because regional-level governments, both as they are emerging within unitary-style states and as they exist in federal countries, represent major territorial schisms that can, ultimately, threaten the territorial stability of the state. In this chapter we shall turn our attention to sub-state, and particularly local, governments (counties, urban jurisdictions, etc.) and examine their role as service providers. This function does not exhaust the responsibilities of local government — it is also involved in the regulation of the local space through planning and zoning powers and more directly in fostering production and capital accumulation through the provision of infrastructure, for example — though there is no doubting that the service function is an important one. (Empirically the analyses of inter-jurisdictional variations in service spending patterns will touch upon some of these other functions, for example expenditure on planning, but at an aggregate level and based on revenue, rather than capital, spending programmes.) The service function of local government is a vital and growing one; as the state has become ever more involved in providing goods and services, for whatever reason, so local government has often been used as a vehicle for their delivery.

There are several reasons why the study of local service provision should be an important field to the political geographer. Firstly, as measurable items they provide a means of studying the output behaviour of local governments — that is, what local governments do and the reasons underlying the behaviour. In a simple descriptive sense, studying local service provision is an explicitly geographical task because of the commonly observed pattern of territorial variation in how services are provided. Though the incidence of variation may vary between countries — as, for example, between federal and non-federal states because of the differing degrees of centralization — it is still true that in the centralized state the pattern of spatial variation is repeated. In other words, citizens living within different jurisdictions receive different mixes of goods and services. This may be justifiable in terms of different patterns of need and demand, but such variation often raises equity considerations, besides demanding an explanation.

Analysing the reasons for such variation takes the political geographer closer to the factors underlying policy-making and to questions with which social scientists generally have become more concerned. Within political science the growth of policy studies — what governments do and why — has sought to look at the relationships between governments and their environments by focusing on the outputs of the political system, lending weight to what Lasswell (1936) had suggested should be the agenda for the discipline, paraphrased in his well-known dictum, 'the study of who gets what, when and how'. The extension of this to include the spatial dimension, pioneered by the work of D. M. Smith (1974), is another reason why political geographers might study local public services. By looking at the factors underlying spatial variation, political geography can feed into a mainstream theme of human geography — the patterning of spatial welfare (Cox, 1979). Nor is there any doubting that the services that political scientists and geographers have analysed under this heading have welfare impacts. Governments, and what they do, are instrumental in influencing life-chances; indeed their role is potentially crucial insofar as the public sector can become a useful vehicle to compensate for the inequalities created by dependence on the market-place economy.

One of the models frequently used to help explain differences in service provision between jurisdictions, and the one we shall be most concerned with here, is the systems framework. The basic assumption of this framework is that the outputs of the system, in this case the spending patterns of local governments on specific services, are in some way determined by a set of input factors mediated through the political and administrative institutions of the authority. Systems models are no stranger to the political geographer (Cohen and Rosenthal, 1971) and their application to output studies has resulted in a large and steadily growing body of research (for a recent review of European work see the book edited by Newton, 1981). It is important, however, to realize the limitations of the systems model; at best it provides an organizing framework within which systematically to examine the influence of certain variables on spending patterns. Its theoretical underpinning is tenuous while, as we shall see, the level of explanation it achieves is suspect in a number of respects.

Another reason for the importance to the political geographer of variations in service provision in the fragmented state stems from the wider questions that local delivery raises for the state. These problems essentially result from the interaction between fiscal variables and local autonomy. Briefly, the argument is that local governments in the industrial nations have become increasingly charged with the responsibility for providing a growing number of services, while at the same time they have suffered from an increasing inability to meet their spending needs from the local fiscal base. Sharpe (1981) argues that at root the problem stems from the 'disparity between responsibility and power . . . [which is] . . . endemic to local government in the modern democratic state' (Sharpe, 1981, 6). On the one hand, local government is constitutionally not in a position to limit the range of functions for which it is responsible, while, on the other, it generally does not enjoy buoyant local tax systems growing in line with the development of the economy. Thus local government can become increasingly dependent upon central government grants.

This is not the only source of fiscal strain or the only reason why local government becomes fiscally dependent upon the actions of the higher jurisdiction. The territorial fragmentation of the state and the resultant spatial disparities in fiscal resources and needs have meant that in many countries some form of fiscal equalization programme, however fully developed, has been introduced. The dependence upon extra-local sources of revenue need not of itself erode local autonomy. But it is a potential danger in that local governments heavily dependent upon the centre for fiscal support may find that a central government intent on cutting public expenditure attempts to control local spending by reducing the level of grant support. Precisely because of its dependence and because of its inferior constitutional status, local government will find itself in a weak position. How services are financed by local government, therefore, becomes intertwined with the larger fiscal crises of the state, thus heightening conflict between the different levels of government.

Before looking at these broad questions, we need to outline briefly the major responsibilities of local government.

THE SERVICE FUNCTIONS OF LOCAL GOVERNMENT

Whatever other importance is attached to local government, such as Mills' idea of it as a training ground in political education, for the majority of citizens a (if not *the*) prime function of it is as the provider of goods and services. This is perhaps understandable when the absolute growth of spending by local and intermediate governments is examined: in Britain between 1890 and 1975 local government current spending *per capita* and capital expenditure rose in real terms by 850 and 2,100 per cent respectively (Foster, Jackman and Perlman, 1980). (*Per capita* spending is a better measure than total spending in that it gives a better indication of the total amount of services consumed by the average citizen.) In America, looking at domestic expenditures, the states and local governments are considerably more important over a whole range of services than is the federal government.

Not unexpectedly the range of functions over which sub-state governments have responsibility varies between countries. The picture is further complicated by the overlap or sharing of functions between different levels of government. Nevertheless there are a number of services for which sub-state governments are usually responsible, a list that includes those essential to the maintenance of law and order, property and environmental amenity, public enlightenment and certain social welfare functions. Table 5.1 compares the major functions of metropolitan local governments in the United States with those of English local government. In both cases there are major responsibilities for protection and maintenance services and, to varying degrees, improvement of the jurisdiction, combined with the provision of a set of services, such as education and welfare programmes, whose benefits can be ascribed more specifically to the individual.

TABLE 5.1   Types of local government functions, United States and England

United States	England
1. Caretaker services — protecting and managing the local environment, e.g. police and fire protection, upkeep of local roads, traffic control measures.	1. Protective services, e.g. police, fire, civil defence, public inspection.
2. Promoter services — enhancing the local environment so as to improve the tax base, e.g. town planning.	2. Environmental — controlling and improving the environment, e.g. highways, town planning, street lighting, housing, water supply, public health.
3. Amenity services — more 'desirable' than 'essential', e.g. social welfare functions.	3. Personal services, e.g. education, children's services, individual health services.
4. Education.	4. Cultural and recreational, e.g. swimming pools, libraries, art galleries and museums.
	5. Trading operations, e.g. bus services, airports.

Sources: Williams and Adrian (1963); Stanyer (1976)

These classifications of the service functions of local government can be recast within O'Connor's (1973) typology of state expenditures; in this way the functions of local government can be seen more closely within the role of the state. O'Connor argues from a Marxist perspective that the capitalist state needs to fulfil two different and often contradictory functions — ensuring the profitability of the economy and maintaining social cohesion and legitimacy. These objectives are met through different types of expenditure — social investment expenditures to ensure a propitious environment in which capital accumulation can prosper; social consumption expenditures aimed at the reproduction of the labour force; and social expenses expenditure directed at the means both of coercion (maintenance of law and order) and of legitimation (such as welfare programmes). Drawing upon O'Connor's typology and the work on the local state by Cockburn (1977), Saunders (1979) has developed the following taxonomy of the functions of British local government:

1. Functions necessary for supporting private production and capital accumulation ('social investment' expenditures):
   (i)   the provision of necessary urban infrastructure, e.g. roads and bridges
   (ii) reorganizing and restructuring space so as to meet the needs of private production, e.g. through planning
   (iii) maintaining the stock of 'human capital' through education, especially technical education.
2. Functions necessary for the reproduction of labour-power through collective consumption ('social consumption' expenditures):
   (i)   through the material conditions of existence, e.g. low-rent public housing
   (ii) through the cultural conditions of existence, e.g. libraries, museums, recreation.
3. Functions necessary for the maintenance of order and social cohesion ('social expenses' expenditure):
   (i)   through the means of coercion, e.g. police
   (ii) through the support of the 'surplus population', e.g. social services and welfare concessions
   (iii) through the support of the agencies of legitimation, e.g. schools, public participation.

EXPLAINING INTER-JURISDICTIONAL VARIATIONS IN LOCAL
   SERVICE OUTPUTS

The way in which public services are delivered usually differs between jurisdictions. Summarizing a great deal of the available evidence, Fried (1975) argues that for the majority of countries that have been studied (mostly in North America and Europe) substantial variations are apparent not only in how public services are delivered but also in the delivery of individual policy items. Looking at one type of local government unit, the English county borough (as it existed prior to the reforms of the 1970s), Danziger (1978) shows that these variations were common — he considered the variations to be salient where the coefficient of variation was greater than 10 per cent — and that their incidence varied according to the type of service (see table 5.2). Spending variations tended to be greater within the personal social services and on certain environmental services, notably town planning, sewage and sewerage. Conversely, spending on education and police — in both of which, particularly education, there have been strong attempts by the centre to ensure local authorities meet certain standards of service — is marked by much lower variation.

While it is easy enough to cite evidence alleging public service disparities, the problem is that there is no generally accepted methodology by which their distribution should be assessed. Very often reliance is placed on *per capita* spending on a specific service, if only because of the relative accessibility of such data. In keeping with other studies, we use the term 'outputs' for these spending levels though they are only crude measures of performance. To say that £x was allocated to education says nothing about how that money was spent, which would give a more accurate assessment of service quality; in fact, rather than being an output, the budgetary allocation could more realistically be considered as an input measure.

Though the use of expenditure variables is unsatisfactory on several counts, a point to which we shall return, as far as the evidence on public service disparities is concerned it is reassuring to find that where more refined performance measures have been analysed the pattern of territorial variations is repeated. Meacher (1971) examined the extent of the variation in how social services are delivered in England using a variety of performance measures specific to each type of service (see table 5.3). Allocations in the most generous authorities can be over eight times the median performance. The more careful and detailed work by B. Davies (1968; 1971) on the variations in certain personal social services used specific measures of performance and again was able to highlight the widespread existence of inter-jurisdictional differences.

TABLE 5.2   Variability in service provision: expenditure per head in the English county boroughs

		Coefficient of variation (%)[1]			
0–10	10–20	20–30	30–40	40–50	>50
	Police, primary and secondary education	Highways, fire, ambulance, parks, libraries	Midwifery, domestic help, health visiting, mental health	Children's homes	Sewage and sewerage, town planning, welfare services for the blind

[1] The coefficient of variation expresses the standard deviation as a percentage of the mean. It is a measure of relative variability.
Source: Adapted from data in Danziger (1978)

TABLE 5.3   Variations in local authority performance in England, selected social services

Service	Highest	Median	Lowest	% of median Highest	% of median Lowest
No. of home helps per 1000 population	1.83	0.77	0.23	238	30
Nursery places: pupils <5 as % of births 1965–66	33.0	3.9	0	846	0
Special housing for elderly persons: accommodation per 1000 aged over 65	118.0	16.7	0	707	0

Source: Adapted from Meacher (1971, 1085)

The basic systems model

A variety of models have been developed to explain such differences in resource allocation. Expressed as an exercise in budgetary decision-making, Danziger (1978) tested several alternative models concerned with the working of the local government as an administrative organization. Resource allocation by decision-makers (elected representatives, bureaucrats) might be based on some incremental or satisficing approach so that future allocations are based largely on past experience, resulting in only marginal changes of spending. Alternatively allocations might be more determined by the 'internal operating procedures' by which the local authority functions. These explanations, though probably more powerful in explaining differences of resource allocation, are of less concern to our present argument than are those ecological models that have sought to trace links between policy outputs and the environment within which the decision-making processes occur.

The idea that the outputs of government can be linked to some initiating set of input factors has attracted considerable attention among political scientists within the last two decades. Usually this input–output approach is tied to a rudimentary systems model according to which decisions on resource allocation are triggered by certain inputs from the environment mediated through a set of political institutions and processes that constitute a 'black box'. In its bare essentials such a model is represented by the three elements shown in figure 5.1, together with the effects of the local and extra-local environments and the existence of a number of feedback loops linking output behaviour to the other components within the system. Unlike in some input–output studies, in this model those environmental

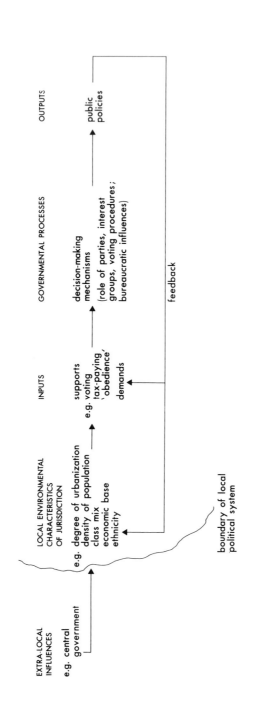

FIGURE 5.1 A simplified model of the local political system

factors frequently described as input variables in their own right (urbanization, class structure, etc.) actually form part of the operating environment; they are of importance in articulating certain demands and supports to which the political system will respond.

Among the components of the local environment the socio-economic character of the governmental unit and the influence of political cultures are fundamental. Within the first would normally be included factors measuring the economic and demographic make-up of the unit; it is presumed that differences in these will have an influence on the demands made of the political system. Measuring the influence of the environment is usually achieved by taking a bank of social and economic characteristics, treating these as independent variables, and using correlation and regression techniques to test for the existence of significant relationships between these and differences in spending patterns on particular services across a set of local governments. This is equivalent to arguing that spending patterns are a response to various 'needs', the existence of which is indicated by differences of socio-economic make-up. But these responses are conditioned by a number of other factors not least of which is the influence of the local political culture which, although a less tangible element of the environment than the demographic or economic composition, is nonetheless a pervasive force. Thus the value commitments of political communities will vary and give rise, as we have shown earlier of the separate states within America, to different types of responses, which are measurable in legislative terms and by other forms of output.

Besides the influence of the local environment, extra-local forces will have a bearing on how the local political system operates. The extent to which these forces influence the local system reflects the autonomy of the local or regional government; this can vary from being considerable (as in the case of the constituent states of federal countries or regional devolution) to cases where local government actions are strongly circumscribed by a higher level of government. Hansen and Kjellberg (1976) show, however, that the constraining influence of central government on local government actions is a complex phenomenon; the autonomy of the locality is measurable in terms both of policy definition and of spending. Thus among Norwegian municipalities there is relatively little flexibility in defining policy goals for education but much greater autonomy in terms of the financing and spending policies on it, while the opposite is true in the case of social welfare.

This analytic distinction between goal-setting and standardization has been extended by Hansen (1981) in a subsequent study of output behaviour in Norwegian municipalities. Goal-setting refers to the basic 'desired state of affairs in terms of local government activity, standardization [to the] regulation of the decision-making rules by which these objectives ought to be pursued' (Hansen, 1981, 35). Thus central government may set certain goals that local authority outputs should strive to achieve for the care of the elderly, while standardization refers to the criteria to be employed to decide who is eligible for assistance. Services vary according to whether central government lays down the basic goals and/or standards for service provision and hence the latitude the local government has in its budgetary behaviour. Some services — primary education in Hansen's analysis — are closely regulated, while others, such as cultural activities, are free of either goal or standardization constraints. Thus when looking at the association between socio-economic and political variables and spending on the regulated service we should find a higher degree of overall association (measured by R^2) than would be the case for the unregulated activity, which Hansen's findings largely corroborate.

Where a higher level of government, very often the central government, is a major influence on how the lesser jurisdiction operates, explaining why public service outputs should differ between jurisdictions will place a heavier reliance on extra-local factors. But the degree of central control over detailed local administration is something that is keenly debated among political scientists. In Britain, Robson (1966) has argued that central control has become increasingly salient in the present century, in part arising from the mismatch between the responsibilities of local governments and their financial resources, which results in a growing dependence on non-local sources of revenue. Other observers of British local government have attacked Robson's thesis of central domination — that the local authorities have become 'mere receptacles for [central] government policy' — arguing that, although the centre does exercise some degree of control over the locality, local governments themselves, when deciding on financial allocations, are more concerned with the demands of their proximate environment (Stanyer, 1976). Nevertheless, for a number of locally administered services the appropriate central government departments stipulate the minimum standards at which services should be delivered, which, though by no means universally adopted, effectively reduces the autonomy of the local government.

These questions of central control and local autonomy have received renewed emphasis in Britain with the policies of the post-1979 Conservative government, one of whose specific objectives has been to reduce the volume of local government spending as part of a wider strategy of reducing the total size of the public sector. As the greater proportion of local expenditure is borne by central government grant, the centre is in an apparently powerful position to control local spending. An important element of the new block grant (the previous rate support grant is described later in this chapter) is an assessment of local spending needs by the centre; failure to comply will entail a loss of grant. Such changes have heightened centre–local conflict — local governments resent the alleged erosion of their autonomy, particularly in the higher-spending Labour-controlled authorities that, anyway, are opposed to the national government's spending cuts policies. In Scotland this has already led to direct conflict between the centre and the Labour-controlled Lothian region, though the effect of the penalty clause led to the eventual reduction of the local budget in line with the centre's assessment. While these measures do appear to have reduced local autonomy, particularly as further legislation was envisaged to prevent local governments from raising extra finances through higher rates charges, it remains to be seen what effects are experienced in inter-authority service delivery patterns.

From a politico-geographic viewpoint we might ask whether there are any spatial regularities underlying these patterns of central influence. Two questions arise: whether the effects of central control are greater nearer to the centre and whether the territorial configuration of authorities, reflected for example in the differences in their population size, has any systematic bearing on the relationship between centre and locality. In neither case are there sufficient hard data to enable proper evaluation and in any case it is extremely difficult to separate these spatial effects from the other factors that influence central–local relations. Clark (1974) suggests that proximity to the national capital does influence local autonomy (see figure 2.8), though he is unable to provide adequate data to support the claim. While it is true that in a number of countries — federal states are a special case in this respect, as has been seen — there are stronger linkages between the centre and the government of the capital city, whose existence should not be interpreted as involving detailed control over specific services, it is rather unlikely that there is any systematic distance–decay effect in the influence of the centre. Similarly, arguments concerning the effects of the territorial configuration on local autonomy need to be approached with caution. Thus the population size of a local jurisdiction has at most probably only a minor influence on improving the locality's bargaining strength with the centre (Ashford, 1980), while Boaden (1971b), looking at some of the available British evidence, concluded that smaller authorities, where they disagree with the policies central government is attempting to impose upon them, are not more likely to submit to the demands of the higher jurisdiction. However, the sheer complexity of the territorial division of the state hinders detailed scrutiny by the centre. Even in the reduced network of authorities following the 1972 reorganization in England, the ability of central government to have an accurate picture of what local governments are doing is limited because of the very number of subordinate jurisdictions (CPRS, 1977).

Before looking in greater detail at the findings of the input–output models, we should note some of the general criticisms that have been levelled at such studies (Coulter, 1970; Newton and Sharpe, 1977). The most serious of these concerns the models of explanation used by such studies and the inadequate treatment of process variables. The first concerns the almost quantum jumps that are made between environmental variables and their effect in producing particular demands; there is little theory to suggest why (for example) in two jurisdictions — one with a mixed social structure and the other more homogeneous in terms of its class or ethnic composition — the demands and hence the policy outputs of each will differ. Related to this is the danger of applying simple cause–effect arguments. Recognizing this, Danziger (1978) prefers the idea of labelling the environmental factors as 'constraints' that might influence spending allocations. The models can be further criticized for concealing the nature of the political processes influencing allocations — the role of pluralist influences, bargaining, etc. — within the black box.

Other limitations of the model concern measurement problems, which have already been mentioned. Outputs considered in terms of government expenditures provide only a superficial indicator of spending effort, concealing the programmes and policies to which the allocations are to be directed. Just as important is the distinction between outputs and outcomes: an outcome refers to the consequences of an output, so there is little doubt that its measurement would give a better indication of the impact (and hence quality) of spending policies (Levy *et al.*, 1974). To know that separate local governments spend different amounts on the library service begs the question whether the readership or book turnover rates differ accordingly. Outcomes rather than outputs will lead to a better understanding of the effect of policies on wellbeing, though the availability of suitable and accessible data represents an obstacle to the greater measurement of outcomes.

Basic findings

Input–output studies have been analysed within a considerable variety of different types of political systems, at both regional and local level. An early study by Fabricant (1952) had suggested that environmental differences, notably differences in *per capita* income, population density and urbanization, helped explain differences in government spending. It was Dawson and Robinson (1963), in an examination of welfare spending in the American states, who explicitly brought in political as well as socio-economic variables: measures of state wealth and social structure were used to indicate the levels of demand and support for welfare spending, while factors related to the party structure, notably the degree of competitiveness between the parties, were intended to reflect the political processes by which the conversion of the inputs to outputs actually took place. Such a framework, although somewhat modified, was subsequently applied to local government both within American metropolitan areas (Dye, 1967) and within European local government systems (Boaden, 1971b; Fried, 1974).

Working within the context of the county boroughs of England and Wales, Boaden (1971b) used three basic sets of variables to explain the differences in spending patterns:

1. Needs. Though an ambiguous term, needs can be defined simply as objective conditions that demand ameliorative action by governments. These should include conditions generated by the physical and socio-economic character of the jurisdiction that arise either within the community at large or from a specific area or demographic sub-group within it.
2. Resources. These are essentially the various means that the local jurisdiction has at its command and that will ease solution of its problems. Resources are of several kinds including, besides fiscal wealth, the jurisdiction's 'supply of leadership' and its territorial extent, which influence the degree to which it can meet problems (attracting industrial growth, rehousing slum populations, etc.) within its own boundaries.
3. Dispositions, giving a measure of the preferences individually or collectively expressed about how services should be provided. Boaden identifies three questions to each of which attitudes may well vary between the principal actors in the local political system — politicians, bureaucrats and the citizen:
   (i)   the perception of needs and the level at which services are to be offered relative to some minimal standard;
   (ii) attitudes towards groups in need within the local community; and
   (iii) attitudes towards the desirability and legitimacy of government action to deal with these needs.

Combining these three dimensions, 'activity in any service will depend on the incidence of *need* for that service, on the *disposition* of the authority to provide that service and on the availability of *resources* with which to provide the service' (Boaden, 1971b, 21).

Table 5.4 summarizes the results of several studies showing the influence of needs, resources and disposition variables on county borough spending. While all three show significant associations, their incidence varies both generally and specifically according to the type of service. Differences of need are the most consistent in influencing spending allocations, particularly in the case of housing. Labour representation tends to play a larger part in education, which is one of the other major redistributive items within the local authority's budget. Boaden's conclusions are that the principal variations in spending are attributable to party politics —Labour-dominated councils tend to spend more on the more expensive services — and that the way in which councils respond to social needs reflects the influence of party control. It is not, however, a conclusion that is shared by other workers in the field. Oliver and Stanyer (1969), looking at the

TABLE 5.4 Resources, needs and dispositions, and expenditure patterns in English county boroughs

	RESOURCES				NEEDS					DISPOSITIONS
	Rateable value/ head	% domestic rateable value	High social class	Low social class	% population 5–14	Population	Density	Amenities	Crowding	% Labour party on council
Protective:										
Police			−			+				
Fire			−	+						
All education							−			
Environmental:										
Highways	+									
Planning	+									
Public sector home building	−	−	−	+	+	−	+	−	+	+
Personal services:										
Local health services		−	−	+						
Children's services		−	−			+	+	−		+
Recreational:										
Parks	+									+

Note: +/− indicates a significant degree of association (Pearson's 'r' $\geq$ .22); in other cases there is no significant relationship.
Source: Adapted from Alt (1971); Boaden (1971b); Danziger (1978)

variation in general financial expenditure in the county boroughs, conclude that socio-economic factors, rather than party political influences, are the most important, while Danziger (1978) argues that Labour representation and other political variables — the electoral marginality of the ruling party and the extent of party competitiveness — have only a moderate influence on resource allocation.

The argument over whether political or socio-economic variables are the dominant influence underlying resource allocation has preoccupied much of the debate on the analysis of spending variations between the American states. In a classic study of Southern politics, Key (1949) suggested that, in state elections characterized by competition between two parties, each party will make appeals to the 'have nots' within the electorate, thereby raising the level of spending subsequently. Lockard (1959), working within New England, shows that spending on welfare programmes is greater in the states where elections are competitive (Massachusetts, Rhode Island and Connecticut). However, Dawson and Robinson (1963) argue that, while party political and socio-economic variables are associated with welfare spending when social and economic conditions are held constant, the influence of competitiveness on spending is insignificant. Expanding the range of spending fields, Dye (1966) has argued that neither party nor structural factors — voter turnout and legislative apportionment — have any systematic independent influence on expenditure patterns.

While Dye's conclusions were disturbing to the political scientist, subsequent workers have tended to qualify his findings. Sharkansky and Hofferbert (1969), in a study of state spending, show that political system variables (defined in terms of two components based on a factor analysis of state socio-political structures, labelled 'competition/turnout' and 'professionalism/local reliance', the latter reflecting the degree of professionalism in government and the use of non-local sources of revenue) correlate highly with welfare and education spending measures but less so with expenditures on highways and natural resources programmes. Part of the explanation for these differences arises from the way in which certain issues and not others tend to be more confrontational between socio-economic and ethnic groups.

The evidence on the independent effect of political variables within different geographical contexts on local outputs, however, remains contradictory. Concluding his synthesis of more than 50 studies of urban output behaviour, Fried argues:

> in many, probably most cases, some socio-economic variable has been found more useful in explaining the variance in outputs than any political variable. The implication of these findings is that most forms of political activity are either futile or marginal . . . it makes little difference for urban policy who controls local government, what their values are, who turns out to vote . . . (Fried, 1975, 337)

Nevertheless, subsequent studies of local government within Italy, France, Norway and Sweden have emphasized that social democratic or leftist control results in higher levels of spending and a greater attention to redistributive programmes.

Systems within systems

Most of the studies referred to in the previous section treat each jurisdiction as an 'isolated' political system; one of the few extra-local influences that is admitted is the centre. However, regional and local jurisdictions do not exist in geographical isolation. They are members of the total system of sub-national governments. Viewed in this way we can look at the spending patterns of one jurisdiction as related to its functional–economic position within the national space-economy; in other words, different types of jurisdiction grouped according to function, economic status or some other defining characteristic will have different types of spending behaviour. This approach to examining variations in spending differs from the earlier type of study not only in analysing groups of authorities but also in looking at spending across bundles of services.

Newton (1979; 1980) has explored two ways by which urban local governments can be classified — their position within the national system of central places and their functional–economic base. The lines between central place status and public spending follow several paths (see figure 5.2). Higher-status central places will need to spend heavily on services critical to their centrality, which are in many cases services used by commuters and other non-residents. Certain types of services, such as major libraries, museums and galleries, can be termed 'central place services' because their usage is directly linked to the city's centrality, while others, the protective services for example, necessitate higher expenditures to maintain a conducive environment within which the commercial sector can thrive. Taking just two services, fire and libraries, table 5.5 suggests an

TABLE 5.5   Spending differences and central place status in Ireland

Type of central place[2]	Service expenditure (£/cap.)[1]	
	Fire	Libraries
National (1)	0.57	0.60
Regional (3)	0.47	0.23
Sub-regional (6)	0.37	0.32

[1] Data on expenditure for 1966.
[2] Numbers in brackets refer to the number of centres involved.
Source: Unpublished research, based on Department of Local Government (Ireland) information

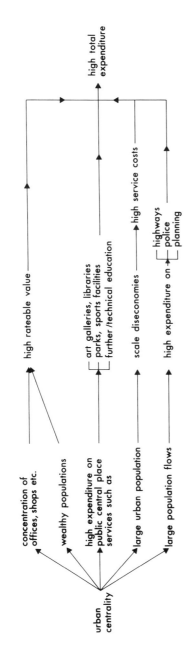

FIGURE 5.2   Some possible relationships between urban centrality and local public expenditure (from Newton, 1980)

overall, though not perfect, relationship between central place status and spending effort among the larger Irish urban local governments.

The idea that the type of city will have an influence on its public service expenditures is intuitively attractive. Just as the spatial division of labour groups urban (and rural) governments into certain functional–economic types, so the differing needs linked to these city types will influence spending. The older, industrial city with a decaying physical fabric will need to spend heavily on urban redevelopment programmes and local housing, while a seaside resort will probably devote most of its resources to leisure and recreation activities, policing and other services necessary to maintain the tourist economy (table 5.6).

City-type explanations of local output variations are not substitutes for the types of variable introduced earlier. Aiken and Depré (1980), in a study of Belgian cities, help put the factor into perspective. They differentiate between the cities on the basis of their 'ecological centrality' — the importance of the city to the state in terms of its consumption and production activities. Three other influences — local electoral competitiveness, socialist control and population stability — were considered likely to lead to higher overall expenditures, while Catholic control over the city would have the opposite effect. As table 5.7 shows, the centrality of the city is consistently the most important variable across a variety of services.

LOCAL SERVICES, FISCAL DEPENDENCE AND FISCAL CRISES

To the local jurisdiction the availability of sufficient financial resources to meet the service needs and demands of the locality is obviously of prime importance. The philosophy underlying the local provision of services was originally that the necessary revenue would be raised locally. One advantage of each local jurisdiction operating as a more or less self-contained financial unit was seen to be that taxing and spending policies could be closely tailored to local needs, while another advantage was the greater autonomy that such 'independence' would foster.

The argument for the fiscal independence of the locality confronts two sets of problems. The first set arises from the spatial mismatch between fiscal resources and needs resulting from the act of territorially dividing the state into a system of local governments. The second set follows from the relationships between central and local government. These two factors intermesh and contribute to the fiscal problems characterizing local governments. In effect, local governments — though not all of them and certainly more in some countries than in others — find it increasingly difficult to provide services in line with their needs or locally expressed

TABLE 5.6 Service spending and city types, England and Wales, 1960–61

Spending 10% above/below average	County towns (12)	Commercial cities (5)	Large free-standing industrial cities (8)	Metropolitan capitals (5)	Secondary capitals (5)	Industrial satelites (26)	Small free-standing industrial cities (5)	Suburbs (2)	Seaside resorts (8)
Above	Libraries Sewerage Planning	Planning[1]	Sewerage Planning	Libraries[1] Parks Public health Highways Housing Police	Sewerage Parks	Housing	Sewerage Public health	Parks Public health Police	Parks Public health Police
Below	Parks	Housing Fire		Sewerage Welfare Planning	Planning[1] Fire	Libraries Planning[1]	Libraries Parks Planning[1]	Libraries[1] Sewerage[1] Welfare Highways Housing[1]	Sewerage Housing[1]

[1] Spending 30% above/below average.
Source: Adapted from data in Newton (1980)

TABLE 5.7 Regression of selected spending categories on four independent variables, Belgium, 196 cities of 10,000 or more population[1]

Spending categories	Ecological centrality[2]	Political competition[2]	Catholic control[2,3]	Population stagnation[2]	R² adj. (%)
Total city spending	0.662***	0.082	−0.146***	0.150	64.6
Administration:					
General administration	0.693***	0.083	−0.158***	0.091*	65.7
Social control:					
Police/security and fire	0.759***	0.102*	−0.030	0.091*	72.7
Social welfare:					
Public assistance	0.529***	0.118*	−0.156*	0.195***	52.6
Public education	0.493***	−0.026	−0.367***	0.166***	50.1
Other basic services:					
Roads/public works	0.382***	0.024	0.078	−0.073	13.0
Art, leisure, popular education	0.535***	0.062	−0.016	0.176***	41.4

[1] Spending data, 1965–66; other data, 1968.
[2] Figures shown are standardized regression coefficients
* $p < 0.05$; ** $p < 0.01$; *** $p < 0.001$ (one tail test of significance).
[3] Socialist control not shown.
Source: Adapted from Aiken and Depré (1980)

preferences. In Britain, as in a large number of other countries, the solution to these spatial disparities has been sought through various types of fiscal grants from the central government, particularly those aimed at establishing greater equality of fiscal potential. What is striking about the British case is the marked dependence of local government on these fiscal transfers from the centre. It is important to emphasize, however, that the incidence of local fiscal crises varies considerably between countries and, though not exclusively, much of the discussion in this section will deal with the British case. (Indeed, the term 'crisis' may overstate the case.) The volume of essays edited by Sharpe (1981) shows how different the picture is within Western Europe. (In the next chapter the fiscal crisis is discussed in relation to the city, when we shall pay particular attention to recent American experience.)

The impact of territorial fragmentation

Enough was said when discussing outputs to show that how public goods and services are provided within the state is partly a function of location. Services are not uniformly provided, nor should they be, given the different needs of separate localities; indeed, the argument favouring local decision-making is that each jurisdiction, acting as a 'local service club' (Buchanan, 1950), is able to articulate its service preferences in line with local demands. Nevertheless, in decentralizing service provision, we need to consider the effects of jurisdictional fragmentation, particularly on the ability of the sub-state government to provide services according to its needs, and the attendant implications this has on spatial welfare.

Two effects of fragmentation are relevant in this respect. Firstly, the division of the state creates sub-areas with varying needs and preferences but also of varying fiscal potential. There is usually a mismatch between fiscal resources and fiscal needs, the product of superimposing jurisdictional networks on the regional and local surfaces of economic inequality brought about by the spatial division of labour. Where these inequalities are salient, and particularly where the disparities between areas are widening, the mismatch will lead to demands for fiscal correction. Secondly, territorial fragmentation exacerbates the spillover problem where there is a mismatch between areas providing (and paying for) a service and those benefiting from its provision. Even the simplest of territorial divisions of the state, the 'least fragmented' option, will create some spillover effects because of the high levels of mobility characteristic of industrial nations. Both of these effects have fiscal implications and in fact are interrelated problems. We shall look at the second within the context of the American metropolitan area in the next chapter. The first will be examined through fiscal equalization programmes, particularly within Britain. Before looking at the operation of such programmes in practice, we need to examine more closely the basis of the fiscal mismatch and some of the arguments for and against inter-jurisdictional equalization.

Fiscal disparities and the case for territorial redistribution   In the establishment of local government and in the delegation of specific functional responsibilities to it, the right to collect a local tax to underwrite the provision of these services was usually also sanctioned. Local taxes are of a number of different types, though a very common one is some form of property tax. In Britain this property tax, called rates, is based on the rental value (as opposed to the capital value) of the property, and accounts for the greater proportion (60–70 per cent) of locally raised revenue. In the United States a greater variety of local taxes is found: property taxes are the most important in terms of absolute revenue raised, but the need to find revenue through other means has led to local income taxes and various sales taxes. (This conceals considerable variation — property taxes are more important to certain types of local government, especially the towns and townships, school districts and counties, but much less so to the special districts; income and sales taxes tend to be more common in certain regions, the former being confined to the eastern half of the United States.)

Normally the tax-raising abilities of intermediate and local-level governments vary (Bennett, 1980), so that governments differ in the extent to which they can meet fiscal needs from their tax resource base. In Britain, these differences of fiscal capacity are expressed by substantial variations in rateable value between authorities as a result of the differing mixes of residential and non-residential land uses and of income groups between the jurisdictions. In England and Wales, rateable values per head among the non-metropolitan counties vary from £173 in Hertfordshire to £69 in Mid-Glamorgan. Within Scotland, valuations tend to be higher in the more heavily industrialized regions and where there is a stock of highly valued domestic property, while they are lowest in the peripheral, dominantly agricultural areas, largely because of the 'de-rating' of agricultural property in Britain.

Fiscal capacity can be assessed in several ways. *Per capita* incomes give an approximate measure of resource potential and, as figure 5.3 suggests, differences in personal incomes will correlate with more direct measures of the tax resource base. In the United States, the Advisory Commission on Intergovernmental Relations (ACIR) developed a measure of fiscal capacity (among the 50 states) based on the yields of a 'representative' set of state and local tax systems (ACIR, 1963). Fiscal capacities below the US average were most pronounced in the Southeastern states, Alaska and Hawaii, while most states in the Southwest, Rocky Mountain and mainland Far West regions had relatively high fiscal capacities.

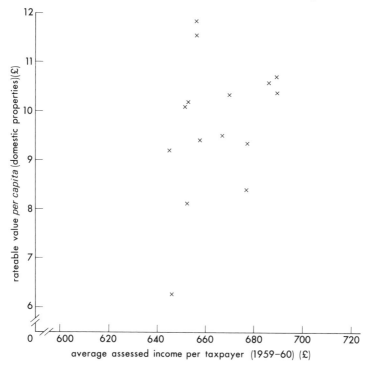

FIGURE 5.3   Domestic rateable values and personal incomes in the Scottish counties
(from Boyle, 1966)

Differences of fiscal capacity become much more important where the poorer jurisdictions are also ones whose expenditure needs are likely to be greater. This gives rise to the problem of fiscal mismatch, a feature common throughout the hierarchy of sub-national jurisdictions. Looking at the American states, Musgrave and Polinsky (1970) compared fiscal capacities (measured as outlined above) with spending needs, based on the output of an 'average' suite of state and local programmes. Many states with relatively low fiscal capacities have the higher spending needs; this is most pronounced in the Southeastern states, except Florida, together with several of the New England states. Conversely, some states — notably Wyoming, Nevada, California and Montana — have fiscal resource bases greater than the average spending need. However, it is not always the case that the jurisdiction with the higher-than-average fiscal needs has below-average fiscal capacity, while the incidence of mismatch as a problem underlying disparities in service provision tends to be more critical at the metropolitan, rather than the regional level.

The existence of these fiscal mismatches has encouraged the development of inter-governmental fiscal transfers in which assistance is channelled to lower from higher levels of government (or through the pooling of resources between affluent and less affluent jurisdictions). One of the means by which transfer is effected is through the payment of grants, of which there are two basic types (Musgrave and Musgrave, 1976):

1. the categorical grant, tied to particular spending programmes (urban renewal, highway construction, etc.) — its allocation can be fixed by a variety of methods: by the use of some formula measuring needs (based on the jurisdiction population, quality of housing stock, etc.), or inversely to the jurisdiction's fiscal ability, or as a matching grant so that the recipient authority has to make an equal financial commitment;

2. the general or block grant, not earmarked for specific programmes — its distribution is often (though not always) based on some geographically expressed needs formula. Revenue-sharing, as introduced in the United States by the State and Local Finance Act of 1972, is a variant of the block grant, differing from it by the assurance of a fixed percentage allocation paid to the lower jurisdictions and by the greater independence from federal (central) control that they enjoy.

Such fiscal transfers serve a number of purposes, the most important of which are to enable the poorer jurisdictions to pay for a minimum or standard level of services, to compensate authorities for differences in their need to spend and to reduce inequalities in tax burdens. But grant payments by central government also help ensure some degree of control over the activities of the lower jurisdictions; specifically this control can be used to ensure that service provision meets at least certain national minimum standards. (In fact, as we have suggested earlier, this control may sometimes be more apparent than real; indeed, the existence of grants-in-aid programmes in the United States gives the locality the opportunity, through lobbying and other tactics, to influence federal agencies — Farkas, 1971.) Another argument frequently used is that because of inter-jurisdictional spillover effects, particularly where there are benefits spilling into neighbouring jurisdictions, there may be a tendency for local governments to under-invest in service provision. Education is one kind of service in which the benefits of provision extend considerably beyond the providing jurisdiction (Weisbrod, 1964). Financial assistance is predicated on the expectation that jurisdictions will not invest in education sufficiently where local politicians and voters see some of the benefits flowing away from the community.

Fiscal equalization transfers are based on the need to meet equity objectives. A persuasive argument has been proposed by Buchanan (1950) based on the principle of fiscal equity: namely, that there should be equal treatment of equals whatever their geographical location. Inequities are created by the partitioning of the state that would be less likely were there to be only a single government: the existence of jurisdictions with different fiscal resource bases means that two citizens with identical service preferences but living in separate authorities, in which the unit costs of provision are the same, will have to bear different tax burdens. According to Buchanan, an equitable fiscal structure is defined where the fiscal residuum, the balance between contributions made and benefits received, is equal for persons of 'similar situation'.

While Buchanan's fiscal equity principle provides the rationale for inter-governmental transfers to offset the fiscal pressures experienced by residents in low-income jurisdictions, some writers have argued that 'an extensive system of centrally organized redistribution of income between individuals would enable some to by-pass the need for inter-authority redistribution' (Prest, 1978, 77). In the absence of effective income redistribution between individuals, inter-jurisdictional transfers are a 'second best' (Musgrave and Musgrave, 1976). However, the two may be complementary and insofar as many services (such as housing, recreation, etc.) are areally defined, giving benefits spatially as well as to individuals, there is a certain justification for the geographically based redistributive measures (Bennett, 1980).

Scott (1952), in a well-known rejoinder to Buchanan, argues that while fiscal equalization between jurisdictions may be desirable on equity grounds it is not so on those of efficiency. Transferring funds is likely to be inefficient insofar as it channels scarce resources to the poorer, lower-productivity regions. In part it is a criticism that can be countered: if the fiscal transfers are used to improve services such as education, transportation and other 'productive' services, then because of the considerable spillovers that these generate the benefits are also enjoyed by the 'efficient' regions. However, the resolution of the contradiction between equity objectives and those of efficiency requires a political decision. As we have already argued in the discussion of federal countries, there are strong political pressures underlying demands for inter-jurisdictional equity, and in the last resort this is a cogent reason for central governments to meet the equity case. Certainly territorial fiscal redistribution has been used to raise the level of services in those areas that, left to free market forces, would enjoy substantially lower standards of service provision.

Fiscal equalization — the British rate support grant In Britain, fiscal transfers from the centre to the localities account for the greater proportion of local government income; if by the latter we measure income only from central government grants and local taxes the transfer element accounts for over 60 per cent. This dependence on central government transfers reflects the steadily widening disparity between the range of duties devolved to local governments and their capacity to provide for these from locally raised income.

By far the greater proportion of grant income (86 per cent in 1976–77) comes in the form of a block grant known as the rate support grant. (The RSG to be described here was replaced by a different equalization scheme following the 1980 Local Government Planning and Land Act.) In 1979–80 the RSG met 61 per cent of the total services expenditure covering the major fields of spending — except housing, transport and police, which are met by categorical grants. In part this dependence on central government grants is rationalized on equity grounds: that is, the cost of local government services is borne by income taxes plus grants rather than exclusively by rates because income is thought to be a more equitable tax base than property values.

Another objective of the rate support grant is to reduce the inequalities between local authorities. Two of the three elements into which it is divided are specifically aimed at territorial justice (B. Davies, 1968): a needs element is designed to compensate authorities for their differences in

TABLE 5.8   The rate support grant, 1976–77

Element	England & Wales £m.	%	Scotland £m.	%	Great Britain £m.	%
Needs	3,565	60.2	624	75.8	4,189	62.1
Resources	1,716	28.9	156	18.9	1,872	27.7
Domestic	640	10.9	43	5.3	683	10.2
Totals	5,921		823		6,744	

Source: Government publications

their need to spend on services, while the resources element is aimed at reducing the disparities between local authorities in their capacity to pay taxes. The third and financially least important part, the domestic element, is designed to reduce the tax burden on the householder, so that this, ideally, will keep pace with the growth of the national economy. Table 5.8 shows how the relative importance of these elements varied between Scotland and the rest of Great Britain in 1976–77. The make-up of the regional budgets in Scotland varies in terms of the proportion from locally raised taxes and from the rate support grant (see figure 5.4). Local taxes account for a higher proportion in the more industrial and populous regions. The needs element, calculated on the basis of such variables as those shown in table 5.9, accounts for especially high proportions in the more sparsely populated regions.

The resources element of the grant allows for a 'levelling-up' of the poorer authorities by bringing their rateable value per head up to a

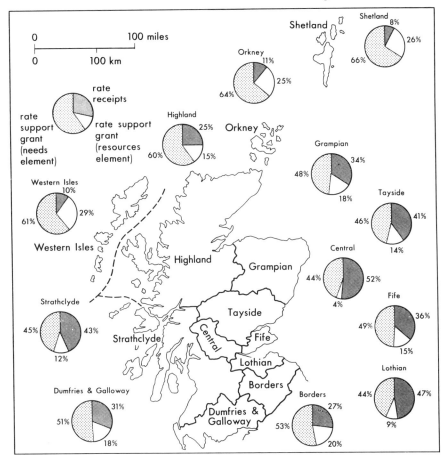

FIGURE 5.4   Sources of local finance in Scottish regional authorities

national standard level. The definition of the national standard is decided by central government following consultations with a number of organizations. The result, however, is only partial equalization because it does not level down those authorities whose *per capita* tax capacity is above standard; after distribution of the resources element, then, considerable disparities remain between jurisdictions. Only in the area served by the Greater London Council, where a separate system exists, is there a greater levelling process between richer and poorer boroughs (Southron, 1972).

Measured by monetary value, the needs component of the rate support grant is the most important. Fiscal distribution according to need is based on the recognition that costs of providing services to a reasonable standard will vary between jurisdictions because local governments differ in their demographic and geographical make-up. Above-average numbers of schoolchildren or elderly, or a large, sparsely populated rural jurisdiction are the kinds of disabilities that will raise an authority's spending needs. (Not all the sources of differences of spending between jurisdictions should be compensated for, however, for example where a local authority decides to provide a service at an above-standard level — Foster, Jackman and Perlman, 1980.) Without some form of grant to high-need jurisdictions and/or to those that have imposed costs, such as the sparsely populated district, the tendency would be for under-provision of services or, where their provision did meet national standards, for the imposition of excessive tax burdens on taxpayers.

The needs element is distributed by establishing the statistical association between a number of needs-related variables and the previous year's expenditure in over 100 local authorities using multiple regression analysis. Only the statistically significant factors are actually included within the

TABLE 5.9   Variables examined and selected in the calculation of the needs element, 1979–80

Total population*
Persons aged over 65
Persons aged over 75
Persons aged 1–4
Single parent families with dependent children*
Large families
Primary school pupils aged 5–10*
Secondary school pupils aged under 16*
Pupils and non-advanced further education students 16–18
Supplementary benefit recipients
Mortality/life expectancy
Labour costs*
Acres per person*
Persons living in households lacking basic amenities*
Persons of pensionable age living alone
Lower income
Unemployment*
Road mileage
New permanent dwellings*
Ratio of population to housing stock
Persons per acre

* Factors actually chosen for needs element.
Source: Local Authorities Association (1980)

distribution formula, and each factor is weighted according to its importance. (Table 5.9 shows which factors were chosen in 1979–80.) What is apparent is that the method of calculating the needs element is based on a circular argument — 'it is assumed that authorities will spend what they need to spend, and that need can be measured by expenditure' (Newton,

1980, 108) — and the reliance on expenditure data to estimate needs tends to reinforce spending patterns regardless of any inequities that they might contain. Nevertheless, one advantage is the use of objectively defined needs criteria, however crude they might be.

Like fiscal equalization programmes in other countries, the way in which the rate support grant is ultimately distributed can be (and is) biased by the administrative and political channels through which it is processed. Changes in the weighting of the formula used to calculate the needs element can bring about substantial shifts of resources, and, as in the case of the revenue-sharing formulae in the US, localities will lobby the centre to gain benefits. The localities in Britain have been able to secure a reasonable level of continuity in their needs-element payment through the process of 'damping'; that is, in the 1979–80 grant, for example, only one-fifth of the needs element was determined by the formula for that year, the remainder being divided equally among the formulae of the preceding four years. The effect of the damping process is to reduce the likelihood of major shifts of resources away from jurisdictions on a year-to-year basis which, because of the heavy dependence of the localities on the grant, would tend to lead to greater tax burdens in order to maintain services.

The distribution of the grant is also open to political, notably porkbarrel, influences at the centre. A number of studies (Alt, 1971; Godley and Rhodes, 1972) have suggested that fiscal flows flavouring the more rural county authorities have been characteristic of Conservative governments while Labour administrations have favoured urban areas. Godley and Rhodes highlight the correlation between the degree to which English county boroughs gain or lose as a result of certain anomalies in the distribution of the grant and their party political colour (see figure 5.5).

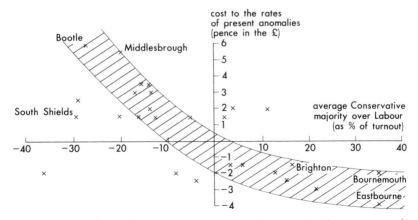

FIGURE 5.5   The relationship of the rate support grant to local party support in England, 1971
(from *The Times*, 22 November 1972)

On the more substantive question of the equity achievements of the rate support grant, most observers have been cautious (LeGrand, 1975; Newton, 1980). The resources element, for example, incorporates a 'poverty trap': jurisdictions that qualify for the topping-up payment but that are successful in attracting industry or other high-valued uses can find themselves little better off financially in that they are no longer eligible for a resources element payment. Furthermore, the basis on which the resources element is paid — rateable valuation — is unsatisfactory because of the fluctuations between authorities in assessment. It has also been quite easy to show that the needs element could be distributed differently and (apparently) more equitably. A study of the county boroughs in the English North West (Northwest Interprofessional Group, 1974) compared needs-element payments with the ranked positions of the urban areas measured against ten indicators representing a wider range of conditions than those upon which the grant payment was based. According to this, some boroughs are unfairly treated, notably Wigan, Salford and Oldham, while others such as Wallasey appear to fare unjustifiably well (see figure 5.6). The report claims that the distribution of the grant is regressive and reinforces the 'cycle of inequality': looking at education spending, in the higher income jurisdictions the residents 'have a high demand for education; so children stay on at school; so the RSG makes substantial payments; the well-endowed educational climate . . . encourages more to stay on, who in turn "earn" the authority more RSG' (Northwest Interprofessional Group, 1974, 15). Overall, however, there is a weak correlation between the alternative needs indicators and the distribution of the needs-element grant in the boroughs.

Several general points may be drawn in conclusion. Fiscal equalization between local governments is a complex technical problem. Where needs payments are based on expenditure as a proxy variable, the calculation of jurisdictional requirements necessitates a detailed data base and an acceptable statistical methodology: it was precisely these sorts of problems that hindered the Australian Labour government's attempt to extend fiscal equalization payments to the local authorities between 1972 and 1975. Secondly, fiscal equalization is not usually synonymous with attempts to establish uniform service levels between jurisdictions; rather, it is a form of compensation whereby poorer authorities have the potential to provide services at a certain minimum standard. This is not to say that the local jurisdiction does not provide a service at a lower or higher standard; such freedom is the basis of local autonomy. Thirdly, the extent to which such programmes achieve full rather than a partial equalization varies. Newton (1980) argues that the rate support grant is not markedly redistributive, being more in the nature of a fiscal transfer between the centre and the localities. Furthermore, because the resources element does not siphon off above-average fiscal capacity from the richer authorities, inequalities

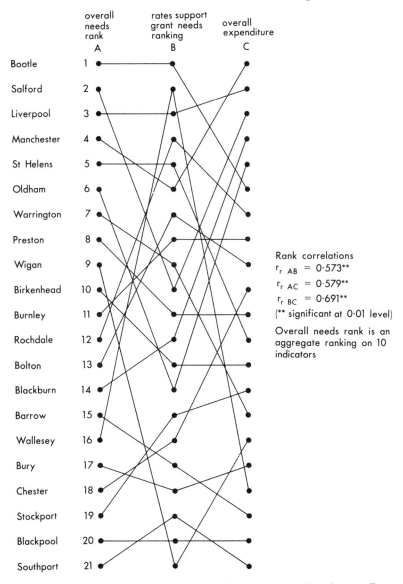

FIGURE 5.6   Alternative needs-related rankings and overall local expenditure
in northwestern towns in the United Kingdom (from Northwest
Interprofessional Group, 1974)

between jurisdictions remain. Nevertheless, the UK rate support grant and
its French and Italian counterparts are markedly more redistributive than
revenue sharing has been in the United States (European Economic

Community, 1977), where the effect of federal transfers on state equalization has been slight (Musgrave and Polinsky, 1970). The absence of a fiscal equalization mechanism — a situation that existed in Ireland until recently — will be even more inequitable. Services will be unequally delivered and rate burdens will be higher in the poorer jurisdictions, reinforcing the regional differences of economic and social wellbeing.

From fiscal dependence to fiscal 'crisis' — British local government

Though not unique within Western Europe, one of the striking features of British local government is its high degree of dependence on grants from central government. Depending on the actual measure examined — the total income of local government, its total spending or its expenditure on current items — the relative contribution of central government transfers will be seen to vary, though within each of these it represents a proportion that has increased from about 10 per cent to 50 per cent or more during the present century. As we have seen, the reasons for the growth of central government grants are grounded in large part on equity arguments — the objectives of reducing differences in the resource base of the localities and of compensating for their varying service needs. This dependence has highlighted certain weaknesses of local government relating to its local democratic accountability and autonomy, which pluralists would tend to see as part of its *raison d'être*.

The issue of accountability was one of the main themes identified by the Layfield Report (Layfield Committee, 1976). The Layfield Committee of Enquiry into Local Government Finance had been set up in the wake of widespread protest against the unprecedented rate increases of 1974. These were largely brought about by inflation, which because of the labour-intensity of local government hit the localities especially hard, but also by the costs incurred in the reorganization of local government and also certain separately administered utility services, notably water and sewerage. The Committee argued that there was a demonstrable confusion over who was responsible for local spending — central or local government — partly brought about by the importance assumed by the rate of grant. Thus the growth of central government grants obscured the real cost of providing an ever-expanding range of services from the local electorate, particularly as the domestic element of the rate support grant was specifically designed to shield the private householder from shouldering the true burden of extra service provision. At the same time central government had no absolute means of ensuring that local spending conformed to its own plans. Layfield argued for clarification so that decisions on policy, spending and taxing should be taken by the one unit, either by central government — a move that would give considerable impetus to the already strong centralizing tendency within the state that the Committee observed — or by local government. By locating these three aspects in the same government, the Committee argued, public accountability would become more meaningful.

The housing of these powers within the localities — something the decentralist would support — has its problems because of what Sharpe (1981, 5) calls the 'central and ineradicable ambiguity to the status of local government in a democratic state'. On the one hand, local government is constitutionally subordinate to some higher level of government, while, on the other, because it was elected, raises its own taxes and employs its own staff, it has the 'potential for independent power'. Its subordinate position means that the centre will be able to influence (or effectively determine) what functions the localities will or will not be responsible for and how these are provided (particularly in relation to the socially vital services, such as education), while it can also constrain the tax-raising powers of local government.

(Interestingly, the Layfield Committee investigated the feasibility of an intermediate position between its centrist and localist alternatives, neither of which was likely to be politically acceptable, the one because of its erosive effects on local democracy, the other because, together with the Committee's proposals for a local income tax, it was only feasible given the political will of the centre to devolve meaningful decision-making powers to the localities. The intermediate position investigated was that central government would pay for the provision of services within each jurisdiction up to a minimum standard, and the local authority could at its discretion 'top up' provision from its own resources. Such a solution would be likely to meet some severe problems, however. Methodologically, the measurement and identification of appropriate service standards is strewn with difficulties. Politically, the solution would impose a number of costs — in particular, it would inevitably bring greater central involvement within the localities.)

Within Sharpe's argument, the fact that tax-raising by local government in Britain has been restricted to the non-progressive property tax partly helps explain the apparent fiscal strain experienced by the local jurisdictions. Rates as a tax do not grow in line with the development of the national economy. It is, perhaps, no surprise that in the Scandinavian countries, where local government has been given access to income as the basis for local taxation, the financial problems of local government are more subdued than elsewhere in Western Europe. In Britain there has been a considerable history of attempts to implement local fiscal reform by seeking alternatives to the rating system, but successive governments have failed to make any major changes. The most recent attempts (1981–82) by the Conservative government, following publication of their discussion paper *Alternatives to Domestic Rates* (1981), appear likely to falter in spite of the electoral gains such a move would attract. While there are a host of reasons why the different alternatives would be difficult to implement, which are too technical to discuss here, one unstated reason why the most feasible substitute, some form of local income tax, is unlikely to be established is that the centre is reluctant to allow local government access to the more buoyant, income-elastic, forms of tax that, in Britain, are exclusively enjoyed by central government.

There is no doubt that the replacement of the rating system would be a popular reform. Opposition to the existing system has become more vociferous within the last decade, both private householders and industry and commerce vocalizing their complaints against the large rate rises of the 1970s. Private industry claims that it is forced to shoulder a disproportion-ate burden — non-domestic users are charged differently and usually at a higher rate — and that rates are in any case an unsuitable tax because they bear no relation to profits. Furthermore, business interests argue, rates are a form of taxation without representation.

The evidence suggests that rates are becoming an increasing burden on both types of groups. In the wake of the current recession, industry has seen its profits fall but its rates burden rise. Similarly, while rises in personal disposable income have been slowing down, rate payments are accounting for an increasing proportion of household incomes. Indeed, since the late 1970s it would appear that rate increases, while very much influenced by inflation, are themselves contributing to it. Thus between 1978 and 1981 domestic rates in the UK rose by an average of 91 per cent compared to a rise of 51 per cent in the retail price index. Thus, whereas in the 1970s rates were static at about 2.2 per cent of personal disposable income, in 1982 the figure climbed to 2.9 per cent. Such a rise is small and, as Newton (1981) has argued, in comparison with the other taxes the citizen pays (income tax and VAT), rates are of fractional significance. Nevertheless, the visibility of the property tax — the lump-sum form of payment —and the belief that rates are a real and ever-growing burden underlie its widespread unpopularity.

However, opposition within Britain to local property taxing in the form of local tax revolts has nowhere reached the degree of success that it has in the United States. Apart from local lobbying and the very occasional court case — as in the citizen group action brought against a London borough for 'overspending' — property tax revolts have failed to materialize in Britain. In the United States, on the other hand, and particularly following Proposition 13 in California, fiscal limitation laws that limit the taxes that can be levied by local governments by various means have become widespread (Danziger, 1980). By 1979 some 23 states had enacted such legislation, though the movement's diffusion has not conformed with any recognizable trend. Prior to Proposition 13, fiscal limitation laws, dating back to 1916 in the case of Oregon, were found in states with traditionally high tax burdens and rapidly growing public service expenditures. More recently the movement has touched a wider cross-section of states — urban and rural, high and low tax-leviers (Pascal and Menchik, 1979).

In Britain local fiscal limitation has taken a different form and has been instigated directly by the central government rather than as a response to grass-roots demands. Following the return of the Conservative party to national office in May 1979, the centre has introduced several programmes specifically aimed at reducing public expenditure in general, and by local government in particular (Meadows, 1981). A start in this direction had in fact been taken by the previous Labour administration, though the replacement of the traditional Keynesian approach to macro-economic management by monetarist doctrines greatly accelerated the trend.

As part of this change in economic philosophy, considerable emphasis has been laid on the need to reduce public spending, by both central and local government. Indeed, in the electoral manifesto of the Conservative party, particular attention had been drawn to the need to curb local spending, to achieve better value for money and to avoid the profligacy represented (for example) by the building of a second town hall in a London borough.

Though the objective of reducing local spending has been pursued through a number of policies, the most important and contentious of these has been the replacement of the rate support grant system by a new block grant. The actual working of the new grant is extremely complex and need not concern us; the crux of the system is that the block grant payable to each local authority is determined on the basis of its spending needs, as assessed by central government. A corollary is that localities that 'overspend' will be penalized by having the grant withdrawn. The penalty clause was aimed particularly at the 'big-spending' authorities, often as we have seen Labour-controlled, who had enjoyed a more open-ended grants payment system under the resources element of the earlier rate support grant.

The contentiousness of the new block grant system largely arises because of the way in which central government has inevitably extended its influence into the individual local authority. As Stewart (1980) has argued, central government was hitherto primarily concerned with the local government system, whereas now it was seen to be involved with individual local governments, and sometimes over particular decisions within these. Whether or not the new relationships between central government and the localities contained within the block grant system represent an erosion of local autonomy is, however, more problematic. It is certainly something on which there has been considerable rhetoric, particularly from local government itself, which claims that the new powers contained within the act undermine the meaning of locally representative and accountable government. Meadows (1981) argues that the centre's policy has been to consider local government as very much part of the state and only secondarily as a system of government in its own right. Page (1981) suggests that we need to be cautious before assuming that the legislation spells the demise of local governments as decision-making bodies; in effect, it will pose an additional constraint on local budgetary behaviour rather than anything more fundamental.

While the effect of the new grant on the somewhat hazy concept of local autonomy is problematic, one of its undeniable effects has been to heighten central–local conflict. This conflict has not arisen exclusively as a result of the change in the grant system; other policies, particularly the more partisan-based (such as the sale of council houses), that Conservative legislation has attempted to foster have exacerbated local opposition and heightened inter-governmental conflict. But such conflict — and this is a general point relating to representative democracies in which there are central and local governments that are both popularly elected (but possibly even more to Britain where there is a 'lack of any formal constitutional entrenchment' for the sub-state governments) — reveals a contradiction within the pluralist account of the state (Dunleavy, 1980b). Pluralists espouse the virtues of local government as being based on its responsiveness to the demands of its local citizenry through the holding of local elections. If local politicians are pursuing policies that are at odds with the wishes of the central government, both are able to claim legitimacy for their actions. Labour-controlled councils intent on expanding the range of public services in defiance of the centre's demands for cutting services — in effect the position adopted by Lothian regional council in 1981 — can claim legitimacy for their actions through the local electoral chain of command, much as the centre is able to claim a mandate for its actions. This conflict has become intensified to the extent that there are local governments, frequently Labour-controlled, intent on retaining the existing level of service, and in some cases on expanding them, while at the same time central government is pursuing a policy of expenditure cutbacks.

This is not to imply that conflict between central and local government is new, but rather that the process of cutting back on public services is a politically sensitive and difficult task in which there is scope for disagreement both on how the cuts should be implemented as well as on the more fundamental question about the need for them in the first place. The objective of the centre to cut public spending has intensified the fiscal strain that other factors, notably inflation, had initiated. (The term 'strain' is perhaps preferable to 'crisis' as applied to British local government, in that its fiscal problems have not reached the dramatic state attained in some North American cities. Nevertheless the fiscal problems of local government in Britain have been such as to lead to demonstrable cutbacks in public services with often inequitable results.)

So far the argument of this section has been that local governments face difficulties in meeting their function as service providers because of the constitutional and institutional framework within which they operate. Fiscal strain is a product of such features as a relatively weak tax base and an over-dependence on transfers from central government, which during times of financial stringency can be cut back.

In concluding this section we might draw attention to a different explanation of the problem, particularly as it has been developed by O'Connor (1973). According to O'Connor, the state exists to fulfil two essential, but sometimes contradictory, functions: the provision of an environment in which capital accumulation can occur and the maintenance of social harmony. These objectives, as we noted previously, are met by different types of expenditure — social capital outlays (divided into social investment and social consumption expenditure), which lay the basis for capital accumulation, and social expenses expenditure, on projects and services that are necessary to maintain social order but that do not produce capital accumulation. (The classification of services into one of these three types is not easy, as O'Connor himself recognized; for example, water and transport services aid the means of production when used by industry but are consumption goods when utilized by households.)

The crux of O'Connor's argument is that the 'fiscal crisis of the state' results from the fact that, while the state has effectively socialized the costs of monopoly capital, it has failed to socialize the surplus; together with the rising demands there have been for social expenses expenditure, this has resulted in a growing gap between spending demands and the revenues able to meet them. O'Connor's argument, then, exposes a contradiction of values within the advanced capitalist state — the rising demands for equality in the manner in which the state provides its various services, while concurrently meeting demands from the economy to maintain the conditions in which accumulation, and hence inequality, can develop. Faced with the increasing budgetary deficits that result from the fiscal crisis, the state will be tempted to cut back on its spending, especially in the social security and general services sector, moves that will affect local spending as well as generate political conflict.

CONCLUSIONS

This chapter has sought to unravel some of the factors underlying the functioning of local governments as public service providers and the fiscal constraints under which they operate. Both of these were seen to impinge on the autonomy of local government. In Britain we might argue that local government has discretion rather than autonomy in the way in which it provides services (Goldsmith, 1980). Other types of sub-state governments, not discussed here, such as the separate state or provincial governments within a federation, will typically enjoy greater autonomy. Nevertheless, all types of sub-state governments need to be seen within the context of the state of which they are a part.

The other basic question of this chapter — the difference in service delivery provision between jurisdictions and their determinants — raised important questions of explanation, which political scientists, as well as political geographers, have studied. The systems model clearly has its limitations and, even accepting its methodological basis, its explanatory power has achieved mixed success. In part, this may be a problem of over-emphasizing the statistical approach to understanding spending patterns. What is needed is a complementary range of more behaviourally focused studies to examine the factors covered under Boaden's 'disposition' category. Political scientists have increasingly stressed the role of perception and the importance of ideology and values amongst local decision-makers. It would also be a fruitful road for the political geographer.

6

Cities, Services and Political Fragmentation

Cities are an inescapable product of the advanced capitalist state. Though current rates of urbanization are markedly greater within the developing countries, and despite trends towards 'counter-urbanization' within the developed countries, the high level of urbanization is one of the more striking features of the structure of the advanced industrial societies. The basic reasons for the growth of cities in the capitalist society are easy to outline: 'urbanisation and the structure and functioning of cities are rooted in the production, reproduction, circulation and overall organisation of the capital accumulation process' (Hill, 1977, 78). To these we can add the advantages that economists suggest are harnessed by the concentration of economic activities represented in the city — those of agglomeration and external and scale economies.

If so much is an obvious truism it is equally true that the management or government of cities has proved to be one of the more difficult, but also one of the more pressing, problems of the contemporary state. In the first place, an urbanized society will demand more government intervention than will a non-urbanized one. In an urbanized population, citizens become more dependent upon one another and more affected by the actions of one another, if only because of the greater density of population. Both features imply a need for greater structuring and regulating. Characteristically, then, the influences of government activities affect, if not to some extent control, how the citizen lives out his everyday routine.

In this chapter we shall examine some of the ways in which these governmental influences impinge on the distribution of services within the city, paying particular attention to the equity dimension. This discussion of the city is a partial one in that we shall be examining only part of the field of what we might call urban political geography (Paddison, forthcoming) — the study and interaction of political processes within the city that have recognizable spatial impacts. It is nevertheless an important discussion, because it brings together two essential elements of urban politics — the importance of governmental intervention and the idea of the city functioning as a large resource system. Most of the city's resources — schools, recreation facilities, hospitals, transport networks — are 'man-engineered' and because, as Harvey (1973) has argued, real income is determined by command over all types of resources, location, or accessibility to these resources, becomes a determining factor influencing the life-chances of the citizen. Given the importance of location within the urban system, a good starting point for analysis might be to examine the factors underlying the distribution of fixed-site facilities within the city. After looking at some of the alternative theories that help to explain the distribution of services within the city, we shall examine the implications of the jurisdictional framework into which the city is divided and the way in which this influences the distribution of services. Here, our attention is directed specifically to the implications of jurisdictional fragmentation within North America.

THE LOCATION OF FACILITIES: PUBLIC GOODS AND PUBLIC BADS

Many public services are delivered through or from fixed sites. Examples would include public libraries, health care facilities, parks and recreation centres. Because of their externality effects on their environs, most of these facilities will be considered by the local residential population as more or less desirable, depending of course on their character. Most citizens would prefer to be accessible to public parks or schools rather than to so-called noxious facilities, which set up negative externalities because of their noise, smell or the type of clientele with which they are associated, as in the case of mental hospitals or alcoholic treatment centres. (Note that some of these activities are part of the private sector, though the general arguments still apply.) C. J. Smith (1980), classifying the range of facilities into five types, shows how the preferred patterns of proximity to examples of each of these varies from cases where citizens would choose to be near to them to those where they would prefer to have them located well outside the neighbourhood (see figure 6.1).

How public facilities are located within the city provides the political geographer with a rich source of case-study material to illustrate the link between local political processes and spatial wellbeing. A variety of theoretical approaches exist by which we can examine the problem of public facility location and those in table 6.1 provide an extension from the simple division into whether or not the state acts in a neutral, non-aligned capacity balancing different interests. The different approaches outlined in table 6.1 illustrate the range of models with which urban political scientists operate, though the list is not exhaustive. (Specifically, Pahl's managerialist thesis is not included. He argues that local politicians and officials are all-important in determining what happens within the city, though there are certain similarities with some of Harrigan's approach.)

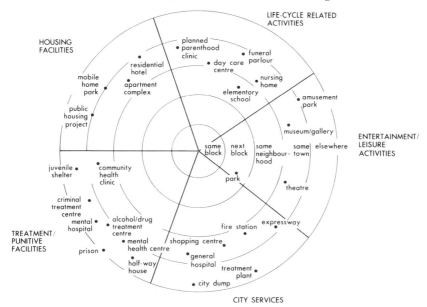

FIGURE 6.1   Preferred residential distance from selected public facilities (from
C. J. Smith, 1980)

At a purely intuitive level it is apparent that within the city the spatial distribution of public goods and bads is biased. If there is such bias, the locational decisions underpinning it probably reflect sectional interests and the influence of elites. It is not unusual to find that decision-making elites within the city are biased in terms of their social as well as possibly their spatial (residential) origins (see figure 6.2). In Britain, the social biases in the composition of local councils — working-class occupations are notably under-represented amongst councillors, for example — are well known, a fact that is repeated in other countries. The system of ward elections helps ensure that the residential distribution of councillors is less skewed than it might otherwise be, though there is no compulsion on the councillor actually to live in the area that he represents. Some observers have been in no doubt that these biases are used to reproduce the patterning of spatial advantage and disadvantage initiated by the operation of the market sector. 'The people who make decisions in Christchurch do not live in the south of the city. That is one reason why Aranui still has its smell to cope with, Woolston still has the Heathcote River in its present state and Opawa has an expressway' (Thompson, 1973, 36). In San Antonio, however, Lineberry (1977) could find only a weak relationship between variables measuring the political power of sub-areas within the city (for example the number of electoral elites resident in the neighbourhood) and their

TABLE 6.1   Some alternative theoretical approaches applied to the problem of urban public facility location

Model	Sources	Basic characteristics	Possible questions[1]
Community elite (stratificationist)	F. Hunter (1953)	1. Existence of a political and business elite widely identified as 'running the town'. 2. Power held by individuals. 3. Pronounced inter-action of economic, social and political elites.	1. Is public facility location biased in favour of the residential patterning of the urban political and/or business elites? If so, why?
Pluralist	Dahl (1961) Polsby (1963)	1. Emphasis on decision-making approach and the contribution of individuals in influencing outcomes. 2. Power held by individuals and is the capacity to influence. 3. Each issue brings in different actors — and ability to influence much more dispersed than in stratificationist approach.	1. Decision-making case-studies of different types of facilities, assessing contribution of individuals and groups. 2. How 'open' are local politicians/bureaucrats to community demands on the location of facilities?
Functional fiefdom (urban bureaucrat)	Harrigan (1976)	1. Dominance of functional special-ization both inside and outside town hall as a force influencing the distribution of public services. 2. Groups functionally organized and include professional bureaucracies, unions, pressure organizations etc.	1. Relative role of specialist professional bureaucrats in influencing location patterns, e.g. are professional norms important in determining facility location? 2. How responsive are bureaucrats to neighbourhood demands?
Political ecology	O. Williams (1971)	1. The control and manipulation of space and place by individuals and coalitions to facilitate/limit accessibility to resources.	1. How do local neighbourhoods attract/deter facilities?

TABLE 6.1 *(continued)*

Model	Sources	Basic characteristics	Possible questions[1]
		2. Accessibility sought through collective action ('coalitions' and 'communities').	
Neo-Marxist	Castells (1977)	1. Urban politics as the study of collective consumption (public services) provided by the state. 2. State intervention to maintain capitalist economic system. 3. Classes as the basis of competition.	1. The role of different types of urban social movements in influencing location patterns associated with collective consumption activities.

[1] These questions will vary with different types of public facilities, sub-areas, etc.

distance from 'desirable' facilities; ecological and socio-economic differences tended to be the more important (table 6.2). Given the traditional importance of the elitist Good Government League to the running of the city, Lineberry's findings are all the more surprising.

Lineberry's analysis is strictly aggregate in approach; even were his findings to be 'positive' it would be rash to conclude that of itself the association was real. More detailed case-studies would help on this point: by following through the history underlying particular decisions, we might be in a better position to be able to judge the relative significance of elites or local interest groups in influencing locational outcomes. This approach carries with it, however, some of the problems typical of community power studies — the problem of measurement, for example. One of the classic methods of assessing the relative importance of specific parties in a community power study is F. Hunter's (1953) reputational approach: a sample of local citizens is asked to assess who exerts most power over decisions that affect their neighbourhood. Suitably modified, this could be applied to understanding some particular locational decision. Hunter's approach has been criticized on a number of grounds (Lineberry and Sharkansky, 1974), not the least of which from our point of view being that it tends to assume that power over decision-making is something that is unequally distributed among the actors involved in the process.

Within the city a sizeable number of decisions influencing where public facilities are located are taken by, or at least influenced by, various types of 'urban manager' (Pahl, 1970). This is an umbrella term used to cover elected councillors, officials and various actors within the private sector,

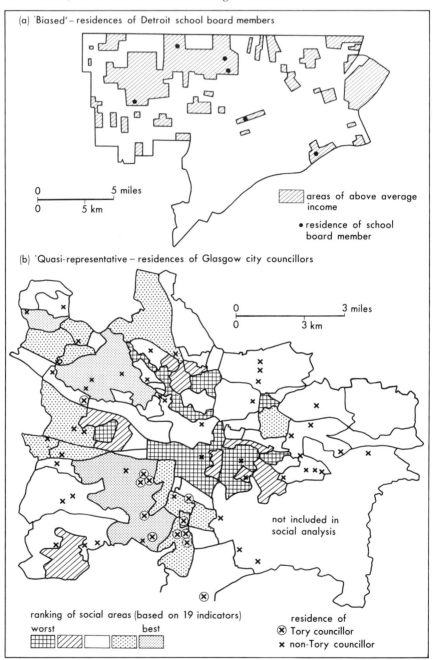

(a) 'Biased' – residences of Detroit school board members

0   5 miles

0   5 km

▨ areas of above average income

• residence of school board member

(b) 'Quasi-representative – residences of Glasgow city councillors

0   3 miles

0   3 km

not included in social analysis

ranking of social areas (based on 19 indicators)

worst   best

residence of
⊗ Tory councillor
✗ non-Tory councillor

FIGURE 6.2   Alternative social biases in representation

TABLE 6.2   Correlations[1] of urban neighbourhood characteristics and average distance from nearest selected public facilities, San Antonio (Texas)

	Public facility		
Neighbourhood characteristic	*Public parks*	*Public library*	*Fire station*
Socio-economic status:			
Median school years	0.498	0.278	0.269
Median family income	0.567	0.354	0.440
Percentage poverty families	−0.414	−0.244	−0.260
Median value of owner-occupied units	0.632	0.332	0.443
Percentage owner occupancy	0.192	0.432	0.397
Percentage overcrowded housing	−0.327	—	—
Ecological characteristics:			
Age of neighbourhood	−0.568	−0.551	−0.619
Density	−0.494	−0.494	−0.476
Racial composition:			
Percentage Negro	−0.166	—	—
Percentage Spanish heritage	−0.428	−0.232	0.01
Political power:			
No. of electoral elites[2] living in neighbourhood	0.162	—	—
Ratio electoral elites to population	0.154	−0.180	—
No. of political elites[3]	0.274	—	—
Ratio political elites to population	0.270	—	—

[1] Correlations measured by Pearson's 'r'. Only significant correlations (at .05 level) shown; non-significant relationships shown thus —

[2] Electoral elite includes city councillors, members of the board of directors of the Good Government League.

[3] Political elite includes senior municipal officers, city councillors, directors of the Good Government League.

Source: Adapted from various tables in Lineberry (1977)

such as building society managers. Urban planners are frequently involved in locating facilities that by their nature generate spatial benefits and disbenefits. Some of the studies that have examined the role of the planner have suggested that what we might call the 'planner's ideology' has been important in influencing policies (J. G. Davies, 1972; Dennis, 1972). In effect, the planner has his own image of the good society, including its spatial form, which influences planning policies. The same appears to have been true in the case of hypermarket development in Britain (Guy, 1981). (The hypermarket is a private retail development.) Originally hypermarket developers favoured low-cost, urban fringe sites that tapped the more affluent, car-owning population of the surrounding suburbs. Apart from the perceived consequences hypermarket development would have on existing suburban, as well as the town centre, shopping areas, the planners saw the hypermarket as a socially divisive facility. Its peripheral location would benefit the already advantaged and because of its competitive effects possibly even penalize inner-city residents. Subsequent developments have tended to emphasize the spatial equity effects of retailing.

Marxist approaches to the understanding of how fixed-site public facilities are located would tend to eschew the behaviouralist's emphasis on values, ideology and images in favour of a more class-based interpretation. Much of the lead here has been given in the work of Castells (1977). Castells argues that the city will become increasingly associated with conflict over collective consumption (the set of social facilities and services provided by the state). Though much of this conflict is not specifically (or, perhaps, exclusively) concerned with the question of 'where to locate' that we are considering, Castells' concept of the urban social movement provides a useful vehicle through which to study these problems.

One of Castells' basic arguments centred on the role he gave to agents of urban social action as a means of materially altering the power structure and pattern of inequalities within the city. The term 'urban social movement' is used to designate groups that, within the context of class struggle, seek to effect a structural transformation of the urban system. (This is a relatively restrictive definition in that most urban action or protest groups operate at a 'lower level' and seeking to reform or alter things within the existing social framework. In contrast to the urban social movement, action or reform groups and other forms of participation are not revolutionary.)

While relatively few local protest groups are in Castells' term proper urban social movements, an unusual and interesting example developed in Australia during the 1970s. The Green Ban movement, which involved local residents' groups working in conjunction with trade unions, was an effective method of halting building in cases where local groups and the unions considered the development in some way harmful to the community. As *ad hoc,* grass-roots activism by the 'less powerful', the movement used direct action as a means to an end. The objective of the movement was usually not one of influencing where a public facility might be located so much as preventing commercial or residential development within areas that it was felt should be conserved or developed for some other use with greater community benefits (Cox and Howard, 1973). The first of the bans focused on a local conservation issue, but also one that was seen as of wider importance. Residential development had been granted for an area of Hunter's Hill, a high-status suburb of Sydney, known as Kelly's Bush, which was one of the few remaining areas of natural bushland within the city. A local resident action group acted in concert with the Building Labour Federation to stop the development, the unions saying that if development was not halted they would impose a ban on all of the developer's other projects within the city. Such pressure proved extremely effective in halting 'unwanted' developments, though the results of the protest were arguably more distributive than they were redistributive (Paddison, 1978).

We have perhaps said enough in this introductory section to show that while these locational questions are important in that they influence the citizen's quality of life, the method of their study is equally important in controlling the type of questions the political geographer will pose. It was inappropriate here to develop a fuller exposition and critique of the different models, but certain of them will be discussed in the next section.

THE DISTRIBUTION OF PUBLIC SERVICES WITHIN THE CITY

Besides the differences in how (and what) public services are delivered between the various jurisdictions of the state, variations are also apparent within the jurisdiction. Such differences are of importance in that the supply of urban public services constitutes part of the totality of urban resources, access to which is commonly recognized as having a direct impact on the real income of its citizens. These questions of who gets what have been studied most frequently within cities, focusing on how specific public services are delivered to different neighbourhoods within the urban area. The reasons for this urban focus are perhaps obvious: not only do city dwellers require more services than do their rural counterparts, but the characteristic subdivision of the city into residential zones of differing class and ethnic composition, itself a product of the operation of largely private market forces, poses the question of how the public sector interacts with this spatial configuration. One particular question has been concerned with the extent to which the way in which public services are provided is spatially discriminatory, in effect distributing the benefits of government disproportionately to the advantage of the already more privileged within the city. Even though this is an issue that has tended to preoccupy researchers to the detriment of the wider questions that intra-jurisdictional service delivery poses, it is evident that the opportunity for discriminatory practices is available. Inasmuch as some kinds of services — public libraries, schools and recreational areas to cite a few — have fixed locations, because of the class and ethnic division of the city 'urban governments have the opportunity to distribute their resources such that some kinds of citizens enjoy more of the benefits of government activities than do other kinds of citizens' (Jones and Kaufman, 1974, 338). We shall concentrate here on the issue of the equitable distribution of services but only within the single urban jurisdiction; the implications of governmental fragmentation within the metropolis, which also impinges on these conditions of equity, is taken up later.

Problems of analysis

To unravel how public services are provided within the city and gain an insight into their impact one needs to confront a series of conceptual and methodological problems, chief among which are those concerned with measurement, the distinction between the production and consumption of services, the criteria by which their performance is to be evaluated and, in particular, the norms against which equity is to be assessed (Webster, 1977). Finally, there is the problem of the method of analysis to be used.

There is little doubt that such analyses require a detailed data base. Aggregate measures, notably crude expenditure allocations to different service types, are too blunt. The criticisms already mentioned in chapter 5 become even more critical when examining the intra-jurisdictional patterns of service delivery; global figures of expenditure conceal how the money is spent, including very often where within the city it is allocated, while saying nothing about outcomes. On the supply side what are needed are more specific indices of service provision that measure both their quantity and quality (Hatry, 1976; Lineberry, 1977). This might include information on the location of the service, staffing inputs, the promptness and regularity of the service and perceived levels of satisfaction among citizens receiving a service. Clearly, the appropriate measures would vary for each service. In the case of the fire service, among the important indices would be the average response time involved in a call-out, staffing and equipment inputs and the distance to the nearest fire station, each of which would be measured for the separate neighbourhoods comprising the city. (The choice of which spatial unit to use — neighbourhood, census tract or other — is itself a problem of the analysis.) As a different example, table 6.3 identifies some of the measures appropriate to assessing the intra-urban distribution of the public library service.

The distinction between the production and consumption of services is important because by measuring consumption it is possible to assess who

TABLE 6.3   Some indices measuring the delivery of a municipal library service

Dimension	Indices (collected for each branch library)
Location of facilities	Number and distribution of branch libraries. Accessibility within transport network.
Quality of facilities	Structural condition of building.
Bookstock	Number of books held, age of bookstock, renewal/purchase rates.
Staffing	Numbers, qualifications.

actually uses or benefits from the provision of a service. It need not follow that because a service is provided in a locality the benefits following from provision fall only on residents in the immediate neighbourhood(s). In their study of Oakland, Levy and his colleagues (1974) show that the beneficiaries of the street improvement programme — those actually using the roads — were more likely to be non-residents in some areas. Webster (1977) argues that this mismatch between service provision and outcome will vary according to the type of service. In the case of services delivered direct to the individual the distinction is redundant, while for those provided for the entire jurisdiction (for example, main road construction, art gallery) or specific groups (for example, schools) the distinction is meaningful.

Any analysis of the intra-jurisdictional distribution of services will need to be evaluated against pre-defined criteria. Local governments as providers of services commonly subscribe to a number of interconnected goals concerned with efficiency, responsiveness, effectiveness and equity. Looking at equity there are several ways in which a fair distribution of services can be defined. In the Oakland study three standards of equity were identified:

1. market equity, in which services are distributed proportionally according to the taxes citizens pay;
2. equal opportunity, where services of a given financial value are distributed equally to all citizens; and
3. equal results, in which a local government 'should allocate its resources so that all people are in equal condition after the money is spent' (Levy, Meltsner and Wildavsky, 1974, 16–17).

In effect the three types are arranged on a scale of increasing redistribution, the last signalling where resources are allocated according to need and where there would be substantial intra-jurisdictional transfers between rich and poor areas. The second highlights the contradictions between the concepts of equality and equity: delivering identical levels of services to citizens who are at the outset unequal will only exacerbate inequities.

How municipal services are allocated to various neighbourhoods within the city can be studied in several ways (Antunes and Mladenka, 1976). Apart from looking at the actual distribution of services (in several respects the most satisfactory approach and the basis of the findings reported in the next section) other methods have included measuring the consumption of, and satisfaction with, services. Benson and Lund (1969) looked at the consumption rates of municipal services among different income and racial groupings. Their basic finding — that consumption varies by income and race grouping, low-income neighbourhoods using poverty and health care-related services disproportionately and affluent groups consuming more education — has not gone unchallenged; Jacob (1972), in a study within

Milwaukee, concludes that differences of wealth appear unrelated to service consumption. The other survey approach, which has been extensively used, has sought to identify levels of perceived satisfaction with service provision. In the wake of the urban riots of the late 1960s, the Kerner Commission (1968) gathered additional evidence on service delivery patterns in 15 metropolitan areas. Its findings are representative of other similar surveys, namely that a majority of citizens, regardless of income or race category, feel that services are about equally provided in their own neighbourhood compared to others with the outstanding exception of the police service in the black ghetto.

Both these approaches harbour certain problems and assumptions. Measuring the consumption of services by the individual inevitably draws in complex questions of motivation, desires and information flows. Consumption, too, is often influenced by spatial opportunity; that is, lower consumption rates of services may be explained simply by the fact that, for example, libraries or recreational areas are less accessible to certain neighbourhoods. Equally, asking the citizen to assess the quality of his own and other neighbourhoods' service delivery is probably unrealistic, given the amount of information he is expected to know, and, not surprisingly, there can be discongruities between image and reality (Schuman and Gruenberg, 1972). Nevertheless, images rather than reality itself are often the springboard for political action and demand-making.

Are services inequitably distributed?

Among the growing body of literature examining whether municipal services are differentially allocated to various neighbourhoods there is an implicit assumption that discriminatory practices are widespread. In the United States, where most of the empirical work has been done, there have been several well-publicized court cases upholding the guarantees of the Fourteenth Amendment's equal protection clause — 'nor [shall any state] deny to any person within its jurisdiction the equal protection of the law' — as applied to the delivery of public services (see table 6.4 for some examples). Besides a number of public school finance decisions, beginning with *Serrano* v *Priest*, which outlawed the dependence of educational provision on local wealth alone, the Fifth Circuit Court of Appeals found constitutional violations in how public services were being provided in the Mississippi town of Shaws (*Hawkins* v *Shaw*), where the city council had long provided paved streets and road lighting only within the white neighbourhoods. A study of another, but larger, Southern city, San Antonio (Texas), also found evidence of systematic racial discrimination: streets in the Black and Chicano neighbourhoods were consistently dirtier and less likely to have effective kerbing.

Though these cases highlight the existence of intra-urban disparities,

TABLE 6.4   Some examples of public service equity law suits filed under the equal protection clause of the Fourteenth Amendment

---

1. *Hawkins* v *Town of Shaw* (Mississippi) — blacks receiving unfair treatment across a whole variety of services, e.g. sewers, lighting, streets. Case dismissed by trial court but appeal upheld in US Court of Appeals for the Fifth Circuit because race is a 'suspect classification' under equal protection clause.

2. *Hobson* v *Hansen* (Washington DC) — blacks claim inequities in educational spending. Case upheld and ordered that *per capita* pupil expenditure variations between neighbourhoods be no greater than 5%.

3. *Burnett* v *Washington* — discrimination between racially different neighbourhoods in allocation of police and fire service, street maintenance, refuse collection. Dismissed on grounds of insubstantial evidence of input variations.

4. *Beal* v *Lindsay* (New York City) — Puerto Rican group claimed that their parks and their upkeep were inferior to the situation in white neighbourhoods. Case dismissed on grounds that these differences were due to vandalism and that inputs were substantially similar.

5. *San Antonio Independent School District* v *Rodriguez* — are public services a 'fundamental interest', i.e. are they implicitly guaranteed by the constitution, as in the right to vote? Following the US Supreme Court's rejection of education as a fundamental interest, other cases in state courts, affecting fire protection and rubbish collection, have been likewise dismissed.

Source: Adapted from Rubinfeld (1979)

there is somewhat contradictory evidence about whether urban services are allocated so as to discriminate cumulatively against areas or groups. What evidence there is, and this is limited, suggests not that either lower-income and/or ethnic neighbourhoods are systematically discriminated against — the so-called 'underclass' or racial hypotheses — but rather that the intra-urban allocation of services varies service to service and between towns. The municipal library service is one of the few services that is reasonably consistent in favouring upper-income areas: bookstock acquisition rates, for example, are higher where circulation and readership rates are greater, which tends to be in upper-income areas. Nevertheless, accessibility to libraries may not always favour such (income) groups, particularly where they tend to move to the periphery of the city as there is a marked lead time in the establishment of new branch facilities.

The pattern of service delivery is further complicated by differences in how particular aspects of a service are provided. In a comparison of four 'underprivileged' areas of Los Angeles, including Watts in which there had been recent rioting, with 'privileged' areas, Martyn (1965) found substantial disparities in educational service provision. Frequently these were to the advantage of the underprivileged areas — where the pupil–teacher ratios were more favourable, more was spent on textbooks, and so on — but in some critical aspects, notably the quality of the teaching staff and its turnover, conditions were better within the privileged areas. What this study also shows is the important distinction between 'input' and 'output' equality and the latter's relationship with the problem of equity. Thus, federal programmes of financial assistance have aimed at ensuring greater inequality in the inputs to the service in order to reduce output inequalities, so that schools, for example, are equally effective. On the basis of the equity criteria defined above, equal results (output equality) inevitably entail input inequalities.

Explaining service distributions

In looking for factors that help explain the distribution of public services within the city we can make a convenient division between those forces related to the characteristics of the neighbourhoods comprising the city and their needs, and the political and administrative processes through which these needs are channelled. Jones and Kaufman (1974) develop a basic model of such factors (see figure 6.3), the general thrust of which is not dissimilar from the systems framework outlined in chapter 5, in that environmental factors, combined with certain demands and supports, are mediated through political and bureaucratic influences resulting in service provision.

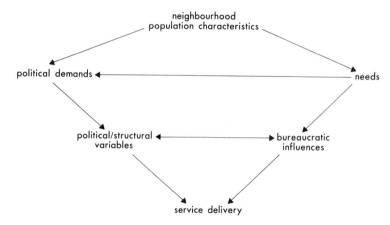

FIGURE 6.3   Factors underlying urban service distributions
(adapted from Jones and Kaufman, 1974)

Two closely interrelated sets of factors are the demographic and structural characteristics that define the type of neighbourhood and the various needs that these set in train. The demographic composition of a neighbourhood will directly influence service needs: key measures will include age structure and ethnicity; similarly, structural-type characteristics of each area — the condition of the housing stock, streets, schools and so forth — will generate needs. Different groups and, insofar as they are spatially segregated, different areas of the city consume varying amounts of public services and meeting these needs means in the first instance that municipal governments must be adequately aware of them.

One type of channel through which this information flows will be various demands, the object of which is to influence how public services are delivered. These demands can be articulated through electoral challenges, either by the individual or by interest or local pressure groups, but while urban governments and their bureaucracies are more or less open to influence through these channels, much depends on the responsiveness of the machine whether change is effected.

Most studies of citizen-contacting suggest that only a minority of individuals attempt to influence service provision. In part we can explain this through the problem of accessibility: citizens find it difficult to 'penetrate' bureaucracies, though urban governments can reduce the difficulty by earmarking officials within each department (housing, planning and so forth) as the primary public contact points. Where contact is made, most demands tend to concern specific matters that directly influence the individual — complaints about, say, street repairs or cleansing directly within the citizen's immediate residence — rather than more general issues relating to service provision within either the neighbourhood or the city at large.

As responsiveness is closely allied to equity, the question of whether urban bureaucracies respond differently to class and racial groups is important. Because of differences of resources, bargaining weapons and skills, some political scientists have suggested that municipal bureaucracies are less responsive to working-class citizens (Lipsky, 1970). However, what hard evidence there is tends to provide a contradictory picture: responsiveness varies in different cities and for different types of services. But specific cases of discriminatory responsiveness are evident. Thus, in Oakland, street improvement expenditures were in part based on the distribution of citizen complaints; as most of these came from upper-income residents, the allocations tended to be skewed.

Neighbourhood pressure groups provide another means through which demand-making can be channelled. Indeed, the intra-urban community as a political pressure organization, which in some countries has been given statutory recognition, has enjoyed a renaissance in both America and Europe (Kjellberg, 1979). Part of the reason for this lies in the demands for greater participation within the urban policy-making process (including service distribution), though we need to treat with caution exactly how much participation such bodies are to be designated with. Attempting to influence how services are provided, if only by acting as an information mediary through which collectively expressed demands are transmitted to the service delivery agency, is considerably lower down the 'ladder' of participation (Arnstein, 1969) than the aspirations of other attempts at local participatory democracy. In America, the community control movement, for instance, had sought to deliver its own services, providing it was given the financial resources. (As equity is influenced by institutional arrangements, neighbourhood governments do have a place within the overall analysis of service delivery.)

As far as urban bureaucracies are concerned, one of the advantages of demand-making through the neighbourhood group is that it reveals local preferences. Furthermore, where these groups are able to claim justifiably to represent their turf and where they are 'recognized' by the city government, the demands made through them will carry greater weight. Elected politicians, especially where elections are organized on the basis of a ward, all or part of which contains the neighbourhood council, will pay greater heed to such bodies. In Glasgow, city councillors normally attend meetings of the community councils, which act as intermediaries between the neighbourhood and the municipal bureaucracy (Paddison, 1981).

As with citizen-contacting, the responsiveness of urban politicians and administrators to demands made through neighbourhood-based groups is the key factor influencing outcomes. Looking at neighbourhood organizations in South Hampshire, Burnett and Hill (1982) argue that demand-making has resulted in changes in service provision. Equally, the community council in Glasgow has managed to 'win' concessions from the city council and other public bodies in such matters as the routing of municipally operated bus services and the provision of social and shopping facilities in areas relatively under-provided with these. But, however vociferous, community activism is only one of a number of factors influencing outcomes — others include political and bureaucratic factors discussed below — and it is difficult to disentangle the separate effect of neighbourhood power. Also, the effectiveness of the neighbourhood organization will vary according to the 'scale' and 'sensitivity' of the issues; neighbourhood groups will tend to be least effective in cases where the issue has substantial extra-local implications or where it is politically sensitive.

If there is evidence to substantiate a link between neighbourhood demand-making and service provision, there is only patchy data to support any systematic trends underlying which neighbourhoods are likely to be the more effective. *A priori*, neighbourhoods with more political clout will tend to be the more successful in winning concessions (Rich, 1980), but so many factors determine local power — leadership, 'size', class composition, voting strength, electoral marginality and so on, which can exist in any permutation — that the concept is inevitably diffuse. Neither is it true that neighbourhood organizations in lower-income areas will be less effective; while some studies have argued that municipal bureaucracies tend to be less responsive to the poorer neighbourhoods, others have found little difference in how higher- and lower-income areas are treated. On the other hand, there is little to support the idea that urban councils are using these neighbourhood organizations to meet redistributive goals. It is the elected politicians and their officials who have responsibility for providing services and it is their responsiveness to political demands that is instrumental to the equitable distribution of services. Conventional wisdom assumes that politicians, mindful of their next election, will tend to be responsive to local demands, particularly if their constituency is marginal. Vote-buying is a feature of intra-urban politics and indeed, through the distribution of patronage in the form of jobs as well as services, it was the basis of urban machine politics, which characterized the large Northern cities of the United States until World War II. Thus in Chicago, one of the last bastions of machine politics, services were delivered disproportionately to areas electorally supporting Mayor Daley (Kasperson, 1965).

There is some evidence to show that the reform-style governments that replaced the urban machines tend to be biased towards certain class and racial groups. The urban reform movement in the United States was based on such ideas as good government through the application of business-like procedures, the need to depersonalize politics (one of the hallmarks of machine politics), and the use of politics as the arena for the realization of moral principles. Certain features of reform — the emphasis on non-partisan elections and the organization of the election on an at-large basis — tend to reduce the electoral power of lower-income and minority groups, and favour those groups identified with the reform movement. In at-large elections, councillors are not elected by wards but by the total community. So long as there is no pronounced spatial segregation of race or income groups, which will be truer of small cities, the at-large election poses no problem. In larger cities, however, minorities tend to become under-represented, particularly Black candidates who can find themselves having to appeal to the white electorate to gain office. Equally, upper-income groups tend to be over-represented: in an extreme example in St Paul, at-large elections and a commission style of government combined 'to produce a city council in which five of the six members lived within a few minutes drive of each other in an area that comprised about a sixth of the city's land area and contained about a seventh of its population . . . and the more affluent sections [of the city] (Harrigan, 1976).

These are input inequalities and so what we have to show is that these characteristics of reform-style governments impact on spatial patterns of responsiveness and service delivery within the city. Lineberry and Fowler (1967) provide the most sophisticated answer to this. Looking at 200 cities with populations of 50,000 or more they found that reformed cities did tend to be less responsive to sharp ethnic and socio-economic divisions in the city:

When non-partisanship is combined with election at-large, the impact of residentially segregated groups or groups which obtain their strength from voting as blocks in municipal elections is further reduced . . . [These reforms] make public policy less responsive to the demands arising out of social conflicts in the population. (Lineberry and Fowler, 1967, 716)

Political scientists have suggested that it is through the requirement to hold periodic elections that local political elites will be responsive to their electorate, but several aspects of the operation of local government elections, at least in Britain, cast doubt on this assumption (Dunleavy, 1980a). The nationalization of local government voting — in which there are electoral swings to parties of either the left or right across different jurisdictions within the country as a whole, often counter to the ruling national party — suggests that purely local factors play a relatively insignificant part in voting choice (Newton, 1976a). In particular elections a party may be successful in mobilizing support for local issues, as notably in the capture of Liverpool by the Liberal party through the emphasis on the community; similarly in the marginal ward, where turnout will tend to be higher, local issues and the performance of the ruling party and the incumbent politician in providing services to the local community can influence the vote. Nevertheless, the thrust of the nationalization argument is that voting choice is influenced less by factors that local politicians can themselves influence than by factors that are effectively beyond their control. But this argument can be countered. Thus, while electoral reaction to the Conservative government's public expenditure cuts generated national opposition in the 1981 elections, with widespread gains for the Labour party, we lack evidence of how much the electoral switch is to be explained by how individual local authorities implemented the service cuts in their areas.

Arguably more important is the fact that in a large number of authorities one-party rule is dominant, which undermines the effectiveness of party competition as a vehicle for giving the local elector real choice in deciding between policies. Dunleavy estimates that as much as 75 per cent of the population of England and Wales lives in areas dominated by either the Conservative or Labour party (table 6.5). The implication of this — that the policies incumbent parties devise will have little effect on their re-election — belies the need for the party to 'cultivate the vote' and the existence of intra-authority variations that measure reaction to the provision of services within individual neighbourhoods. Many mundane decisions on service provision are in fact made by the city's officials rather than by its elected members, and some writers have suggested that municipal bureaucrats are more important. Because the bureaucrat is not directly affected by the voting, the problems of both responsiveness and accountability are real and this is compounded by the monopolistic character of local governments as service providers.

Table 6.5   One-party rule in various types of local governments, England and Wales, post-1974

	Likely Conservative control[1]		Likely Labour control[2]		Totals	
	No.	Pop. (millions)	No.	Pop. (millions)	No.	Pop. (millions)
Non-metropolitan counties	25	26.8	3	1.5	47	30.6
Metropolitan districts	2	0.5	14	4.1	36	11.6
London boroughs	5	1.2	14	2.9	35	7.0
All governments	32	28.5	31	8.5	118	49.2

[1] Where Labour gained fewer than one-third of all seats in 1973 (a relatively bad year for the Conservatives).
[2] Where Labour retained control in 1976 and 1977 elections (both relatively bad years for Labour).
Source: Dunleavy (1980a)

Urban bureaucrats generate 'decision rules' and procedures to provide the basis on which resources are allocated. Very often these 'rules of thumb' are influenced by the standards of the profession of which the officer is a member. (In Britain nearly all the local government departments have become professionalized, with a national institute setting down 'guidelines' for services.) Levy and his colleagues (1974) illustrate how important these professional influences can be in establishing techno-rational rules by which resources will be allocated. In Oakland's street department, allocational decisions are dominated by professional (engineering) criteria of flows, design speed and safety, so that streets giving access to freeways or acting as cross-town arterials are earmarked for funding before neighbourhood streets. In Britain, the procedures underlying the allocation of council houses are based on such criteria as the length of residence in the area, size of family and present conditions, the kinds of largely bureaucratically determined rules that materially influence life-chances.

Urban bureaucrats frequently act as gatekeepers (Pahl, 1970), particularly where they have discretionary power over the allocation of services. These include the street-level bureaucrat (Lipsky, 1976) — employees who deal extensively with the public and who work relatively independently in the city; teachers, the police, social workers and environmental enforcement officers are all examples. Their more overt influence within the city comes as a result of stereotyping an area, or an income or racial group, which can easily influence how they respond to service demands.

Origins

The impact of jurisdictional fragmentation is exemplified *par excellence* in the American Standard Metropolitan Statistical Area (SMSA) (Barlow, 1981). Most metropolitan areas are governed through a bewildering maze of overlapping but independent local governments and, though not unique to America, governmental fragmentation is at its more extreme in that country. In part this proliferation of governments is a response to meeting the complex and frequently competing interests of different, especially class, groups within the city; in part it represents a response to the problem of providing city residents with essential services. Historically the trend has been towards greater fragmentation, more or less in parallel with the growth of the metropolitan population, so that the number of jurisdictions increases with the size of the SMSA. Indeed, the balkanization of the city has tended to foster its own further subdivision; the special district, which is now by far the most important unit numerically, and which has greatly expanded the complexity of the governmental systems, has been used as a device to enable essential services to be provided without the need to reform the existing structure (Harrigan, 1976).

The overall complexity of the metropolitan government structure is matched by the variety of different types of unit and by the variations in their geographical incidence. In 1972, at which time there were 264 SMSAs, the number of local governments totalled 22,185; 42 per cent of these were multi-purpose jurisdictions — counties, municipalities and towns and townships (table 6.6). The bulk of the remainder comprised single-purpose governments, either school districts or special districts, of which the chief types were fire protection (1,547 of the total 7,492 units in 1972), natural resources (1,371), utilities (939), sewerage (866), housing and urban renewal (731), school buildings (619) and parks and recreation (378). Each of these operates within unique geographical territories overlying the existing complex of multi-purpose governments, but of greater importance than this 'territorial confusion of boundaries' is that in most cases these units have separate taxing powers.

Jurisdictional fragmentation is not of equal incidence in the SMSAs. It is generally greater in the older SMSAs of the North East (except New England) and North Central regions, Chicago heading the list in 1972 with 1,172 units, followed by Philadelphia (852), Pittsburgh (698) and New York (531). Conversely in the newer cities of the South fragmentation is

TABLE 6.6   Types of governmental units in SMSAs, 1962–77

| | 1962 | | 1967 | | 1972 | | 1977 | |
	No.	%	No.	%	No.	%	No.	%
Municipalities	4,903	22.4	5,319	23.9	5,467	24.6	6,444	24.9
Counties	447	2.0	447	2.0	444	2.0	594	2.3
Towns and townships	3,282	15.0	3,485	15.7	3,462	15.6	4,031	15.6
School districts	7,072	32.4	5,421	24.4	4,758	21.4	5,220	20.2
Special districts	6,153	28.2	7,569	34.0	8,054	36.4	9,580	37.0
Totals	21,857		22,241		22,185		25,869	

Source: US Bureau of the Census, *Census of Government*, Volume I, 1972 and 1977, US Government Printing Office, Washington, DC

less pronounced. These basic differences in fragmentation, particularly in the frost-belt and sun-belt split, were measured by Ziegler and Brunn (1980) in their index of geopolitical fragmentation, which was based on the combined measure of the number of local government units per 100,000 population and the percentage of the metropolitan population resident in the central city. The index is lower in Southern and Eastern SMSAs where annexation and city–county consolidation have been used to ensure that the central city incorporates a greater proportion of the metropolitan population.

Historically, the origins of governmental fragmentation in the older, generally larger, SMSAs is to be explained initially through the failure of the city to annex the suburban population growth that was extending the city limits through the nineteenth, and particularly in the present, century. This had not always been the case, and up till the end of the nineteenth century the industrial cities of the North had been able to annex the burgeoning population: on the one hand peripheral residents were anxious for city services, while on the other city politicians were in favour of the political boundaries being extended where growth was seen as inherently 'good'. But the emergence of the large, socially heterogeneous, machine-controlled urban governments, divided along class lines, in which the machine gained its greater support from lower-income groups, led to growing anti-urban feeling among the 'middle-class on the periphery [who] concluded that the only way to save themselves from domination by the core was to separate their neighborhoods from the inner city' (Danielson, 1972, 149). Subsequently, attempts at annexation were to meet increasing opposition from the suburbs, whose political muscle had been strengthened by state governments hostile to the city. Through legislative and judicial means annexation was made more difficult, as through the requirement for example to hold a local referendum.

While class interests together with an underlying belief in the virtues of local self-government help explain the political separation of city and suburbs, it is administrative factors that help account for the popularity of the special district. Usually responsible for only one function, special districts are 'limited purpose governmental units which exist as corporate entities and which have substantial fiscal and administrative independence from general purpose local government' (ACIR, 1973a, 20). They offer a convenient way of providing services that for various reasons — fiscal inability or inappropriate geographical territories — existing local governments are not able to meet. However, it is the proliferation of special districts in particular that has added to the fragmentation of government — of the total 1,172 units in Chicago, no fewer than 470 are special districts, of which 402 act as separate taxing authorities — bringing in its train problems of coordination and accountability. Thus, in spite of their ubiquity and their importance in providing services, they tend to have low political visibility for the average citizen.

Fiscal implications

Two main fiscal implications are associated with the proliferation of governments within metropolitan areas — the exacerbation of inter-jurisdictional spillovers and of fiscal disparities through the separation of public needs from available resources. Both contribute to what Hirsch (1971, 4) has described as the fiscal crisis of the central city — 'the imbalance between people's aspirations for public services and their willingness and ability to pay for them'. Though this ties the question to the central city, these spillovers and fiscal disparity problems also affect the suburban municipalities, which increasingly, as the city has grown and the processes of residential, industrial and commercial decentralization have gathered momentum, have themselves become economically stratified.

Just as cities encourage spillover effects because of their greater densities and mix of population, so will the fragmentation of the metropolitan area into separate jurisdictions. *A priori,* the greater the number of jurisdictional boundaries in a given area, the greater the potential for positive and negative externalities to 'escape' across the governmental units. Vincent (1971) has suggested that within the metropolitan area there are three main causes of spillover — commuting, migration and 'non-movement' — the effect of which varies according to spending category (table 6.7). In theory, as we have already suggested, these externalities prevent the efficient production or consumption of public goods, so that a jurisdiction losing some of the benefits of provision will under-produce the goods. However, the empirical evidence on the connection between fragmentation and such inefficiency is inconclusive (Adams, 1965).

Of the various types of spillover effects resulting from governmental fragmentation, most interest has centred around the interaction between

TABLE 6.7   Types of benefit spillovers in urban areas according to expenditure category

Expenditure category	Mechanism causing benefit spillover			Effect on income redistribution
	Commuting	*Migration*	*'Static'*	
Education	No	Yes	Yes	Major
Public welfare	No	Possible	Possible	Minor
Highways	Yes	No	No	Minor
Police protection	Yes	No	No	Minor
Fire	Possible	No	Yes	Minor
Housing and community development	Possible	No	No	Minor
Health and hospitals	Possible	Possible	Yes	Major

Source: Adapted from Vincent (1971)

the central city and the suburbs through the 'exploitation thesis'. It was in a study by Hawley (1951) that the argument that the suburbs were exploiting the central city was first outlined. Hawley had found that the *per capita* public expenditures of cities with populations of 100,000 or over correlated positively with the size of the suburban population of the metropolitan area: central city residents were paying for services that were being used by commuters not contributing to their cost. Subsequent studies extending Hawley's analysis, such as those by Margolis (1961) and Brazer (1959), generally confirmed the earlier finding, though there has been a greater reluctance to conclude that these results spelt out central city exploitation.

Neenan (1972) is one of the relatively small number of workers providing evidence to support the thesis, though not in terms of the commuting population but in terms of the net welfare gain the suburban municipalities as a whole experience. Neenan examined the fiscal interactions between Detroit and six municipalities that represent a variety of different types of suburb (table 6.8). His method involved firstly the measurement of public sector net benefit flows across a variety of services, for example libraries, street and traffic control, poverty expenditure. Taking poverty expenditure, the measurement of the benefits enjoyed by the suburban jurisdictions was based on the difference between the *per capita* contributions of the 'non-poverty populations' (families with incomes of over $5000) of each municipality and the average *per capita* spending within the SMSA; where the average was $6.58 and Detroit's contribution was $12.90, the only case above the mean, each of the municipalities was benefiting. These benefits, summed across the services (column 6 in table 6.8), were then adjusted on a willingness-to-pay basis by a multiplier that took account of the argument, for which there is some empirical support, that higher-income residents perceive greater benefits from public service provision than do lower-income citizens, so that their willingness to pay will be greater. Subtracting from these adjusted benefits, the revenues flowing to Detroit showed that each municipality enjoyed a net gain, though its incidence varied.

What other workers have suggested is that, though suburban residents do benefit from services provided by the city, the relationship is hardly one of exploitation, given the effect that commuting has on raising the tax base of the central city. Certainly the evidence is far from conclusive and, as we can see from Neenan's analysis, only half of the municipalities would have enjoyed a net subsidy had the benefits not been weighted by the welfare criterion used.

By contrast, the effect of fragmentation on fiscal disparities is more straightforward. The separation of the central city from the suburbs, and of one suburb from another, has meant that the city and the low-income older suburbs have high service demands but lack the financial capacity to meet these, while there are other jurisdictions that have low demands and excess fiscal resources. Among the causes of the fiscal problems of the central city, much emphasis is given to the effects of decentralization, particularly of businesses and of middle- and upper-income households, which especially in the case of industry and commerce will tend to depress the city's tax base. Thus, as indicators of the overall trend towards urban decentraliza-tion, the growth rates within recent decades of total employment, manufacturing employment and retail sales have been consistently higher outside the central city. But while the central city has been progressively losing some of the fiscally more 'profitable' uses, it has retained its traditional role of housing low-income and racial, often migrant, groups whose need for public services is greater across a number of the major spending fields. Consequently, the tax rates needed to meet service demands will be struck at ever higher levels, leading in turn to substantial disparities in tax burdens between the city and its suburbs — over 50 per cent in some metropolitan areas. The relatively greater tax burdens of the central city are an incentive for further decentralization of businesses and upper-income groups, completing the 'fiscal impoverishment cycle' of the central city.

This general picture needs qualifying. Firstly, there has clearly been a large-scale, though selective, economic and social decentralization of businesses and households, but the evidence on whether fiscal factors have been, or will continue to be, important to the 'flight to the suburbs' is inconclusive (Bradford and Kelejian, 1973; Oakland, 1979). For both firms and private households the decision to relocate is multi-faceted and it is difficult to separate out the effect of the 'fiscal push' factor. Suburban autonomy and the fiscal advantages that this bestows are undeniably a potential attraction to migration. On the other hand, rather than the

TABLE 6.8 Detroit and six suburban municipalities: social characteristics and public sector benefit and revenue flows

(1) Municipality	(2) Population (1965)	(3) Per capita property values ($)	(4) Median family incomes ($)	(5) % of families with income $15,000 or more	(6) Benefits measured by cost of service ($/cap.)	(7) Benefits adjusted for willingness to pay ($/cap.)	(8) Revenue flow to Detroit ($/cap.)	(9) Net subsidy from Detroit ($/cap.)
Detroit	1,538,487	3,085	6,350	4.6	—	—	—	—
Allen Park	38,336	2,943	9,420	9.4	4.77	7.06	4.36	2.70
Birmingham	24,684	4,077	12,850	38.2	4.39	8.87	6.32	2.55
Dearburn	112,571	6,438	8,500	10.1	5.05	6.77	2.42	4.35
Grosse Pointe Park	15,030	4,103	13,250	42.1	6.33	13.23	10.53	2.70
Highland Park	36,666	4,525	5,620	3.3	3.68	3.28	2.18	1.10
Roseville	56,780	2,378	7,870	5.1	6.97	8.63	3.32	5.31

Source: Various tables in Neenan (1972)

central city being a victim of 'natural' spatial processes, it is argued by some that the fiscal crisis is due more to overspending by central city governments. Several variants of the overspending thesis have been suggested — that it is due to: the higher wage rates paid to public sector employees, largely because of the greater unionization of the labour force than in the suburbs (Peirce, 1975); poor management and lower labour productivity (Netzer, 1977); or, the excessive raising of expectations among the lower-income groups following the 'Great Society' programmes of the 1960s (Peterson, 1976). Very probably both of these basic arguments, though in varying mixes in different cities, have acted as causal agents underlying the fiscal problem. The real point is that their fiscal consequences are similar: 'from a locational stand point, it matters little to business firms and upper-income groups whether their city taxes are used to support the services of poor city households (the outcome of selective decentralisation) or the higher wages of city government workers' (Oakland, 1979, 332).

Secondly, the continuation of the basic segregation forces — spatial socio-economic differentiation and jurisdictional autonomy — has meant that, as the metropolis has grown, inter-suburban differences have become salient alongside the central city–suburban dichotomy. The suburbs have become differentiated into rich and poor jurisdictions, and the ability of middle- and upper-income municipalities to zone out public housing and other 'undesirable' uses and zone in light manufacturing has had a similar effect in separating fiscal resources from needs as had been the case earlier between the central city and the suburbs. To the Advisory Commission on Intergovernmental Relations, the fiscal prognosis for the poorer suburbs is arguably worse than it is for the central city:

> The older, suburban communities are taking on the physical, social and economic characteristics of central city [but] this type of community is especially vulnerable to fiscal distress because it lacks the diversified tax base that has enabled the central city to absorb some of the impact of extraordinary expenditure demands. (ACIR, 1967, 6)

At the extremes, between the industrial suburb with a small residential population and the low-income suburb, the disparities are striking: Vernon municipality in Los Angeles county had nearly $13,000 revenue available *per capita* while Baldwin Park had $35. More usually, the *per capita* taxable resources in the wealthier jurisdictions will be three to five times higher than in the low-income suburbs.

Thirdly, figure 6.4 shows that, in line with the regional differences in political fragmentation, central city–suburban disparities vary inter-regionally. Central city hardship and its converse, 'suburban superiority',

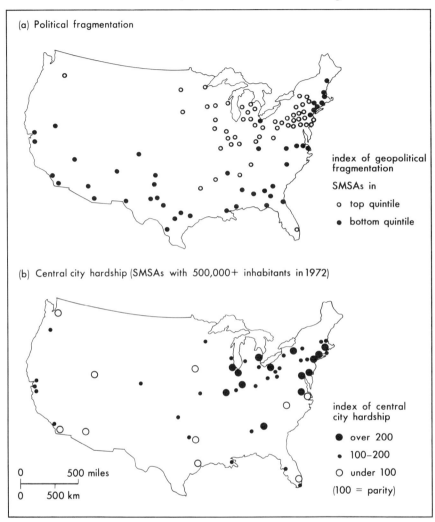

FIGURE 6.4 Metropolitan political differences in the United States
(adapted from (a) Ziegler and Brunn, 1980 and (b) Nathan and
Adams, 1976)

differ between metropolitan areas, as Nathan and Adams (1976) have
shown, based on the measurement of six socio-economic variables
(unemployment, demographic dependency, real *per capita* income, over-
crowding, education and poverty). Again, the older industrial cities,
particularly of the North and East but also in various geographical isolates
such as San Francisco and St Louis, have the more emphatic disparities.
However, these regional differences are less important than the racial and

personal income characteristics of the metropolitan area in explaining variations in jurisdictional inequality. Apart from the strong positive relationships between racial heterogeneity and income inequalities, governmental fragmentation is also important — the larger the number of jurisdictions in a given population, the greater will be the variation in inter-jurisdictional incomes (see figure 6.5).

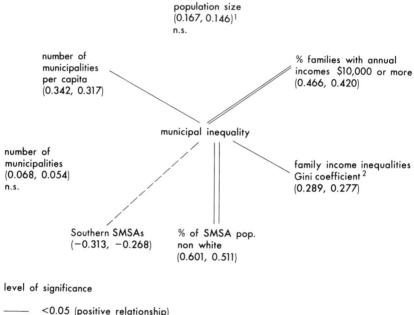

level of significance

——   <0.05 (positive relationship)

═══   <0.01 (positive relationship)

— — —   <0.05 (negative relationship)

n.s.   not significant

[1] First figure in brackets is the standardized regression coefficient, or beta weight, which can be directly compared so as to give an indication of the relative importance of the independent variables; the second is the partial correlation coefficient, which indicates the relationship between x and y holding other independent variables constant.

[2] Income inequality measured by the standard deviation of the median family incomes for municipalities of over 2,500 population (1960) in each SMSA.

FIGURE 6.5   The effect of structural and social variables on inter-municipal income inequality in 63 SMSAs, 1960 (adapted from Hill, 1974)

Outcomes and palliatives

The superimposition of separate political jurisdictions upon the class- and racially-segregated city, combined with the heavy reliance on local property taxes as the basic source of revenue, not only underwrites the separation of fiscal needs from resources, but, more substantively, generates a system of urban stratification. R. C. Hill has extended the sociologist's concept of stratification to the polycentric city, defining it as 'the institutionalization of social arrangements that generate and perpetrate inter-generational inequality in the distribution of scarce economic, political and social resources among collectivities in the metropolis' (Hill, 1974, 1558). Class and status groups compete for access to resources and this is institutionalized through the competition to gain control over governments whose task it is to distribute these resources.

The political fragmentation of city and suburbia along class and ethnic lines is the primary means by which the system of urban stratification is maintained. Suburban incorporation ensures the protection of class interests: just as the patterning of residential areas into homogeneous class and ethnic zones is a means of maintaining 'life-style values', so suburban incorporation, particularly through the zoning power that local jurisdictions enjoy, is a means of cementing this socio-spatial arrangement. The tax-base question is very important within this equation; a basic goal of each jurisdiction is the minimization of its tax rate, which leads to attempts to zone in and out uses that have positive and negative fiscal externalities respectively (Cox, 1978). However, the competition is inherently an unequal one, because of the tax and other advantages of the wealthier jurisdictions and their zoning behaviour, so that the stratification is perpetuated.

In their effect on the provision of public services these inequalities have been highlighted in the case of education. The notion of 'separate but equal', struck down in the school desegregation ruling, was to be contested in a slightly different format in the 1970s, in that separate school districts, because of the reliance on the local tax base as the primary means of funding, meant unequal resources. In 1971 the California Supreme Court declared that the system of financing education — two-thirds locally derived and one-third from state aid — 'invidiously discriminated against the poor [in that] the quality of a child's education [is] a function of the wealth of his parents and neighbors' (*Serrano* v *Priest,* 1971). Although the California precedent failed to secure federal support — the Supreme Court ruled against education being a fundamental right — other state judiciaries individually (e.g. Michigan, New Jersey) have ruled in favour of greater equalization. Nevertheless, as we have argued previously, equalizing inputs, given unequal service needs, is likely to be inequitable. A preferable method is programmes that effectively redistribute the property tax resources of the city, as has been the effect of the pooling system instituted in the Twin Cities by the 1971 Fiscal Disparities Act.

A variety of methods exist by which greater equity, notably in reducing fiscal disparities and in improving the access to resources, could be achieved. Some of the possible policies, grouped under four headings, are:

Legal: Securing equity in service provision through the equal protection clause. Reducing zoning powers, notably to disperse public housing.

Fiscal: Financial aid from higher-level governments. Replacement of property tax by income tax (taxing suburban commuters). User charges, especially for transportation, water, sewerage, cultural facilities. Metropolitan base sharing, i.e. pooling of fiscal resources.

Functional: Transfer of selected functions, including those with high income redistribution effects, e.g. education, to higher-level governments.

Structural: Metropolitan government alternatives.

Some brief observations might be made on these. Legal redress has been sought through two channels — invoking the equal protection clause of the Fourteenth Amendment to achieve the equalizing of service provision, and securing a Federal Supreme Court decision to outlaw exclusionary zoning. Both goals have proved elusive, service equalization because of the failure to establish services as a fundamental right, while the attempt to get a general Supreme Court ruling against suburban zoning also failed (Danielson, 1972). Some of the fiscal policies, notably programmes under the 'New Federalism', have had an ameliorative effect on fiscal and service disparities, though they have been insufficiently radical to meet the disparities existing between the central city and the suburbs. The functional-assignment alternative, the transfer of functions to metropolitan or state-level government, raises the question of the advantages and disadvantages of centralization, which together with the issue of structural reform are discussed in the next chapter.

SYNTHESIS: THE URBAN CRISIS

During the last two decades the problems of the American city have reached crisis proportions. The crisis has taken several forms (Castells, 1977). Most dramatically, it has been associated with a breakdown of social order, the eruption of street rioting and a general increase in violence and crime, together with the development of urban social movements designed to effect change. Secondly, it has affected the provision of collective consumption activities, notably education, public transport and housing. Thirdly, there has been a developing fiscal crisis of local government, particularly within the inner cities of the older metropolitan areas.

This fiscal crisis stems partly from the political fragmentation of the city — the 'barbed wire mentality' of the separate suburbs — but it is also 'a particular expression of the overall fiscal crisis of the state, that is of the increasing budgetary gap created in public finance in advanced capitalist countries because of the historical process of socialisation of costs and privatisation of profits' (Castells, 1977, 415). Castells goes on to argue that during the 1950s local governments in the inner city were able to cope financially with the demand for public and welfare services, but that mass protest in the 1960s led to an increased expectation of local jurisdictions in the provision of services. The resulting increase in the municipal labour force and its unionization, leading to successful demands for wage rises, strained the urban fisc. Increasingly cities were forced into debt financing and it was by defaulting on its debt that New York was led into 'bankruptcy' in 1974–75. Under pressure from business interests and the federal government the city cut back services and laid off sizeable numbers of employees; with union acquiescence this successfully staved off actual bankruptcy.

What, then, might be the political consequences of the urban fiscal crisis? Evidently, the idea of simply abandoning the central city is a non-option because of its underlying significance to the US capital market. Nor is it likely that the contradictions encapsulated within the fragmented city will be effectively solved. If they are not, Castells suggests that the consequences will be dire 'because they could threaten the already unstable political legitimacy of local governments as well as their financial viability' (Castells, 1977, 419).

R. C. Hill (1977) develops a somewhat different argument and future scenario, based upon an interpretation of O'Connor's fiscal crisis model. Hill argues that three factors underlie the present fiscal crisis: governmental fragmentation, federalism (the circumscription of local government's tax-raising abilities in spite of the growing spending demands placed on it, a factor discussed in the preceding chapter) and the 'structure of municipal production'. The basic point he is making here is that in the older central cities there are increasing demands for social expenses forms of expenditure 'which are not even indirectly productive of private accumulation . . . [while] they simultaneously experience fundamental barriers to accumulating revenue for social capital outlays requisite to transforming the resident labour force to labour productive of capital accumulation' (Hill, 1977, 84). It is this latter contradiction that underpins the current fiscal crisis of the central city and that also helps explain the rising tide of political conflict.

Hill's futuristic blueprint, the State Capitalist City, attempts to show how the city might be ideally organized so as to enhance accumulation and overcome the contradictions of the existing urban forms. State Capitalist City is an integrated political, geographical and economic unit, corporately managed so as to maximize productivity and increase profits in the private sector. Two features of it are especially relevant to our earlier discussion. Firstly, the problems of spillover, inadequate tax base and service inequity are overcome by transferring the fiscal burden to a higher level of government. Secondly, this shifting of the fiscal burden assumes a greater role for metropolitan-wide government and, consequently, the reduced importance of governmental fragmentation. In this respect (as well as others) the newer metropolitan centres of the American South are the closest approximation to State Capitalist City and have, as we have seen earlier, been experiencing the most rapid growth among the nation's SMSAs. Even so, State Capitalist City is not the only way out of the fiscal crisis — as New York's experience illustrates. From a territorial viewpoint, however, what is of particular interest in Hill's model is that metropolitan fragmentation is an inefficient structural form for monopoly capital. This introduces the question of reorganizing the territorial state, to which we turn in the next chapter.

7
Reorganizing the Territorial State

Reorganizing the jurisdictional make-up of the state is in a very real sense a geographical problem. The size of the units to be employed, the delimitation of boundaries, the problems of which *de facto* spatial communities to use for the purposes of establishing jurisdictions — important elements in their own right in the process of territorial restructuring — underpin the spatial organization of the state. Nor have political geographers been unaware of the importance of understanding how the state is or should be territorially organized, partly because of its obvious relationships with the wider question of spatial organization, itself one of the key concerns of geographers. But there are other reasons why territorial reorganization should be high on the political geographer's agenda; as the previous chapter argued, the territorial configuration itself has a bearing on the benefit and burden pattern of service delivery, as well as allowing the student direct insight into how political and administrative factors influence the spatial organization of the state.

Several different approaches can be recognized within the earlier work by political geographers in this field. Much the most common has focused on the outmodedness or otherwise inappropriate character of the existing network of political areas and boundaries. Because the jurisdictional structure characteristically fails to keep pace with socio-spatial patterns — territorial governments have a high inertia factor — reorganization is 'dictated' by the changed circumstances of the social geography. The underbounded city — where, in other words, the city's limits have been overtaken by urban growth — and, more generally, the territorial anachronisms created by an increasingly mobile population are typical examples. Extending from this some political geographers have sought to prescribe what ought to be the pattern of sub-national governments, usually relying heavily on arguments relating to different geographical conditions within the state. Amongst these perhaps Fawcett's study, *The Provinces of England* (1919), is the most celebrated (although Australia through the work of Holmes, 1944, and America in the more recent work by Brunn, 1974, together with a host of other countries, exemplify the popularity of this type of study in what might be labelled applied political geography). Insofar as Fawcett developed a number of geographical principles by which to draw provincial boundaries, so as to establish a preferred order of space, his study provides a classic example of the *genre* and is the forerunner of other geographical 'solutions' to the territorial area problem, such as the city region (Senior, 1965). Other studies (for example Honey, 1981) have analysed the process of reorganization in practice and the problems of redrawing boundaries.

Though to varying degrees, each of these concentrates on reorganization as a problem in terms of its spatial characteristics, particularly its justification and outcomes. Such questions are legitimate because restructuring the territorial make-up of the state is an overtly spatial act.

Nevertheless, and this is a criticism particularly of the purely prescriptive approach to the problem, such studies fail to root the question of reorganization within the wider set of issues that it raises. Redrawing the political map, whether comprehensively within the state or only within a part of it as, for example, in a metropolitan area, is a painful process and not one on which the centre, where it is often the source initiating the process, will readily embark. Thus in Britain local government reform had been on the political agenda for much of the twentieth century though it was not until the 1960s that the process was properly set in train with the setting up of the Royal Commission. Local government areas may not be as immutable as state or provincial units within federal countries because of the different types of relationship with the overriding national government that these two systems of power division enjoy, but all territorial reform, because it alters the pattern of access to decision-making, is a game of 'winners' and 'losers' and in this sense is inevitably an issue that is highly charged politically. National political leaders can find that reforming the periphery might even jeopardize their own tenure, as de Gaulle found in the failure of the 1969 referendum that sought reform of the existing regional machinery and also of the Senate.

As local government reform has been so widely considered a necessity — and since 1945 none of the major industrial nations has not put reform on the agenda (Rowat, 1980) although actual achievement has been somewhat less than the welter of Commissions and Inquiries might suggest — the question why such change is advocated is perhaps obvious. On the one hand the reasons for territorial reform seem straightforward enough, when the argument in so many reports from different countries is couched in terms of the efficacy of service provision — that the existing areas are too small, at variance with the changing socio-spatial patterns, and the like. These arguments have much to say about the size of local administrative units, particularly as they relate to notions of efficiency and local democracy. Nevertheless to some students of local government reform, notably in the British case (Dearlove, 1979), these arguments have become all too readily accepted as conventional wisdom when in many cases the relationships attributed to size have at best only a flimsy empirical basis. The reasons for reform should, then, be sought elsewhere. According to Dearlove, adopting a Marxian perspective, this leads to a consideration of which classes are likely to benefit from territorial reform since this is by its nature a process altering the access to power.

This chapter will be largely empirical and 'implicitly' pluralistic in approach. Two main issues will be discussed. First is the range of factors within which local territorial reform has been discussed, criteria that reintroduce some of the arguments that were touched upon in chapter 2. Much of the argument about how local government should be organized (and reorganized) has hinged around the question of size, particularly as it relates to the efficiency with which services are provided and to the notion of local democracy. Secondly, we shall look at the problem of territorial reorganization in its various forms through a case-study approach. This involves looking at administrative regionalism, as well as local government generally and more specifically within metropolitan areas. Territorial reorganization has become so widespread a phenomenon that political geographers have a problem in trying to separate the general principles that might be held in common from the mass of detail and information contained within each reform attempt. Hence the choice of examples in this chapter, more so than in our preceding discussion, has had to be selective.

For the most part our analysis will address the question 'how' territorial reorganization is approached. In the last section, however, we shall look briefly at the more problematic question, which Dearlove raises, 'why'.

NORMATIVE APPROACHES

Judging by the experience of most industrial nations, the need to reorganize the network of local government areas, or otherwise rationalize the territorial systems of administration within the state, arises periodically. It is the case that particularly in certain countries, such as France, the issues that such reform raises — political centralization and local autonomy, the possible methods by which power might be areally divided — are part of a continuing debate amongst academics and some practitioners about the organization and role of the state (Hoffman, 1959; Gourevitch, 1980). In practice, however, because of the political and administrative complexities raised by reorganization, attempts to alter the jurisdictional map, particularly in any comprehensive strategy, will tend to be sporadic.

Initially the impetus to reform can be traced to the effects the modernization process has on the ability of local governments to function effectively. Thus, during the period since the 1960s in England,

The once common thread running through the decision to examine this or that aspect of local government was simply the alleged inadequacy of the system to cope with the growing demands made on it as governments continued to extend the range of public services and as conditions of daily life were transformed by the increasing mobility and size of the population. (Redcliffe-Maud and Wood, 1976, 2)

On the one hand there are the continually changing facts of social geography, which are a direct result of the development of the urban–industrial society, while, on the other, there is a concern over the efficacy of local government.

According to O'Connor (1973), economic development in the advanced capitalist state has inevitably brought pressures for the centralizing of control and for the delimitation of larger units of administration over which the planning and administering of services might be made more effective. Reorganization has invariably brought about a reduction in the number of local government units and consequently an increase in their size, both territorially and in terms of their population. However, the political reorganization of space lags behind changes in the spatial structure of the socio-economic environment; while the latter experiences more or less continuous change, political space is more static and resistant to change. Even in those states in which comprehensive reorganization has been implemented, as in Britain, the frequency of such alteration has been very limited. In Britain it has been restricted to the reorganizations of the late nineteenth century and, more recently, of the 1970s, though in the intervening period piecemeal alteration of parts of the local government structure had taken place. More generally the industrial nations have attempted to overhaul parts or most of their territorial systems in the post-war period, where in a number of cases the network of units had actually been established in the pre-modern period.

The actual form in which reorganization has been conceptualized and examined has fallen into several stages (see figure 7.1). Firstly, the objectives to which the system of local government is directed are spelt out. From these, specific methods by which these objectives might be attained are developed. In Britain these operating principles were developed partly from the research studies carried out for the Royal Commissions set up to report and make proposals on reorganization, partly from earlier research findings and partly from the evidence of expert witnesses invited to submit comments on the problems of the existing structure and possible palliatives. These sources also contributed to the final stage within which the operating principles were applied to the political map.

The range of objectives raised for local government typically involve

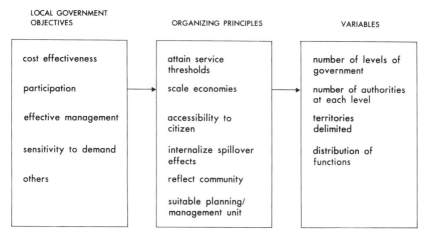

LOCAL GOVERNMENT
OBJECTIVES   ORGANIZING PRINCIPLES   VARIABLES

cost effectiveness	attain service thresholds	number of levels of government
participation	scale economies	number of authorities at each level
effective management	accessibility to citizen	territories delimited
sensitivity to demand	internalize spillover effects	distribution of functions
others	reflect community	
	suitable planning/ management unit	

FIGURE 7.1   Stages in the local government reorganization of England
(from Honey, 1981)

arguments about local autonomy, efficiency and effectiveness, equity, accountability and participation. Thus the Royal Commission on Local Government in Scotland (1969; the Wheatley Report) stated as its four objectives:

1. power, in which local government would have sufficient autonomy to enable it to play a significant role in political life;
2. effectiveness, to ensure that citizens are effectively provided with services;
3. local democracy, to ensure that local decision-making is politically accountable through the ballot box; and
4. participation, to include citizens within the processes of local decision-making as much as is feasible.

This does not exhaust the list of possible objectives — in some cases, for instance, some notion of territorial justice was to be included, particularly in arguing for the equitable distribution of services between localities.

Though restricted to the question of local government design within a metropolitan area, a more concrete example of the way in which normative arguments impinge on structure is developed in the United States Advisory Commission on Intergovernmental Relations report of 1963, *Performance of Urban Functions: Local and Areawide:*

1. Jurisdictions providing a service should be large enough to enable the benefits of it to be consumed largely within the governmental unit;
2. Jurisdictions should have a geographical area large enough to permit effective performance and to harness scale economies;

3. Jurisdictions should have adequate legal and administrative abilities to perform effectively;
4. Jurisdictions should have a sufficient number of functions so as 'to

TABLE 7.1 Some arguments for and against small local governments

Basis of argument	Arguments for	Arguments against
Efficiency/ rationality	1. Small jurisdictions encourage efficiency by bringing closer ties between expenditure needs and revenue decisions. 2. Small jurisdictions make it easier and cheaper for voters to understand issues. 3. A multiplicity of small jurisdictions will foster competition and innovation in the provision of public goods, contributing further to meeting diverse consumer preferences. 4. Easier to coordinate across services.	1. Economies of scale in the provision of many public goods. 2. Large jurisdictions can employ specialist staff and are more likely to attract higher-quality councillors and officials. 3. Supervision of local by central government will be eased the smaller the number of jurisdictions. 4. More jurisdictions mean more boundaries and, thus, more spillovers across boundaries.
Citizen preferences/ community	5. Smaller jurisdictions are more likely to be homogeneous in terms of wants and therefore match citizen preferences more exactly. 6. Smaller jurisdictions facilitate feelings of community, reducing alienation.	5. Small jurisdictions can become dominated by particular factions (e.g. the company town).
Citizen participation	7. Smaller jurisdictions enhance citizen participation and the opportunities for it.	6. Smaller jurisdictions limit the effectiveness of participation by limiting control to only some of the aspects in a given situation (because of, for example, the smaller number of functional responsibilities over which the jurisdiction has control, compared to a larger government).
Redistribution	———	7. Small jurisdictions restrict the opportunities for redistribution between rich and poor areas.

Sources: Adapted from Foster *et al.* (1980); Dahl and Tufte (1973)

provide a forum for the resolution of conflicting interests, with significant responsibility for balancing governmental needs and resources';
5. Jurisdictions should be accessible to citizens;
6. Functions should be allocated to jurisdictions which are able to combine effective citizen participation with service performance.

Such principles are based firstly on a broad consensus about the objectives for local government; from these, certain design criteria have been developed.

These criteria by which local governments have been territorially restructured have also shown a striking degree of consistency between the developed nations. According to Carroll and Carroll,

> The general approach has been to divide services into two categories. Some services have been deemed to be essentially local because demand for them varies greatly from community to community, the 'spillover' from one community to the next is minimal and the service is of a type that may be administered reasonably efficiently within a small community. Others usually have been assigned to a higher level of government because of the importance of administrative or financial economies of scale or because of the probability of significant 'spillover' from one community to another. (1980, 297)

From this it can be seen that the critical criteria by which local governments have been redesigned have been the harnessing of scale economies and the internalizing of spillover effects. Both revolve around the basic variable recurrent in the reorganization process, the appropriate size for the new jurisdictions, though these two factors by no means exhaust the issues that size generates and that have been rehearsed in the reform debates. Table 7.1 lists some of these issues as they are divided between those who have advocated small or large local governments. Most of these arguments are at best only partially verifiable in empirical terms, though this has not detracted from their significance as criteria by which alternative systems can be justified. We shall next explore some of these issues through the two objectives at the centre of the debate, efficiency and local democracy.

Size and efficiency

The idea that local governments should in some way be efficient has attracted widespread support. In part the quest for efficiency stems from the role of local government as service provider in which one interpretation of an efficient local government service could be that no further cost savings could be achieved for a given level of output. This interpretation, however, raises a number of problems. It assumes that meaningful measurement of public service outputs is possible and that, indeed, the concept of efficiency is applicable to the public sector. Defining what exactly constitutes the output of a local government service is as hazardous as it is critical — hazardous where we need to be able to measure the activities of, say, health visitors or teachers, and include within this some evaluation of the quality of the service, and critical where, rather than taking a service as a whole, we need to examine particular activities within it. Studies of the police service illustrate the complications of the latter problem; Hirsch (1970) reported that taking the service as a whole neither economies nor diseconomies of scale were apparent, a picture, however, that altered when specific activities within the service (handling personal complaints, crime solving, i.e. non-routine functions) were examined.

Nor is 'efficiency' necessarily the correct term to apply to local government. In industry and commerce efficiency is meaningful insofar as performance and overall objective — profit maximization — are quantifiable. Ambivalence towards the use of efficiency within local government reform in fact permeated the reports on restructuring in Britain, and 'effectiveness' was preferred to the term efficiency.

Economies of scale   Economies of scale were considered one method by which local government could become more efficient, or effective. If it could be shown that cost savings were possible either by enlarging or by reducing the territorial area and/or population over which a service was presently provided, there would be a strong case for altering the jurisdictional make-up. It was an argument that was all the more persuasive because of the cost of local government and, within some countries (such as Britain), growing public disquiet with the burdens these costs were imposing.

Though in itself a persuasive argument, proving that scale economies could be attached to service provision within jurisdictions of x population or territorial size has been difficult to establish (Massam, 1975). Methodologically, there are several problems, particularly those concerned with the measurement of the two basic factors — costs per unit of production and output. Overall, Alesch and Dougharty (1971) argue that economies of scale analysis will be easier in those services that involve routine tasks and that have relatively standardized resource inputs and measurable outputs. Most utilities — sewage treatment and water supply, for instance — together with streets and highways would fall into this category. By contrast, services such as education and welfare programmes are much more complex, frequently non-routinized tasks involving variable resource inputs and outputs.

The problems of analysis are matched by the ambivalence of the findings themselves. Hirsch (1970) summarized the findings of 19 studies completed between 1959 and 1970 covering education, police services, hospitals and utilities. It was particularly in the latter (electricity, sewage plants, gas) together with fire protection and certain parts of the educational service that average unit cost curves declined or were U-shaped, suggesting scale economies. In Britain, attempts to equate population size with performance have been similarly inconclusive. In a survey of 73 studies, Newton (1976b) noted that 38 found no statistically significant correlation and only 17 found significant associations of between 0.40 and 0.59. Firm evidence for the operation of scale economies in local government is lacking.

Even were the evidence to favour the scale economies argument more positively, as B. Wood (1974) points out the translation of these findings into proposals for territorial reform would inevitably involve a number of value judgements:

1. assuming that the larger jurisdictions do offer scale economies, it still remains to decide what is a satisfactory level of service to which it would then be possible to attach a given population size;
2. scale economies have been identified with particular aspects of a service rather than with the whole of the service, raising the problem of how great an importance to attach to these parts;
3. as different services would be associated with different 'ideal' populations, the question of their relative importance is likewise a problem, i.e. do certain 'key' functions exist that will dictate the administrative positioning of others?
4. evidence of scale economies relates to what *is* rather than what could be. Improved technologies might radically alter how a service is provided and therefore the conditions under which scale economies would operate.

Furthermore, the scale economies argument can be sidestepped by 'separating the provision of local services from their production' (Foster *et al.*, 1980, 569). This is a strategy that has been barely considered in Britain, while in America, through contracting schemes between local jurisdictions, it has become quite widespread. Some 42 states have enabling legislation permitting jurisdictions to enter into contracting arrangements with other units whereby services in the one are provided by the other. Such agreements were first introduced between Los Angeles county and neighbouring municipalities at the beginning of the century and by 1954 400 separate arrangements had been contracted. In 1954 the idea was extended following the incorporation of the City of Lakewood, comprehensive service packages being offered by Los Angeles county. The 31 Lakewood Plan cities within the county have contracted for the provision of such services as law enforcement, fire protection, street maintenance, building inspection and engineering services. This still leaves the city in control of services over which it wants to retain responsibility, such as zoning and, in many cases, parks and recreation.

In spite of such possibilities as the Lakewood Plan and the value problems identified earlier, and in spite of the inconclusiveness of the research, much emphasis is still placed on the scale economies argument. This was particularly the case in the recent British reforms. As Dearlove (1979) has pointed out, although the Commissioners (in the English reform) had to admit that size and performance were only barely related, the overall truth of such a relationship was accepted. However ambivalent the research, acceptance of population size as a critical variable had a strong tradition within British local government with which it was difficult to break; since the nineteenth century the idea of a minimum, if not an optimum, population suitable for a local authority with a given range of functions had become a commonly accepted method for defining jurisdictions. With the aid of expert witnesses — representing the separate functional activities of local government and drawn from central government and the localities as well as the professional associations — the Redcliffe-Maud Commission proposed populations of 250,000 and one million as the ideal lower and upper limits for the new jurisdictions, though their reasoning for this was one of the less well-argued proposals within the report.

The benefit area criterion   The other economic criterion usually linked with the functional assignment problem (the allocation of services to the different levels of government) is the question of benefit spillover effects of public service programmes. Allocation is typically considered to be efficient where the benefits of service provision are totally internalized within the producing jurisdiction. Ideally the costs incurred in production and the benefits of provision would accrue to the same population. In fact, because of the complexity of tracing such benefits and the 'openness' of the economy, allowing movement across jurisdictional boundaries both of fiscal resources and of population, identifying the appropriate jurisdictions is a herculean (and to some, fruitless) task. It can also be argued that were the internalizing of benefits as a deciding criterion to be persistently pursued there would be a strong centralist push — that is, services would become administered by higher levels of government than might otherwise be the case. The benefits of education (for example) flow relatively freely because of migration, so that logically the service should become a responsibility of the national government. In the United States in particular, where there are over 5,000 separate school districts, but also in most of the other industrial nations, the fact that education is locally controlled, although within varying degrees of central control, puts the externality argument into perspective.

It is widely assumed that public goods are classifiable into a hierarchy of

TABLE 7.2 Public services classified by the geographical scope of their benefits

Local[1]	Intermediate[2]	Federal[3]
Fire protection	Air and water pollution	Education
Police protection	Water supply	Parks and recreation
Parks and recreation	Parks and recreation	Anti-poverty
Public libraries	Public libraries	programmes
Water distribution	Sewage and refuse	Communicable disease
City streets	disposal	control
	Mass transit	Research
	Arterial streets/inter-city	
	highways	
	Airports	
	Urban planning and	
	renewal	

[1] Services with only marginal benefits beyond the local level of government.
[2] Services with significant spillovers beyond the local level but not beyond intermediate/regional level.
[3] Services with significant spillovers beyond intermediate/regional level.
Source: Break (1967, 69)

spatial units according to the benefit area criterion. Break (1967) has illustrated the types of functions that could be suitably allocated to local, intermediate and federal governments in the United States according to this factor alone (see table 7.2). Such a classification is at best approximate; each service is likely to have a unique benefit area associated with it so that the aggregation represented in the table inevitably involves a compromise. Also some services — parks and recreation, for example — are difficult to classify because they can be divided into a hierarchy, local versus national parks and the like. Different aspects of a service, therefore, may have different benefit areas. In other cases, notably inter-city highways, as Break acknowledges, there is inevitably a degree of arbitrariness in the final classification.

In the British reform, the objective of internalizing spillover effects was to be sought through defining jurisdictional boundaries on the basis of commuting patterns, so that commuters would be shouldering the costs of city services for which they received the benefits. However, just as the scale economies argument could be supported only loosely, so Honey (1976a) has shown that internalizing externalities was only partly achieved in the actual reform. His analysis was based on the number of misallocated districts, defined as where a district and its principal commuting destinations (given by the 1971 census) were assigned to different counties. Most of the district authorities were not misallocated by this criterion and, as table 7.3 shows, 'incorrect' assignments were less likely where the primary commuting flow was particularly dominant (more than 15 per cent of the workforce commuting to it). Moreover, there were marked differences between the reorganization proposals: the Conservatives, lending less support to the argument, preferred to maintain the advantages gained by separating suburban jurisdictions from the urban core.

TABLE 7.3 Commuting externalities: misallocated districts in English local government proposals

| | Misallocated districts[1] | | |
	Metropolitan ring[2] No. %	Outer ring[3] No. %	Total No. %
Redcliffe-Maud	18 0.03	95 0.24	113 0.12
Derek Senior	9 0.02	29 0.07	38 0.04
Labour White Paper	10 0.02	88 0.22	98 0.11
Conservative White Paper	45 0.09	92 0.23	137 0.15
Local Government Bill	53 0.10	96 0.24	149 0.16
Local Government Act	55 0.11	102 0.26	157 0.17

Note:
[1] A district is misallocated if assigned to a different county from the one containing the district's chief commuting destination.
[2] The metropolitan ring includes those districts with at least 15% of the workforce commuting to an employment centre, and with no more commuters going to any other centre.
[3] The outer ring includes districts with less than 15% of their workforce commuting to a centre, but more workers commuting to that centre than any other.
Source: Honey (1981)

Size and local democracy

Apart from efficiency criteria, another factor on which reorganization has been popularly argued is the need to foster local democracy. In Britain, several arguments were usually cited to show that such a need was real, amongst which were low electoral turnouts in local elections, particularly by comparison with national elections, the increasing tendency to switch the administration of functions (such as health and water supply) to *ad hoc* indirectly elected bodies and a growing appreciation of the need to introduce more citizen participation, especially within such services as land use planning. Some of these are more disputable than others; low electoral turnouts may not mean apathy as much as satisfaction with the operation of local government, or, as lower participation in local than national elections has been observed in many countries, this may be because of the greater importance rightly attached to the latter and is to that extent inevitable.

These different criticisms of local government are matched by the different interpretations that can be attached to the term 'democracy'. Four different interpretations were apparent in the British debates (B.

Wood, 1974). Representationally, democratic arguments were linked to the preferable size of the electoral districts, the number of representatives these would return and their population or territorial size. Secondly, democracy was associated with the 'small' jurisdiction or with areas that were meaningful geographical communities. A third meaning was conveyed within the need for local government to be responsive and accountable, while, lastly, democracy was also equated with the need to allocate services to the lowest possible administrative tier.

A popular claim linking size with democracy is that smaller jurisdictions will enhance local democracy. Several intervening processes are normally included within this overall claim. Thus small jurisdictions, it is argued, will encourage greater community feeling and in turn influence attitudes towards local government, its political representatives and local officials. The small jurisdiction, by virtue of its smallness, is less likely to be split by 'them' and 'us' attitudes than is the larger jurisdiction.

Some of these relationships were tested empirically by survey work commissioned for the British local government reports. Questions were asked on the citizen's home area and on various attitudes towards local government, notably those covering the confidence a respondent had in his local councillors, satisfaction with the extent of his knowledge about the operation of the local council, his involvement in local organizations and knowledge of local government. Some of these were aimed at assessing a citizen's alienation from local political processes, while the home area question sought to determine whether citizens did identify strongly with a territorial unit. Tables 7.4 and 7.5 show some of the findings of the surveys in England and Scotland classified by the population size of the jurisdiction. The basic finding of the surveys, particularly in the English case, except for the home area question, is a surprisingly small variation among the indices between the different sized local governments. Where we might expect the trend to be upwards — that, for example, citizen knowledge of local government would tend to be greater in the smaller jurisdiction because communication 'costs' and obstacles will be less — the statistics reveal only slight differences. The influence of size is more apparent on the more geographical questions: local isolation — the proportion of citizens saying that they did not identify with any home area (which may, of course, not be coterminous with the local government itself) — was greater in the large urban authorities, something that relates to the lower social attachments of citizens within the larger towns. Length of residence is a factor that strongly correlates with home area identification, and population stability negatively correlates with urban size. Equally, the influence of distance decay effects is suggested in the variations between visiting patterns to the City Chambers (in the Scottish sample) and urban size: in the small burghs, where in many cases the City Chambers would be physically nearer, visiting patterns were markedly different from the large burgh.

TABLE 7.4   Some relationships between local government size and citizen attitudes in England (excluding Greater London)[1]

Item	County boroughs[2]		Large towns[3]	Medium-sized towns[4]	Smaller towns[5]
	Conurbation	Free-standing			
1. Confidence in local councillors %[6]	50	45	49	50	54
2. Satisfaction with knowledge of local government %	50	62	63	56	55
3. Involvement in local organizations	45	48	54	46	50
4. Knowledge of local government %	46	49	57	52	52
5. Local social attachment %	42	42	35	44	56
6. Interest in local and public affairs %	47	44	53	48	52
7. Local isolation %	21	24	30	20	18
8. Relative size of home area (proportion of large to small)	0.56	1.00	0.84	1.80	2.09

Notes:

[1] Except for item 8, figures give the percentage of respondents scoring above the 'pass mark' for the questions. (The pass mark was chosen to divide the number of 'passes' and 'fails' into two equal halves.)

[2] County boroughs generally have populations of above 100,000.

[3] Over 60,000 (items 1–4); 50,000–100,000 (items 5–8).

[4] 30–60,000 (items 1–4); 20–50,000 (items 5–8).

[5] Below 30,000 (items 1–4); below 20,000 (items 5–8).

[6] Questions on which items 1–4 were based:

A. Confidence in local councillors.
   1. Respondent agrees that people become councillors because they have the good of the community at heart.
   2. Disagrees that people become councillors because they want higher position at work.
   3. Disagrees that people become councillors to make money for themselves.
   4. Agrees that people become councillors because they have a sense of duty to their fellow citizens.
   5. Disagrees that people become councillors because they want people to look up to them.

B. Satisfaction concerning knowledge of local government.
   1. Respondent feels he knows enough about the council to use his vote to best advantage.
   2. Feels he knows enough about the council for his own needs.
   3. Feels he knows enough about the council to know if they are doing the right things.
   4. Feels he knows enough about the council to make use of their services.
   5. Feels that the council run things well.
   6. Claims that he does something to help people in his local authority area.

C. Involvement in local organizations.
  1. Respondent belongs to at least one organization.
  2. Has attended at least one meeting in the last six months.
  3. Takes an active part in running some organization.
  4. Does something to help people in his local authority area.
D. Knowledge of local government.
  1. Respondent can mention one, two, or three local government services.
  2. Knows that the clerk is not elected.
  3. Knows that the housing manager is not elected.
  4. Correctly names his mayor/district chairman.
  5. Knows when the next council meeting will be.
  6. Knows where town hall is.
  7. Has heard news of council during last month.
  8. Knows that councillors are not paid salary.

Source: Royal Commission on Local Government in England (1969b)

TABLE 7.5   Community association, political knowledge and contacting in Scotland —
respondents classified by type of local government

	Type of local government				
	Counties of city[1]	Large burghs[2]	Small burghs[3]	District or County[4]	All
% claiming that they have a 'home area'	82	82	88	88	85
% born in home area and continuous residence	14	20	31	30	23
% correctly identifying authority responsible for 14 local and other public services	74	65	55	54	N.A.
% visiting City Chambers at least once during previous 12 months	17	27	53	13	N.A.
% thinking that City Chambers/main local government offices to be 'very' or 'quite' near	76	90		71	81

[1] Includes urban centres with populations of between 100,000 and 1 million.
[2] Includes urban centres with populations of between 20,000 and 100,000.
[3] Includes urban centres with populations of less than 20,000.
[4] Mainly rural areas.

Source: Adapted from various tables in Royal Commission on Local Government in Scotland (1969b)

These British findings are repeated in surveys done in other countries; jurisdictional size is at best only weakly linked with local democracy but the support there is precludes us rejecting outright the existence of these relationships. In his study of the effects of urbanism on levels of political involvement, sense of political efficiency and electoral participation,

Fischer (1975) concluded that city size had little influence and to the extent that political involvement was higher in the cities then this was due to class factors (which, as a large number of surveys have shown, strongly correlate with various forms of political behaviour). Equally Finifter (1970), though finding significant relationships between urban size and political alienation, suggested that the real causal agent here might be type of city government rather than demographic size. Survey data from Sweden, on the other hand, lend some support to the size factor (table 7.6). Differences in awareness and attitude were greatest between relatively small and large high-density jurisdictions. The Swedish study argued that it was in the densely populated, small communes (less than 8,000 population) that citizens were more likely to talk about political affairs and participation, generally, was greater.

If we look at just voting turnouts, one of the few aspects of political participation for which there are considerable data, evidence on the effect of urban/jurisdictional size is equally ambivalent. In some countries participation does relate to size, in others not. Local voting in the Irish Republic provides one of the better examples of the influence of size (Muir and Paddison, 1981). Turnouts are higher the smaller the size of the jurisdiction, positively correlating with the representation ratio, the number of electors per councillor and demographic stability, which is a measure of the cohesiveness of the community. This agrees with the 'decline of community thesis': 'in the small town social relations are more manageable, the sense of community more pronounced so that the voter will be more knowledgeable as to how the political system operates and whom to contact' (Verba and Nie, 1972, 231). However, as the British data underline, political knowledge is not greater in the smaller local governments.

Dahl and Tufte (1973) argue convincingly that even if in some ways

TABLE 7.6   Political awareness and commune population size and density in Sweden

Awareness factor and density of population	Population of commune			Three largest cities
	under 8,000	*8,000–30,000*	*over 30,000*	
Could name at least one local candidate (median %)				
High	73.0	62.3	49.0	—
Mixed	64.5	68.5	—	
Low	62.4	—	—	
Both knew and had attitude toward at least one official (median %)				
High	54.0	44.7	36.0	28.5
Mixed	54.2	54.2	—	
Low	47.2	—	—	

Source: Birgersson *et al.* (1971); quoted in Dahl and Tufte (1973)

democracy is better served in smaller jurisdictions, participation in larger local governments will be that much more meaningful because such jurisdictions will usually be responsible for a wider and more important range of services. The larger the jurisdiction, the more diverse will be its social and economic composition, so that even within the lowest tier within English local government — the parish council — there is a tendency for the larger councils to discuss a broader range of issues (Royal Commission on Local Government in England, 1969b). Larger jurisdictions, because of their greater functional role, will increase effectiveness, making participation more worthwhile, an argument that, as we saw earlier, might help explain the higher turnouts in national elections.

The size factor — some conclusions

In spite of the importance attached to size within the various national reorganization debates, much of the preceding discussion points to the inconclusiveness of the research evidence. Newton (1978, 27) makes the point more forcefully, concluding 'that size is largely irrelevant to many aspects of functional effectiveness and democracy, and . . . that where it does have some relevance, its effects appear to be beneficial just as frequently as they are the reverse'.

Part of the problem may lie in the methods that have been employed to analyse the effect of size. Assessing remoteness can be taken as a case in point. Following the recent reorganization in Britain, a popular claim is that the new, and always larger, jurisdictions have become more remote. By remoteness we might mean two things — a perception of being distanced from the decision-making locus and, more materially, the failure of the local government headquarters adequately to meet local service needs, because the very diversity of the large jurisdiction leads to the neglect of particular community requirements (Page and Midwinter, 1979). Intuitively, the first appears rational. In physical terms there is no doubt that larger jurisdictions leave citizens more distanced from city or county hall and that as Taylor (1973) illustrated, though within the single confined context of electoral participation, distance decay effects are apparent in political involvement. But we lack variables that sufficiently articulate perceptions of remoteness and whether this has an influence on attitudes. Equally we lack sufficient data to test effectively whether socio-economically diverse, large jurisdictions are less likely to be responsive to different areal needs. Both are linked within Kohr's (1957) dictum that the interest, responsiveness and involvement by the centre in its hinterland decline according to the square of the distance separating it from specific sub-areas. Though it is somewhat unlikely that this gravity model formulation would find much empirical support, the area is in general a promising field for further politico-geographical research.

TABLE 7.7   Classifying public services according to economies of scale, benefit spillovers and political proximity

Service	Economies of scale	Allocation criterion Benefit spillovers	Political proximity	Composite
Local schools	A	A	L	J
Transportation	A	A	?	A
Public welfare	L	A	L	J
Health and hospitals	A	A	A	A
Police — basic services	L	L	L	L
special services	A	A	L	A
Fire	L	L	L	L
Water supply	A	A	A	A
Sewage disposal	A	A	A	A
Refuse collection	L	L	A	L
Refuse disposal	A	A	A	A
Parks and recreation	L	A	?	J
Public housing	L	A	L	J
Urban renewal	?	A	?	J
Libraries — basic services	L	L	L	L
special services	A	A	A	A
Air and water pollution	A	A	A	A
Urban planning	A	A	?	A

A — favours area-wide (metropolitan-wide) control because economies of scale important, or benefit spillovers significant or political proximity unimportant.
L — favours local control for opposite reasons.
J — favours joint control.
? — allocation criterion has questionable implications.
Source: Break (1967, 76)

While the size factor can at best be only partly supported, as we have suggested it has nevertheless played a major part in how our territorial systems have been redesigned. We might conclude by drawing attention to a model scheme for the allocation of functions within a metropolitan area based on the three factors broadly discussed here: scale economies, benefit area and political proximity (see table 7.7). These criteria, it should be noted, are not exhaustive. Also, to the extent that they can conflict, the manner in which trade-offs between the criteria are decided is a problem that again involves value and not positive judgements.

Delimiting local governments

Alternative approaches   Actually delimiting local governments is a deceptively complex stage within the process of reorganization. Local government is premised on the existence of the local community, and, indeed, it is argued that the fusion of autonomy with community is one of the real benefits of such decentralization. But this assumes that we know what constitutes, or should constitute, suitable areas for local government purposes and that, when reorganizing needs are to be considered, such areas will be politically and administratively viable. Excepting the case where the centre dictates in an absolute sense how the state will be divided, the 'Napoleon solution', partitioning the state needs to take account of a variety of local and centre interests. Not only must the new divisions be acceptable in this sense but also they should be rational from a socio-geographical viewpoint, remembering that it has often been the alleged territorial anachronisms that have motivated demands for modernization.

Reorganizing local government is a multi-faceted process. It brings into question how services might be most efficiently provided, the nature of the relations between the centre and its localities and more broadly an ideology of what local government should be; but it also raises the issue of geographical definition. One problem following from this is where within the sequence of operations should the geographical factors be raised, not a trivial point as the debate on English reform illustrated. Hall (1973) shows how the Majority and Minority Reports of the Commission (Royal Commission on Local Government in England, 1969a), the Redcliffe-Maude and Senior Reports, differed in the importance that they attached to socio-geographical factors in delimiting the new jurisdictions. As figure 7.2 demonstrates, Redcliffe-Maud opted for a particular organizational structure, the unitary authority, whose overall size and other requirements would be related to efficiency and democratic preconditions that were to be sought; only at the end of the process did socio-geographical features contribute to the delimitation. By forcing an organizational structure onto the map, the problem was that in certain parts of England it was impossible to find unitary authorities falling within the desired population limits and at the same time meeting the conditions of the local social geography. This led to a number of geographical anomalies, cases where urban centres that did not otherwise have particularly strong connections with one another or were more associated with other centres were joined — for example, Birkenhead with Chester, where its 'natural' connections are with Merseyside — or where existing cohesive units, such as the county of Kent, were dismembered. Senior, on the other hand, began with the socio-geographical map, which together with the needs of functional efficiency and local democracy determined the structure. This map comprised the city regions into which much (but not, somewhat awkwardly, all) of the state could be divided and which, therefore, provided a more rational spatial basis for local government. The point is, however, that these two approaches, varying in the weight of importance to be given to geographical factors, resulted in very different territorial systems.

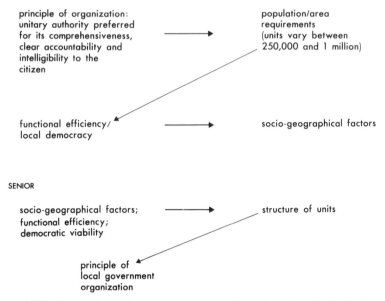

FIGURE 7.2   Alternative approaches to delimitation (from Hall, 1973)

Formal or functional units   Assuming that community is an important construct underlying local government, then establishing spatial units, which are themselves meaningful as communities, is a critical part of the reorganization process. This presupposes that we know what a community is, a term that has given rise to considerable debate among sociologists (Stacey, 1969) but that at minimum would include reference to social coherence, common value preferences and association with a definite territory. (There has been some discussion whether in a highly mobile society communities remain territorially rooted — Webber, 1963.) These three criteria need not be the appropriate ones for defining the local government community; for example, because value preferences are strongly influenced by class does not necessarily mean that only class-differentiated jurisdictions are appropriate in a given situation. Nevertheless, some degree of consensus of interests, together with social coherence and a well-defined territory, spell out the basics of a political community.

Among the ways in which such communities might be geographically traced, the city region concept has attracted considerable support. Senior, one of the idea's more ardent advocates, defines the city region as an 'area whose inhabitants look to a common centre for those specialised facilities and services (social, cultural, professional, commercial, educational and other) whose economic provision demands a user population of large but less than national proportions' (Senior, 1965, 84). The city region is in fact a variant of the geographer's functional or nodal region — the city and its surrounding hinterland. The assumption is that such a unit is the most appropriate for local government, that it represents 'a social entity much more relevant to the concerns of local government than any other now that the motor vehicle has come into general use' (Senior, 1965, 84). In particular, the city region breaks down the distinction between city and country that the Victorian local government reforms had sanctified, a distinction that increasing mobility had eroded. To Senior, then, in a highly urbanized and mobile society to talk of 'city' or 'village' is artificial; even where the built-up limits of cities stop, urban influences are very much apparent in the rural areas beyond — Britain is a nation of city regions.

Though it is true that much of England, with which Senior was concerned, can be subdivided into a set of city regions, it is important to establish whether such a unit could command popular support. Merely because residents commute to, or otherwise use the facilities of, the same city need not mean that this is the basis upon which strong political sentiments will be forged. In the sense that any realignment of local jurisdictions inevitably confronts the problem of reorienting popular allegiances, city regions would need to 'territorially socialize' their citizens much as would any newly defined jurisdiction. (In many authorities this 'reorienting' was achieved through publicity campaigns and other public relations exercises.) The assumption has been that the city region identifies a 'community of interest' but in spite of its frequent usage in the official reports and by political commentators this term has been barely defined. A common interest will be shared in the central city, particularly in its effective functioning so as to meet regional needs; by the same token there may be other parts of the city region (for example, recreation areas) that are part of the regional identity. Both of these involve planning issues and it is physical land-use planning within the British reforms that, according to observers of local government reorganization (Brand, 1974), has been one of the more influential factors underlying change. Planning issues, however, at best only partly contribute to 'community of interest'; they tend to galvanize opinion, and particularly reaction, at particular points in time rather than forge any ongoing relationships between citizen and area, except at the local (for example intra-urban neighbourhood) level. Equally in the case of regional services such as hospitals, though the city region makes geographical sense — enhancing accessibility — as well as hopefully being of sufficient size to meet scale economies and/or spillover effects, the contribution of such regional organization to establishing a community of interest is somewhat more problematic. Very likely, each of these — regionally organized services, city region planning problems and the like — probably contributes to establishing a 'sense of region', which is only built slowly and cumulatively. Like all territorial identities, city regional ones need to be nurtured.

While the city regional solution was not adopted — the Conservative government favouring the enlarged-county-and-conurbation solution (see below) — the new local government system, outside the metropolitan areas, has married urban and rural interests. Sharpe (1978) has argued that dissatisfaction with the reorganization has arisen partly from the size of the new units and because urban communities have been fused with rural areas. Urban areas, because of the density of population, give rise to different problems of service delivery and coordination than do rural areas. This is tantamount to saying that urban areas have different interests and that the jurisdictional structure should take these into account.

Rather than arguing that the functional or nodal region provides a 'community of interest', we can also argue that areas that are homogeneous in their socio-economic make-up provide better material by which to establish political communities. Urban areas have very different characteristics and problems from rural areas; likewise urban areas are internally differentiated by their problems and needs. In Wales, for example, the coal-mining communities mounted a campaign to establish a separate jurisdiction rather than be absorbed as part of a Cardiff-based government, an argument partly based on the different economic problems of the coal valleys (but very important to these numerous campaigns against amalgamation have been perceived fears of urban political domination). Formal, or more homogeneous, units might equate better, then, with community interests (or possibly self-interests). Evidently such units would be more rational to public choice theorists, for greater homogeneity means that local outputs are more likely to be closer to the collective preferences of the citizenry.

These arguments were rehearsed within the Scottish debate on local government reorganization where the city region solution was adopted. The west of Scotland, based on Glasgow, posed a particular problem; were the urban hinterland approach to be studiously followed this would mean a unit stretching from the English border to the Highlands and including nearly 60 per cent of the country's population. Ultimately the Commission favoured the splitting of the area into three city regions, which apart from Glasgow included the 'incipient' Central region based on Stirling–Falkirk, and the dominantly rural region of Dumfries and Galloway. (Even so, with nearly half the national population, Strathclyde failed to meet one of Fawcett's rules, which we have discussed in relation to federal countries — that no single unit be disproportionately large, because of the horizontal inter-regional conflict that this can give rise to.) However, following the first five years of its operation, Page and Midwinter (1979) cite optimistic evidence of Strathclyde being able to forge commonalities between its urban and rural areas. Thus, as one councillor from Argyll, a sparsely populated former county whose economy naturally links it with the Highlands region, put it, 'Strathclyde has not only done everything possible to understand the needs and problems of the area but also has great resources to commit to the area; Argyll has many friends in Strathclyde [a view which can coexist] alongside a perception of loss of identity and a feeling of remoteness from the centre of decision making' (quoted in Page and Midwinter, 1979, 13).

TERRITORIAL REFORM: CASE STUDIES

How territorial reform has been considered — which levels of government, regional and local, have been the subject of reorganization, whether the exercise has been restricted to the creation of an administrative body or has involved the establishment of some representative governmental unit, issues that by no means exhaust the battery of questions to which reorganization is addressed — has varied between countries so that when we look at recent experience cross-nationally territorial reform is seen to be a very complex issue. In some countries, reform has been restricted to consideration of only one level of government or of only part of the national territory, to meet the needs of special areas such as the heavily urbanized region; in others, such as New Zealand, reform legislation covers the entire country, though its implementation has been piecemeal; in others reform has been comprehensive and less gradualist.

In spite of these variations, a number of features are recurrent. Regional reform has been discussed in many countries, but 'region' ia a troublesome, ambiguous concept when we look at it in relation to territorial reorganization: regional reform is used to refer to both administrative and political reorganization. There are also ambiguities in the way in which region is used in a spatial sense; in England (for example) the term is used in relation both to the city region, of which Senior (1965) recognized some 35 units, and to the administrative region, which is closer to Fawcett's provinces, of which there are usually 8–10 units, depending on the definition (see below).

We can use these two concepts of administrative/political reform and spatial scale to classify different types of territorial reorganization. Figure 7.3 combines classification criteria suggested by Gourevitch (1980) and Kalk (1971). On the one hand, reorganization into new territorial jurisdictions can be administrative and non-representative (deconcentration) or more political and representative (decentralization). On the other hand, these reforms are distinguishable by their geographical scale of operation. National–regional units are larger than the local-regional ones, which are particularly associated with local government reform. National–regional units are more associated with deconcentration from the centre, though this scale also operates in regional devolution.

The diagram may help in distinguishing various types of territorial

SPATIAL SCALE

	national-regional	local-regional
deconcentration: administrative non-representative	UK: regional economic planning council, water boards etc. France: regional prefectures	UK: not applicable France: re-emphasis of the department
decentralization: political representative	UK: regional devolution (Crowther Report) France: regional devolution proposals	UK: unitary areas, city regions, enlarged counties France: *communautés urbaines*

TYPE OF POWER DISTRIBUTION

FIGURE 7.3 Alternative types of territorial reorganization

reorganization, but there are also strong links between them that need to be recognized. One of the arguments for regional devolution at the national–regional level is that this would help put on an executive and representative footing the coordination and provision of a whole group of services presently administered on an *ad hoc* and only weakly accountable basis. In this sense regional devolution has followed from the emergence of regional administration. The latter, too, has developed firstly with the emergence of individual deconcentrated services leading to a growing recognition of the need for horizontal coordination of certain, especially planning-oriented, services at sub-national level, in turn leading to the establishment of regional economic planning institutions. Local government reform has embraced the idea of planning at the area-wide level and, though the local–regional unit is typically smaller than the units that have been adopted for regional economic planning purposes, in the English reform this larger unit was to be incorporated within local government reform — the Redcliffe-Maud report recommended that provincial councils be established with overall coordinating responsibilities but whose areas were broadly similar to those of the regional economic planning bodies.

The classification suggested in figure 7.3 applies only to Western Europe and we shall concentrate on the two aspects of administrative regionalism and local government reform using examples mainly from the UK, France and the Irish Republic. (Regional devolution has already been discussed in chapter 3.) As a last case study we shall look at the special problem of metropolitan reform, particularly within the United States.

Administrative regionalism

Administrative deconcentration, particularly through a network of field services, is both a necessary and a natural outgrowth of centralized government. Building a national administrative network ensures that the policies of the centre will be implemented throughout the state. The network of field service units can also be used to monitor and evaluate the impact of such programmes, acting as a feedback channel to the higher jurisdiction. As such they provide an essential method of penetrating the periphery and, as Friedrich (1968) demonstrated in the case of Prussia, the process of replacing local, decentralized power structures with a centrally directed administrative service was an important adjunct of state-building historically.

Two major types of field system are generally recognized — unintegrated functional and integrated territorial — which are dominated by the organizing principles of function and area respectively (Leemans, 1970). Under the functionally organized system, each central government department operates its own network of field services whose territorial structure will be more or less independently determined. Thus the size and the boundaries of the units, because they are strongly influenced by the unique characteristics of each service, will often differ, in some cases from other field services within the same government department. Their strongly 'functionalist' organization emphasizes vertical control of the locality by the centre and, because of the fragmentary nature of the service structure, horizontal coordination between services sub-nationally becomes difficult. Functionally organized field systems predominate in the English-speaking countries, and in federal countries are found at both national and state levels.

Territorially the integrated field system is distinguished by the attempt to establish organization around a common set of units and by their fusion under a local prefect or similar official who acts as a coordinating link both across the services and between the centre and the locality. In the archetypal model, France, the prefect has constitutional standing; as an appointee of the central government, he is the representative of 'the national interest', acting as a lynch-pin between central and local government (Ridley, 1973). As introduced by Napoleon, the system combined deconcentration with integration based upon a network of 95 departments, each prefect being responsible for the overall coordination of services within the department. Recently this integrative role has been somewhat eroded because the field services of central government ministries have increasingly become organized in areas larger than departments, although a system of regional prefectures has been established. Though less marked a problem than in those countries whose field services are functionally organized, administrative growth in France has brought about a confusion

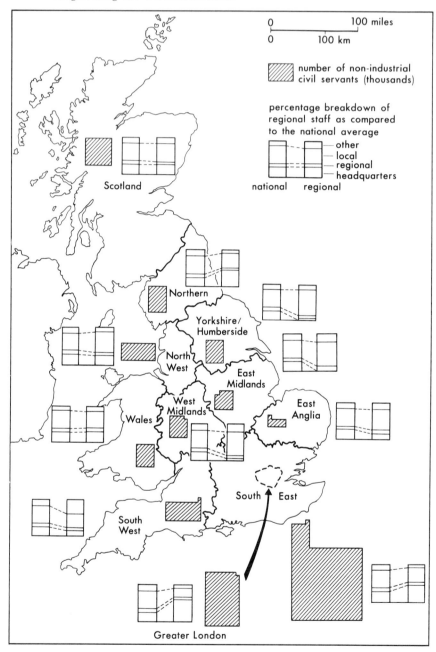

FIGURE 7.4   Civil service employment by standard regions in the United Kingdom, 1977

of areas that restructuring at the regional (multi-department) scale might help to rationalize.

Defining and spatially standardizing a field service system   Before looking at the question of how attempts have been made territorially to rationalize the field services of a country, we need to describe the factors that help account for how individual services are organized. We shall concentrate on the functionally organized system and draw examples mainly from the British Isles.

In Britain, and taking only the non-industrial civil servants, nearly three-quarters of those employed in administering central government services are located outside London. Not unexpectedly, as figure 7.4 shows, the majority of staff in London are classified as headquarters staff; far lower proportions of these are found in the provinces where they generally relate to particular enterprises that have been decentralized, such as the National Savings Bank in Glasgow. The majority of the civil servants are out-stationed staff functioning as part of a central government ministry, the most important of which in employment terms are Defence, Health and Social Security, Inland Revenue and Employment (all over 50,000 in 1977).

In Britain the two recent attempts to unravel the geographical structures of the field services of central departments and national public bodies (British Rail, Post Office, Tourist Board and the like) have emphasized the confusion of areas and boundaries (Thornhill, 1972; Hogwood and Lindley, 1980). Each service has its own territorial limits, which are more or less different from those of others. Hogwood and Lindley (1980) concentrated on the regional level — in many services there is another level below this — and found that even by taking the single type of unit there are considerable variations in definition. Some services operated within England with fewer than five regions, while a few at the opposite end use more than 13; even though there is a pronounced peak within the 7–9 category, the actual areas frequently differ (see figure 7.5). Some idea of these differences is given in figures 7.6–7.8, which show the territorial structures belonging to a number of field services in the Irish Repubic.

The reasons underlying the cartographic complexity, though various, are not difficult to discern. Where 'functionalist' pressures are important they are likely to dominate the other factors that can come into play, such as span of control restraints, organizational history, perceived importance of conforming to existing boundary arrangements, and the optimum workload. In certain services the nature of the function itself will inevitably determine the territorial breakdown: thus the field services of the Irish railway and postal services closely follow the divisions made by the rail network radiating out from Dublin. In others, optimum workload considerations, though closely tied to the type of function, will be the basic

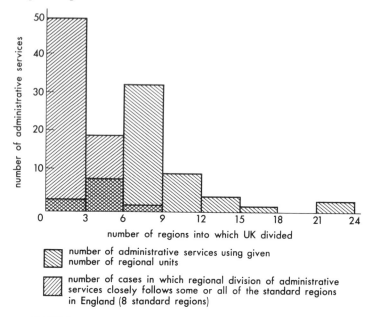

FIGURE 7.5 Regional boundaries and regional overlap —
administrative services in the United Kingdom
(adapted from data in Hogwood and Lindley,
1980)

factor influencing the initial apportioning of territory. Thus, where the target population of the service is trees (Forestry Service) or fisheries protection, the number, size and distribution of administrative units will depend on the characteristics of the target population and on the workloads that a field officer can effectively manage.

While the influence of the function and workload factors tends to be spatially divisive, the control span and, particularly, the boundary conformist influences operate in the other direction. The premise underlying the theory of the span of control is that, because of limited resources, knowledge, energy and expertise and, where a service is spatially organized, because of the frictional effects of distance, a supervisor within an administrative network can be responsible for only a limited number of subordinates. For many services it is not feasible for the centre directly to oversee the localities; in other words, an intermediate supervisory tier controlling the officers in the field and reporting back to the centre is necessary. (Figure 7.4 shows the relative importance of staff classified as intermediate, or regional, who, by definition, are responsible to the centre for the local offices.) Even though the boundaries of the regional units frequently differ, control span constraints tend to dictate the emergence of a regional administrative tier. Furthermore, the number of such regions used by individual field services frequently gravitates towards a reasonably small range: more than half of the services investigated were organized into between seven and nine regions. The upper limit of the number of regions will be strongly influenced by the span of control principle; thus in the United States federal departments generally restrict the number of primary sub-national units to under 20, and it is rare to find more than 25 regions in any country. But apart from this, the peaking apparent in figure 7.5 suggests that national administrators tend to view the state as divisible into a given number of regions. This could merely represent an extension into public life of something that very likely exists as part of the popular culture, the common perception of different regions, albeit one with practical consequences. However, the boundaries of these regions frequently differ, though there is sometimes a conscious effort by administrators to make them conform, if not with one another, at least to existing units, such as the county. It is the attempt to impose a greater degree of boundary conformity between services that takes us closer to the concept of administrative regionalism.

The standardizing of field service and possibly other governmental boundaries eases the problem of horizontal coordination at regional level. (It is not suggested that all boundaries need to conform; as our previous discussion indicates, this would be virtually impossible nor would it be necessary.) In Britain and elsewhere, the significance of coordination at a regional level has shown itself most clearly in times of national crisis. The first appearance of a coordinated system of regional administration in Britain was in 1925 as an emergency measure to minimize the disruption likely in the event of large-scale industrial strikes. By the time of the General Strike a year later, England and Wales had been divided into 10 regions, in each of which there was a civil commissioner overseeing representatives from government departments responsible for transport, the distribution of food and coal and internal communications. The experiment was extended during World War II with the establishment of regional commissioners, in effect prefects, who were to be 'the eyes, ears and mouth' of the central government in the region; in the event of an invasion and the fall of Whitehall, they were to assume total control in the regions. As earlier, individual government departments stationed regional officers who would operate with the regional commissioner.

Wartime experience emphasized the potential of the administrative region and, though the regional commissioner system was to be no longer considered a necessity shortly after the end of the war, the Treasury, the most influential central government department, attempted to establish field services on a similar footing through the establishment of the standard regions. Thus the regional arrangements of the field services of each department were meant to conform to the standard regions, though allowing for deviations where this would mean cost savings or administrative

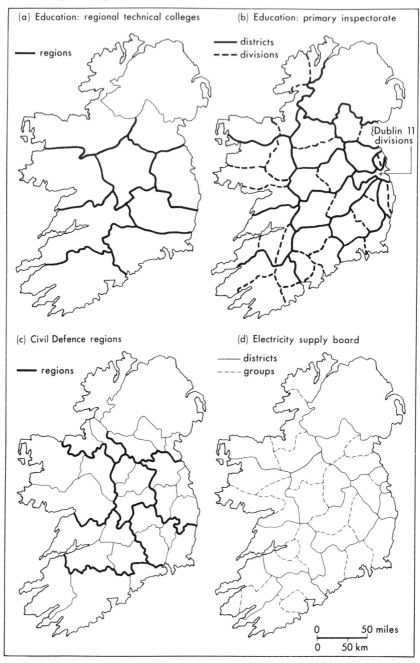

(a) Education: regional technical colleges

—— regions

(b) Education: primary inspectorate

—— districts
--- divisions

Dublin 11 divisions

(c) Civil Defence regions

—— regions

(d) Electricity supply board

—— districts
---- groups

0   50 miles
0   50 km

FIGURE 7.6   Regional structure of Irish field services — education, civil defence, electricity supply

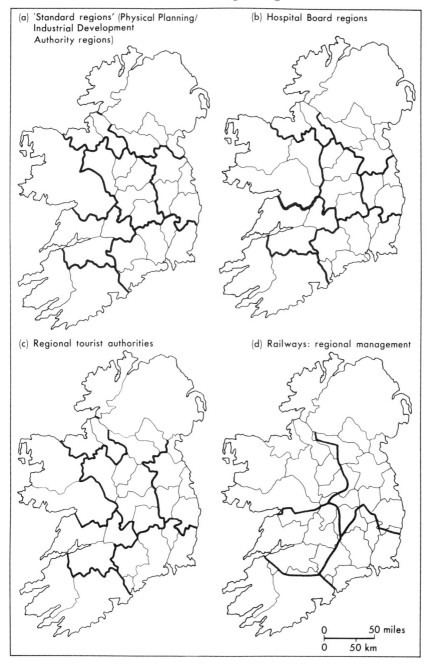

(a) 'Standard regions' (Physical Planning/ Industrial Development Authority regions)

(b) Hospital Board regions

(c) Regional tourist authorities

(d) Railways: regional management

0   50 miles

0   50 km

FIGURE 7.7   Regional structure of planning-oriented administrative services in Ireland

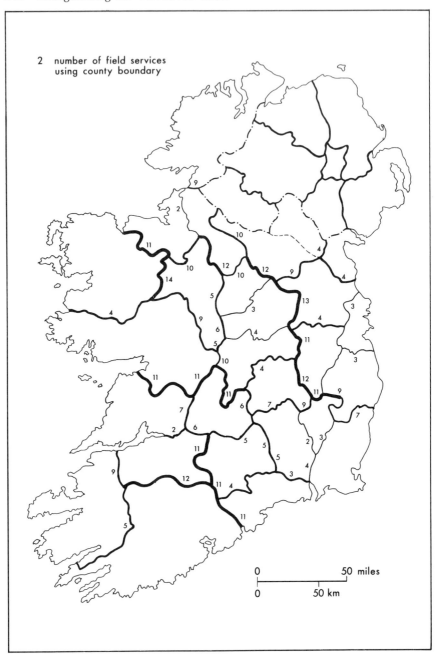

2 number of field services
using county boundary

0   50 miles

0   50 km

FIGURE 7.8 Regional boundary overlap of 18 Irish field services

convenience. An inter-departmental committee, under Treasury chairmanship, oversaw the scheme and during the early period of its operation most departments did cooperate. However, with the return of a Conservative government in 1951, public sector intervention declined and the regional machinery was allowed to lapse, particularly as central government departments themselves were keen to recoup the powers that had been decentralized. After 1956, the insistence that wherever possible field service units should follow the standard regions was dropped, leading inevitably to a proliferation of regional boundaries.

Historically, the re-emergence of regional boundary standardization in Britain as an issue followed from the initiatives by the new Labour government in 1964 to establish regional planning machinery. The Regional Economic Planning Council (REPC) gave expression to a need that was becoming commonly recognized throughout much of Western Europe — the need to prepare a regional physical and economic plan setting out investment guidelines for central and local government and framing regional proposals within those set by the national economic plan. Besides representatives from the centre, such bodies would also represent local government, industry, chambers of commerce and a number of other regional institutions. Of importance from the boundary standpoint was that the Regional Economic Planning Councils, and their associated Boards (REPBs), were to be based on the standard regions. Nevertheless in their 1979 survey, by which time the REPCs, but not the Boards, had been abolished, Hogwood and Lindley showed that only the Boards among 60 field services actually use the standard regions *in toto*, even allowing for minor boundary differences. Some caution is necessary at this point, however, as to the possible effects of boundary overlap on the working of the regional planning bodies; very probably its effects were marginal by comparison with some of the other problems under which the scheme operated, for example its advisory role, its 'lack of political visibility', and so forth. Nevertheless, there are cases where common regional boundaries would have eased coordination.

Experience elsewhere has shown that, if not as unsuccessful as in Britain where functionalist pressures are so dominant, standardizing regional boundaries is a difficult task. In Ireland a set of standard regions were drawn up by the Department of Local Government and much like the British system the Department was meant to act as a clearing house through which all new field service arrangements would have to pass. Even in those services closely connected with regional planning — industrial development, tourism, transport and communications, hospitals — only a minority replicated the standard regions (see figure 7.7).

The problems of administrative regionalism   We have concentrated on the difficulties of establishing a common territorial framework within which administrative regionalism might operate, but as has been suggested this issue needs to be put into perspective. Administrative regionalism involves far more questions than those of regional definition and we should look briefly at these where they relate to questions of local government discussed later.

Administrative regionalism, through the REPC and the REPB, provided in some respects a weak solution to regional planning and coordination (G. Smith, 1972). As an attempt at horizontal coordination, one problem was that central government retained its strong vertical (central–regional) perspective, so that the departmental representatives on the Boards kept their departmental loyalties, for career reasons, rather than developing a strong regional outlook and allegiance. Because of the non-elected nature of the REPCs and hence their lack of legitimacy, where investment priorities of the department, and of central government generally, conflicted with those of the regional councils, the councils were likely to be in a losing situation. Significantly, these problems of horizontal coordination were less outside England; both Scotland and, less so, Wales have enjoyed the amalgamation of a whole series of departments under the aegis of the decentralized Scottish and Welsh Offices, located in Edinburgh and Cardiff respectively.

Another source of weakness stemmed from the relations between the regional councils and the constituent local governments that they embraced. In contrast to the local governments, the councils were appointive, non-elected and advisory, all of which undermined their political stature. The advisory status of the regional bodies meant that constituent local governments, particularly in their capacity as the statutory planning bodies, could block their recommendations, and because regional investment decisions frequently distribute benefits in a lumpy or uneven fashion it was only to be expected that the 'disadvantaged' local governments would be reluctant partners. This opposition, which however it is possible to exaggerate, is all the more understandable, given that these regional bodies were commonly viewed as a potential threat to the local government's own power base (see the Australian regionalist reform discussed in chapter 4).

In contrast to local government, which combines a number of functions within a single geographical unit, the thrust of administrative regionalism has been to emphasize function over area so as to produce a multiple set of overlapping jurisdictions. In large part this reflects the *ad hoc* methods by which bodies have been created, some put on a regional footing because of the geographical inadequacy of the existing local government network (for example, hospitals), others, such as the Countryside Commission, established by the centre because of the apparent unwillingness of the local government planning authorities to take on board such issues. As one of the more vociferous critics of ad hockery, the political scientist Mackintosh

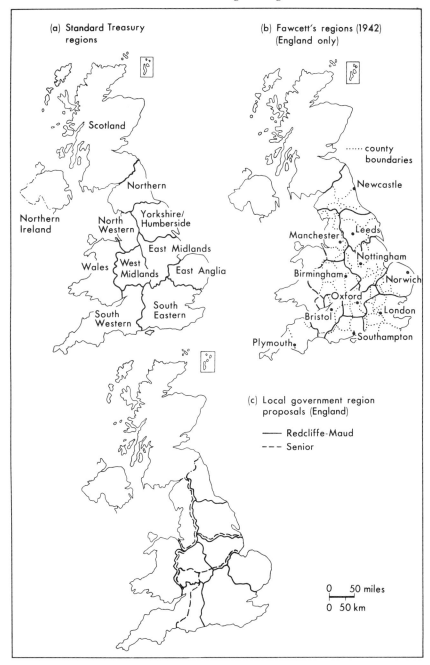

FIGURE 7.9 Alternative regional definitions of the United Kingdom

(1968) points not only to the territorial complexity to which these developments had given rise but also to the lack of local democratic accountability that the system had encouraged. Ad hockery does bring about a confusion of areas and authorities — as the rather different contexts of the present American metropolitan area and late Victorian England illustrate — a problem to which the debate on local government reform was to be addressed.

Reforming local government

Earlier in this chapter we discussed the range of factors that have dominated the debates on local government reform during recent reorganizations; these could be reduced to economic rationality objectives and local democracy. We also looked at the questions underlying the spatial definition of the new units. These describe the conditions under which proposals for reform have been framed — in the case of the British Royal Commissions the proposals were those of the bodies that central government had established. But these proposals need to be framed within legislation and exposed to political influences at the centre as well as in the localities themselves before becoming law. We need, therefore, to look more closely at how these political factors influence territorial reform. We shall do this by focusing on the British and Irish reform proposals.

The Commissions of Inquiry charged with the responsibility of formulating proposals did not work in a vacuum. Once they were given their remit they actively sought opinion from both citizens and public bodies so that there were opportunities for interests to be expressed and discussed. In England, over 2,000 witnesses offered written evidence to the Redcliffe-Maud Commission: 536 were individual citizens (such as academics, town planners, local councillors), 1,249 were local authorities and the remaining 350 were a wide variety of bodies, including national and local associations, amenity groups, industry and professional groups. The opportunities to give oral evidence were effectively restricted to central government departments, the local authorities and the chief local government trade union, NALGO.

The evidence of these groups reflected their interests and preferences, an argument that was true both when evidence was sought during the Commissions' deliberations and also following publication of reform proposals. In the Irish Republic the process of reform differed somewhat in that in the first instance the Government itself submitted proposals that were then commented upon by interested bodies. Submissions following the government proposals varied in their support of these proposals. One of the major recommendations of the government proposals was that the county be retained as the basic all-purpose local government and that the regional dimension, where this had become important administratively but in a poorly coordinated fashion, was only given recognition insofar as advisory regional bodies were to be encouraged. To a number of groups this was suboptimal. The Confederation of Irish Industry (for example), the major employers' association, favoured the region, wanting not only to transfer functions to it from the existing county but also to devolve extra functions to it from Dublin; such an 'authority would have full responsibility for overall regional planning and development . . . and *would be responsive to the needs of industry*' (Confederation of Irish Industry, 1971, 5; emphasis added). Affirmation for the region brought together some unlikely partners. Thus the CII's proposals for a regional government were largely endorsed by the submission of the major union, though its reasoning was not always the same. Apart from the greater efficiency and local democracy such a scheme would allegedly enjoy (the latter particularly because of the devolution of functions from the centre), the union emphasized the advantages of such an arrangement for the mobility of specialist staff.

While avowedly a pluralist exercise, it is likely that greater importance was attached to the evidence of some witnesses/submissions than to others. In Britain, several central government departments were 'key' witnesses, including the Treasury and the Department of the Environment, the ministry responsible for local government. However, it is difficult to separate out the influence of the public bodies on the proposals for territorial reform: thus, in Ireland, a number of submissions supported the idea of establishing some form of local community council of the order of size of an urban neighbourhood or rural parish, but the idea for this was already firmly implanted within government thinking, partly because of the general pressures for greater participation and partly because of their counteracting qualities to the emergence of larger local government units. Also, because of the similarity of the situations found in other countries, the 'community council solution' has spread internationally as a result of a 'demonstration effect'.

If it is difficult to trace out accurately the influence of public organizations and private bodies on territorial reform, the reverse is true when we look at the Government's role. Table 7.8 shows the structural reform proposals of the Labour and Conservative governments following the publication of the Redcliffe-Maud Report. The report had favoured sweeping structural changes: the then existing network of 48 counties, 79 county boroughs, 285 municipal boroughs, 491 urban districts and 415 rural districts (excluding parishes) was to be reduced to 58 unitary authorities and 3 metropolitan areas, which included 20 district authorities. Government reaction to Redcliffe-Maud varied between the Labour and Conservative administrations. While the Labour government largely endorsed Redcliffe-Maud, tinkering with the proposed structure only in that the number of unitary and metropolitan governments were to be reduced and

TABLE 7.8 A comparison of the various structural local government reform proposals in England, 1969–72

	Redcliffe-Maud Report, 1969	Labour government White Paper, 1970	Conservative government White Paper, 1971	Local Government Bill, 1972	Local Government Act, 1972
Metropolitan areas and districts	3 (20 districts)	5 (28 districts)	6 (34 districts)	6 (34 districts)	6 (36 districts)
Councils outside the metropolitan area	58 unitary authorities	51 unitary authorities	38 counties + districts; a boundary Commission to recommend district areas	38 counties + districts, but changes in boundaries	39 counties + 296 districts
Provincial councils	8 indirectly elected	No decision	No decision	No decision	No decision
Local/parish councils	In unitary areas existing authorities to become local councils	As Redcliffe-Maud, except that large cities allowed to subdivide	Existing parish councils to continue	Existing parish councils retained; new parish councils in urban areas possible	Existing parish councils retained; 300 municipal boroughs and urban district councils to become urban parishes

Source: B. Wood (1974)

increased respectively, the Conservative proposals marked a more radical departure from Commission principles and were, in structural terms, a compromise between the existing structure and some of the two-tier ideas outlined by Senior.

These different reactions to the Redcliffe-Maud proposals can be traced to the ideological preferences of the two parties and the implications of particular territorial systems on their electoral fortunes (Brand, 1974). While the Labour party had been a more or less consistent advocate of larger local government units for reasons of efficiency, planning and equity, the Conservatives had championed the local democracy argument and the need to keep local government local. The unitary authorities were by popular consent likely to be remote, particularly in the case of the geographically large units; as one leading local government official put it, because 'the unitary system works for the 81 square miles of Birmingham does not mean that it will work when transplanted to the 2,227 square miles of Exeter and Devon' (*The Times,* 22 August 1969). The Labour government White Paper recognized the problem and suggested that district committees be established within the unitary jurisdictions. To the Conservatives the unitary authority was more clearly seen as antithetical to local democracy, so that the district authorities in the two-tier structure were to be given responsibility for local planning matters, street maintenance, housing and public health.

It is also clear that the Conservative proposals sought to improve the party's electoral chances. The unitary authorities threatened to eliminate the separate rural areas, traditional strongholds of the Conservative party. The demotion of the Labour-dominated county boroughs to district council status within the counties, which were more favourable to the Conservatives, had equally partisan undertones. Finally, the separating out of the metropolitan areas gerrymandered the Labour vote, and whereas Redcliffe-Maud had proposed three such authorities six were finally to be incorporated into the statute book.

Local government's influence on reorganization was apparent in several ways. It could, and invariably did, respond to the initial invitations by the Commissions of Inquiry. Not surprisingly these views reflected the interests of the local government, though generally this was clothed in terms of a structure that was considered suitable for the country as a whole. In Ireland, where the smaller urban district councils (less than 10,000) were threatened with abolition, a common counter-proposal from them favoured the small town + hinterland authority, seen as the 'natural community'. Particular authorities very often reacted to the proposals affecting their area and always so when these involved any loss of territory or functions. Collectively, local governments could express their opinions through their national associations, which would seek to amend or support general principles underlying change rather than necessarily fighting the case for the individual jurisdiction. Collective action by the local authority associations was sometimes aimed at mobilizing public support; hence in Britain the Urban and Rural District Councils Association mounted an impressive campaign against the Redcliffe-Maud Commission: 'Don't Vote for R. E. Mote'. The influence of the associations was on occasions important and sometimes very apparent, as in the Labour amendment of Redcliffe-Maud to include district committees, which were strongly favoured by the County Councils Association.

These associations acted as pressure groups and they were again to be important when the reform legislation was being debated in Parliament. It was at this stage that it was possible to amend the government's proposals, and, in the English Bill alone, 1800 amendments were tabled. Apart from the associations, other groups sought to make changes through lobbying MPs. Boundary changes, in some cases materially altering the intentions of the legislation, were possible at this final stage. In the Scottish reform, new, dominantly middle-class suburban jurisdictions won separation from Glasgow in spite of government intentions, lobbying by the city and some internal civil service opposition within Edinburgh (Keating, 1975).

Ultimately a combination of central and local, partisan and organizational, influences resulted in a new local government map very different from the ones proposed by either the Redcliffe-Maud Majority Report or the Senior Minority Report (see figure 7.10). The latter envisaged a map that was too radically different to be politically acceptable to existing vested territorial interests; quite apart from the complexities that Senior's two-tier system would encounter in the operation of local government, the definition of the units marked too major a departure from county and other governmental boundaries. Local government reform was a political 'hot potato' and no more clearly so than in the case of deciding new boundaries. The Conservatives' reform marked a 'minimum departing' solution from the counties, evidently a point of some importance to Peter Walker, the minister responsible for initiating the 1972 legislation. Also, whereas the new areal units could be introduced and the transition to the new system effected, the question of district boundaries was left to a Boundary Commission because, as they would involve amalgamations between urban and nearby 'rurban' areas, they would inevitably encounter grass-roots opposition. Unlike the rest of the reorganization, district boundaries were to change incrementally. In the conurbations, the pattern of governmental units prior to the reform of 1972 was complex, the counties being punctuated by the county boroughs. The structure of metropolitan areas and districts simplified the pattern, though the 1972 Act areas were drawn round the metropolis much more tightly than Redcliffe-Maud had suggested, largely for party political reasons (see figure 7.11).

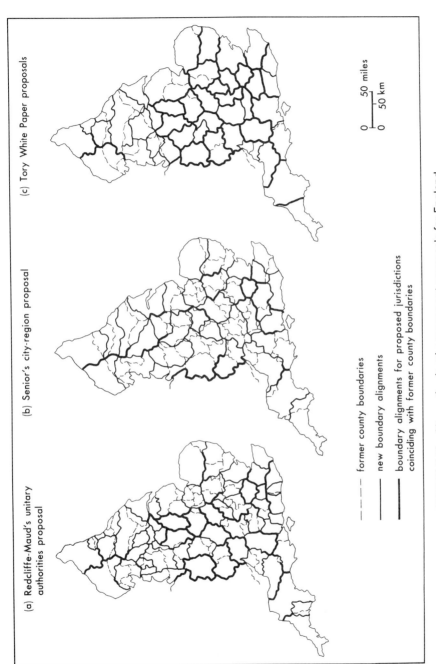

(a) Redcliffe-Maud's unitary authorities proposal

(b) Senior's city-region proposal

(c) Tory White Paper proposals

----- former county boundaries

----- new boundary alignments

—— boundary alignments for proposed jurisdictions coinciding with former county boundaries

0   50 miles
0   50 km

FIGURE 7.10   Alternative local government proposals for England

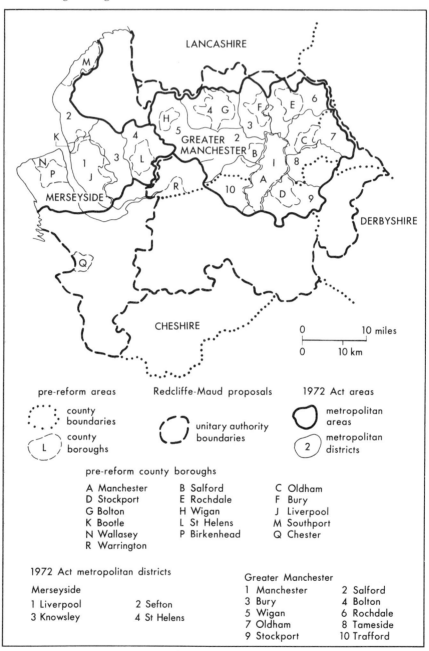

pre-reform areas

: : county
: : boundaries

county
boroughs

Redcliffe-Maud proposals

unitary authority
boundaries

1972 Act areas

metropolitan
areas

metropolitan
districts

pre-reform county boroughs

A Manchester	B Salford	C Oldham
D Stockport	E Rochdale	F Bury
G Bolton	H Wigan	J Liverpool
K Bootle	L St Helens	M Southport
N Wallasey	P Birkenhead	Q Chester
R Warrington		

1972 Act metropolitan districts

Merseyside

1 Liverpool	2 Sefton
3 Knowsley	4 St Helens

Greater Manchester

1 Manchester	2 Salford
3 Bury	4 Bolton
5 Wigan	6 Rochdale
7 Oldham	8 Tameside
9 Stockport	10 Trafford

FIGURE 7.11   Greater Manchester and Merseyside — the pre-reform, Redcliffe-Maude and 1972 Act boundaries compared

Explaining differences in reform achievements between countries When we look at local government reform cross-nationally, it is striking that, while reorganization of some or all of the local jurisdictional map has been considered, actual achievement has been considerably less. Three achievement 'types' can be broadly defined:

1. Maximalist — comprehensive, nation-wide local government reforms have been implemented;
2. Incrementalist/gradualist — local government reform has been considered for the state or for whole areas within it (e.g. an entire metropolitan area) but actual reforms are being implemented in a piecemeal or gradual fashion;
3. Nil — where nation-wide local government reform has been debated by the centre (possibly being accepted) but not implemented.

Examples falling within the last group are comparatively rare — the Irish Republic is one such case — largely because, as we have said, the pressures to modernize local government geographically and functionally have been strong, so that in most countries some reorganization has been attempted. In Western Europe and the English-speaking world, most countries fall into the second category. It is only in a handful of countries, most notably the United Kingdom and the Scandinavian democracies, that comprehensive reform has been achieved within recent decades. However, this typology is by no means exact. Some reforms are difficult to classify: for example, the Italian regional reforms were maximalist in that apart from the 'special regions' all the others gained autonomy simultaneously, but overall the reform was gradualist in that while the 1948 constitution included provisions for regional government it was not until 1970 that this was effected nation-wide. Equally, some countries have changed position even within relatively short time-spans — prior to the recent reorganizations in Britain, territorial changes had been considered in a piecemeal fashion.

The paradox here is that such differences do exist between countries. The need to modernize local government areas has been readily appreciated by the centre and often, perhaps somewhat more grudgingly, by the localities themselves, and local government is constitutionally subordinate; yet comprehensive change has been comparatively unusual. Constitutional relationships matter, but apparently it is the political environment in which local government reorganization is staged that counts even more.

Ashford (1976; 1982) has drawn attention to the differences in political environment between Britain and France and how this might help explain the stark contrasts between the countries, both in their approach to local government reorganization and in actual achievements.

The direct political links between the center and the periphery are readily apparent; an electoral system that imprints the center with local partisan differences; a splintering of parties around regional, occupational, and ideological differences; party organizations that are difficult to control from the center; and the intermingling of political roles at the various levels of government. (Ashford, 1976, 51)

Not only do national and local politics interdigitate, but through its functional organization Paris has extended itself to the localities through the prefectural corps. Thus,

Since the state cannot readily dominate the periphery, it extends itself to the periphery. Once this is done, it becomes virtually impossible to achieve a major reorganization without provoking a state crisis of unmanageable proportions. (Ashford, 1976, 51)

In Britain, by contrast, the centre has been able to 'isolate the periphery'. There is, for example, no close interplay between local parties and the national party organizations, so that policy formation is relatively sheltered from partisan politics. Where local party and national politics do converge, the evidence suggests that the localities play the more subservient role. Indeed, as one study showed, local party agents in Merseyside accepted such a position vis-à-vis their national parties and that they were unlikely to play any significant role in national policy formation. (More recently, however, the importance of the constituency branch has been enhanced with the democratizing of the Labour party.)

The interplay between national and local politicians and their party organizations is arguably a recurrent factor underlying the failure to reorganize local government comprehensively. In Ireland, where the issue was allowed to lapse altogether, the original proposals of 1971 belonged to the Fianna Fail government and their idea of abolishing the smaller urban authorities was opposed by the incoming Fine Gael–Labour coalition of 1973. The reform issue had not been raised in the election campaign — not surprisingly, as it would have been a vote loser. But also many MPs concurrently serve as local government councillors or, at least, local government acts as a stepping stone for the aspiring national politician (Chubb, 1971), so that territorial amalgamations or the abolition of jurisdictions become the less likely.

These arguments do not exhaust the reasons why reshaping the local government map is so difficult. Other factors are suggested when we look at Australia. In each of the separate states (except Queensland), re-organization on a comprehensive basis has been debated, but has subsequently on a state-wide basis been allowed to lapse. Opposition from 'threatened' local governments has been effective in blocking reform, but equally the reform proposals themselves lacked substantive support either popularly or, in some cases, through the state governments. For them, reorganization was not only a contentious issue but one that promised to result in larger local governments posing a potential threat to the state. (The Labour party's regionalist policies in the period from 1972 to 1975 had shown, for example, that by virtue of voluntarily amalgamating into loose regional associations the federal government was willing to fund the bodies direct, thereby eroding the states' positions — in that local government had always been considered an entity of the state.) Thus in those states where reorganization continues this is in an incremental fashion; in the case of New South Wales this means a Boundary Commission examining the pros and cons of local amalgamation where there have been demands for it.

Reforming metropolitan areas

Metropolitan areas pose special problems for governmental organization. The density of population, the close juxtaposition of class and territorial interests, the existence of multiple, overlapping externality fields, the need to coordinate services over large areas while simultaneously ensuring proximity between citizen and the political decision-making processes — such factors need to be taken into account by the jurisdictional draughtsman, though, because they underwrite alternative territorial frameworks, weighed up by politicians. Because cities grow in an incremental, but often patchy form and because jurisdictional change lags behind the growth of metropolitan areas, relatively few of them are administered as a single entity. Even accepting that specific parts of the urbanized area will be separately administered by some lower-tier authority, it is unusual to find that metropolitan-wide interests are catered for by a single jurisdiction with executive authority whose area of charge embraces all of the urbanized area. Most metropolitan areas are fragmented, though the degree of fragmentation varies between, as well as within, countries. In the last chapter we looked at the effect of such fragmentation on service delivery and equity questions, particularly within the United States. Here it would be useful to examine some of the reform proposals and achievements within US metropolitan areas, where the problems and debate over governmental organization have been more wide ranging. We shall finish by looking at metropolitan reforms elsewhere.

To many observers, jurisdictional fragmentation is considered one of *the* root causes of American metropolitan problems. Certainly the list of problems that are blamed on it is impressive — inadequate area coordination, duplication of services, ineffective service delivery, the separation of fiscal resources from needs, inter-governmental conflict and so forth. In the case of some of these, such as the fiscal implications, the effects of fragmentation are well documented, but to some analysts, particularly those from the public choice school, the multiplicity of governments is to be seen as beneficial. Nevertheless, the history of the American city is a history of attempted structural reform; whatever the merits of reform in terms of the kinds of criteria to which we have been referring — efficiency, equity, citizen access and accountability — the thrust of the debate over the last century and more has assumed the 'rightness' of restructuring.

Three basic approaches to reform can be recognized: the consolidation-ist or one-government solution, the federal or two-tier solution and the polycentric or 'multiple jurisdiction with *ad hoc* inter-local cooperation' solution (C. R. Warren, 1974). Within each of these are included a number of alternatives. Federal models, for example, include Toronto-type federa-tions, the comprehensive urban county, state-supported umbrella regional councils and the metropolitan multi-purpose district (ACIR, 1974a).

Of the two basic consolidationist-type reforms that we shall examine — the other is city–county consolidation — annexation is the more histori-cally established and both numerically and territorially still by far the more important. In the nineteenth century and particularly after the Civil War, when a surge in industrialization and immigration brought about rapid increases in population of Eastern and Midwestern cities, annexation was widely used by central cities. Frequently this would be achieved by unilateral action by the state legislature or by a straightforward majority of local residents or a vote of the municipal council. The logic of such annexation was readily accepted in that growth that spread beyond the boundaries of the municipality was urban and should be annexed (see figure 7.12). After 1900 there was increased opposition to annexation from the suburbs, and although the total number of annexations is still large — in 1967 there were as many as 787 — most involve only small areas, and particularly in the older, large SMSAs of the North and East the method holds no potential for gaining consolidation. According to the ACIR study, 'Perhaps its chief use today is to meet, on a piecemeal basis, previously unmet service needs on an urban fringe' (ACIR, 1974a, 84). In Southern states, on the other hand, annexation has been used successfully by medium-sized cities as a means of consolidating the urban area. Oklahoma City provides one of the more extreme examples, increasing in size from some 50m^2 in the early 1950s to 635m^2 before the end of the next decade (see figure 7.12). Other Southern cities, Houston and Dallas among the larger ones and San Antonio, El Paso and Fort Worth among the smaller ones, have annexed large areas so that in such Texan cities as Amarillo and San Angelo as much as 90 per cent of the metropolitan area population is included within the city limits. However, these annexations have been completed under somewhat special conditions, particularly the more permissive annexation laws that are found in Southern states. This

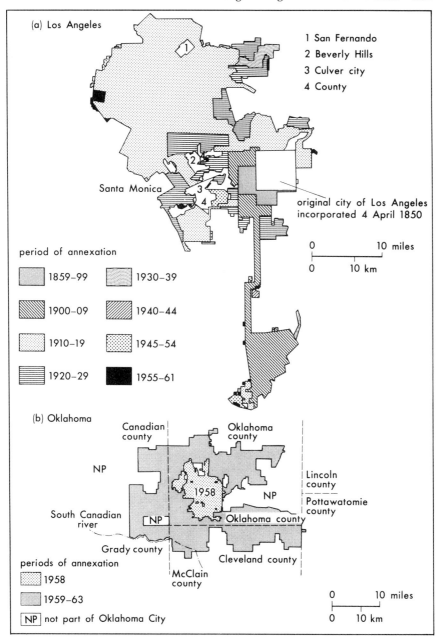

(a) Los Angeles

1 San Fernando
2 Beverly Hills
3 Culver city
4 County

Santa Monica

original city of Los Angeles
incorporated 4 April 1850

period of annexation

1859–99   1930–39

1900–09   1940–44

1910–19   1945–54

1920–29   1955–61

0   10 miles
0   10 km

(b) Oklahoma

Canadian
county

Oklahoma
county

NP

Lincoln
county

1958

NP

Pottawatomie
county

South Canadian
river

NP

Oklahoma county

Grady county

Cleveland county

periods of annexation

1958

McClain
county

1959–63

NP   not part of Oklahoma City

0   10 miles
0   10 km

FIGURE 7.12   Alternative annexation styles in the United States — 'traditional' and
'Southern' (adapted from Crouch and Dinnerman, 1963; Bollens and
Schmandt, 1975

permissiveness effectively allows for annexation in spite of any veto that the affected areas might attempt to block the action, a position which contrasts strongly with the situation in many Northern states where township 'rights' are a real obstacle to annexation.

City–county consolidation has long been debated as one of the methods by which to consolidate the governance of the urban area. Several notable city–county consolidations were completed in the nineteenth century — New Orleans (1813), Boston (1821), Philadelphia (1854) and New York (1898) — though all were imposed by direct state legislation without any local referendum being held. Subsequent state legislation has made the holding of a local referendum mandatory and very often consolidation is only possible if a majority in both the central city and the county separately are in favour of the change. Since the turn of the century only five major consolidations have been completed (Honolulu, 1907; Baton Rouge, 1947; Nashville, 1962; Jacksonville, 1967; and Indianapolis, 1969) from over 20 attempts. In spite of the plausible efficiency, equity and area-wide planning advantages that reform campaigners suggest consolidation would benefit from, there is sufficient reaction to block change, though predictably the level of opposition tends to be higher among county electorates (see table 7.9).

TABLE 7.9 Levels of voting opposition to city–county consolidation

| | | Levels of opposition | |
| | | City | County |
Year	Reorganization referendum	%	%
1959	Knoxville–Knox County, Tenn.	50.8	63.4
	St Louis–St Louis County, Mo.	66.0	75.0
	Cleveland–Cuyahoga County, Ohio	55.5	53.2
1961	Richmond–Henrico County, Va.	30.8	60.6
1962	Columbus–Muscogee County, Ga.	52.0	74.5
1964	Chattanooga–Hamilton County, Tenn.	81.3	83.3
1969	Athens–Clarke County, Ga.	40.2	70.7
	Brunswick–Glynn County, Ga.	62.7	78.1
1970	Columbus–Muscogee County, Ga.	18.3	62.1
1971	Augusta–Richmond County, Ga.	50.3	64.9
	Charlotte–Mecklenburg County, N.C.	56.9	88.1
Averages		49.3	71.7

Source: Marando (1974)

Most twentieth-century consolidations have been within the last three decades and it has been since 1950 that renewed interest in city–county mergers has emerged. Harrigan (1976) argues, however, that, in spite of the greater interest, successful consolidations have emerged under rather particular conditions: when public service provision has met particular problems and possibly broken down, when especially favourable state legislation that is less formidable to consolidation proposals has been in operation, when there is a relative absence of incorporated municipalities within the suburbs. In Nashville, for example, utility services within the suburbs were poor and in one or two cases in danger of breaking down; politically, consolidation was propitious in that county voters, otherwise likely to vote against the proposal, were anxious to vote against the city mayor (who was anti-consolidation) because of his earlier unpopular moves to annex land; finally the area had only a handful of incorporated municipalities, which were allowed to maintain their autonomy.

Federal ideas have particular appeal to the problem of metropolitan governance. As the influential Committee for Economic Development (CED) said in its 1970 report, *Reshaping Government in Metropolitan Areas:*

> All metropolitan areas are affected to a greater or lesser extent by conflicting forces of centralization and decentralization. The inter-dependence of activities within metropolitan areas requires area-wide institutions for some functions or parts of functions of government. Just as clear is the need for units of government small enough to enable the recipients of government services to have some voice and control over their quality and quantity. (1970, 18)

Federalism applied to the city is able to encompass both the city-wide and neighbourhood levels and the CED proposals were for two-tier government.

While theoretically appealing, no complete examples of federation are to be found in the United States metropolitan areas. (This is perhaps all the more remarkable given the length of time over which the idea has been discussed and the number of proposals that have been considered — Hallman, 1977.) The partial federation example usually discussed in this connection is the case of Miami–Dade County. The two-tier government structure that narrowly won support in the referendum of 1957 gave responsibility to the county for area-wide matters (for example, public health, planning, mass transit and certain police and fire services) while responsibility for local zoning, public education, police patrolling and a number of other functions was left to the municipalities, which accounted for over half the county population.

Before looking at the polycentric school's ideas but recognizing that these are a strategy aimed at avoiding metropolitan-wide governments, we could usefully review the achievements of structural, area-wide reforms. Wilken (1974a, b) presents a detailed analysis of the effect of centralization on the different questions of economy, efficiency, equity and citizen access based on the experience of the city–county consolidations and the Toronto and Dade County federations. In general, the verdict is that centralization has led to public services being greatly improved, so that effectiveness tends to be high while economy is less so, in that the cost of providing the services has increased and hence, in turn, the burdens falling on the property tax-payer. Reorganization has been especially effective in dealing with the coordination of public works programmes and the physical development of the metropolitan area. Though the available evidence on the harnessing of scale economies is equivocal, centralization has been efficient in reducing overlap and duplication of services. Also, city–county consolidations have tailored public service provision more closely to tax rates than is characteristic of the unreformed metropolitan landscape; thus the county is divided into several zones, beginning with the rural area where residents receive the minimum package of public goods but pay the lowest tax rate. Wilken also suggests that centralization has brought access gains, though is careful to point out that the available evidence is sketchy. Thus, inasmuch as centralization has become associated with district-based rather than at-large elections — though this is only a partial relationship — access is improved. Moreover, district-based elections favour minorities and there is some evidence to suggest that black political access is improved under the city–county consolidation.

It is on spatial equity questions that reorganization has been less successful. None of the metropolitan areas looked at by Wilken had made any headway in persuading suburbs to allow public housing developments. O. Williams (1971) puts this into perspective by dividing services into two types: system-maintenance functions such as water supply and drainage, and social access services, notably education and zoning. While the first type of service is essential to the physical operation of the city, the second underwrites life-style and class differences. Voters for metropolitan reform have been in support of system-maintenance functions being taken over by an area-wide body, while reserving the social access services to the individual suburbs. In Dade County, for example, the division of functions between the two tiers closely matches Williams' typology. In other words, city–county mergers or federal experiments have not been able to overcome the social equity problems that political fragmentation encourages; indeed metropolitan-wide government is being deliberately used to enable the city to function more efficiently in physical terms while at the same time the suburbs are able to maintain their relative advantages.

Under the term 'polycentrists' we can include a variety of writers who differ by virtue of their theoretical origins but are united in their opposition to metropolitan reform, especially the establishment of area-wide bodies, and who, though to varying degrees, argue that fragmentation has overall beneficial effects. Public choice exponents explicitly favour fragmentation, beginning from the assumption that because citizens have diverse preferences for public goods and services then a multiplicity of jurisdictions will cater for different tastes more effectively than will an area-wide body. Others have begun by being more critical of reform. Some political scientists questioned some of the beliefs that underwrite reform proposals, for example the assumption that central areas of metropolitan zones should by right continue to be *the* focus. Because urban decentralization and the 'multinucleated' city are so common a feature of North America, if perhaps slightly less so in other advanced nations, attempting to ensure that central cities and suburbs are jurisdictionally fused is to that extent questionable. Public choice theorists also question the assumptions on which reform is based. Bish (1971) discusses a number of these assumptions:

1. Majority interests should take precedence over those of minorities, particularly as (he claims) reform is biased to middle- and upper middle-class needs.
2. Jurisdictional fragmentation inevitably leads to administrative chaos. Reform-based attempts assume that only through a hierarchy of governments, area-wide and local, are coordination and administrative efficiency possible. Polycentrists, however, point to the advantages of *ad hoc* coordination, which is possible through the Lakewood Plan, through area-wide special districts, councils of government (groupings of jurisdictions) and other means.
3. Equal service levels are desirable area-wide. Clearly this conflicts with the idea of individual preferences and also that of minimum levels of service provision (see chapter 5). Seeking to establish minimum levels is justifiable on equity grounds, but it does not in itself demand the creation of an area-wide body.

To the polycentrist the choice argument is given direct spatial expression in Tiebout's idea that citizens as consumers will 'vote with their feet' until they find the jurisdiction whose package of public goods and services most closely matches their own preferences (Tiebout, 1956). Tiebout's model is hedged in by a number of substantive assumptions — some of which subsequent workers have released — though its basic thesis has sparked considerable theoretical and empirical debate. Empirically the evidence for Tiebout-type migration is equivocal. Critics of the model emphasize the inequities that it contains — some citizens are simply not in a position to be able to vote with their feet. There is also the argument that Harrigan (1976) raises, that the Tiebout model and public choice theory generally extol the advantages of a free market jurisdictional structure, whereas both theoretically and in practice the so-called free market economy requires considerable government intervention to ensure its smooth running.

In the United States the polycentric metropolis is the norm. Fragmentation has in effect been self-generating and various strategies have been adopted to overcome particular administrative problems while maintaining the overall pattern of fragmentation. Attempts at reform have been conspicuous for their failure, though not always so, and Marando (1974) has summarized the available evidence on city–county consolidations and federation attempts — suggesting the kind of factors that are more likely to lead to successful reform (table 7.10). Reforms have been more

TABLE 7.10　Typical factors associated with reorganization support in US metropolitan areas

Metropolitan area characteristics	
Population size — less than 1,000,000	+
more than 1,000,000	−
Large number of local governments	−
Region — South	+
Voter participation and related aspects	
Size of voter turnout:	×
High city voter turnout	+
High county voter turnout	−
Feared loss of autonomy	−
Anxiety over taxation	−
Possibility of new services	−
Aggressive annexation policy	+
Types of majority requirements:	
Double majority	−
Single majority	+
'Double count' majority	+
Voting patterns	
Political factors:	
Proposal or charter document:	
Quality of research	×
Popular election of officials	+
Large legislative body	+
Citizen awareness	−
Fragmentation: special districts	−
Municipal exemptions from consolidation	+
Prior departmental consolidation	−
Economic factors:	
Possibility of new services:	
To urban residents	−
To suburban residents	−
Cost of new services	−
Taxation anxiety	−
Race, local control and consolidation	
Inner-city black residents:	
Study commission representation	−
Representation in new government	+
Reduction of potential black majority control	−

TABLE 7.10   *(continued)*

Reorganization campaigns	
Citizen apathy	
Type of campaign:	−
Exclusive reliance on mass media	−
Grass roots	+
Get-out-the vote effort	×
Crucial issues	+
Use of public relations firms	?

+ Positive relationship
− Negative relationship
× No relationship
? Uncertain relationship
Source: Marando (1974)

successful in metropolitan areas of less than 1 million and especially in the South but where reorganization has had to meet with voter approval it is obviously crucial to mobilize support for the change. The problem with this is that reorganization campaigns tend to be spearheaded by the few and not the grass-roots; furthermore, the groups supporting change — academics, business and civic groups, professional groups, the media — are less likely to mobilize support than are local politicians to mobilize opposition (table 7.11).

TABLE 7.11   Community elements involved in metropolitan reform campaigns, 1950–61

Community element	*Number of metropolitan areas in which the indicated community elements played the indicated roles*[1]							*Total score*
	+3	+2	+1	0	−1	−2	−3	
Strongly in favour of metropolitan reform								
Metropolitan newspapers[2]	16	−	1	−	−	1	−	47
Leagues of women voters	11	4	1	1	−	−	−	42
Central city chambers of commerce	8	7	1	−	−	−	−	39
Central city commercial interests	6	6	5	−	−	−	−	35
Central city real estate interests	4	9	3	−	−	−	−	33
Radio and television stations	5	5	3	1	−	−	−	28
Banks	5	3	2	2	−	−	−	23
Central city officials[2]	5	3	4	2	2	−	−	20
Academic groups or spokesmen	2	6	2	1	−	−	−	20
Manufacturing industry	4	1	5	3	1	−	−	18
Utilities	4	3	1	−	1	−	−	18
Municipal leagues or similar research groups	5	2	−	−	−	−	1	17
Central city homeowners	2	3	5	−	3	−	−	14

TABLE 7.11   *(continued)*

Community element	Number of metropolitan areas in which the indicated community elements played the indicated roles[1]							Total score
	+3	+2	+1	0	−1	−2	−3	
Ambivalent toward metropolitan reform								
Central city employees	4	1	4	–	1	2	2	7
Suburban chambers of commerce	2	1	1	2	2	–	–	6
Taxpayers groups	–	4	1	1	–	–	1	6
Church groups	–	1	4	–	–	–	–	6
Central city political organizations	–	3	1	2	2	–	–	5
Central city neighbourhood improvement groups	1	1	2	–	1	–	1	3
Labour unions	–	4	2	–	3	2	1	0
Parent teacher associations	–	1	1	–	–	–	1	0
State political leaders	–	–	2	–	–	1	–	0
Government suppliers	1	–	1	–	–	2	–	0
County political organizations	–	3	1	2	2	–	2	−1
County officials[2]	1	2	3	5	2	2	2	−2
Suburban homeowners	2	1	2	3	2	4	1	−3
Suburban neighbourhood improvement groups	–	–	1	3	–	1	2	−7
Minority racial elements[3]	–	1	1	–	1	2	2	−8
Rural real estate interests	1	1	1	–	6	4	2	−8
Strongly opposed to metropolitan reform								
Suburban commercial interests	–	3	2	3	3	3	3	−10
Suburban real estate interests	–	2	3	–	3	3	2	−10
Farm organizations	1	–	1	–	2	2	3	−11
Officials of other local governments	1	–	1	2	2	2	3	−11
Employees of other local governments	–	–	1	1	2	1	3	−12
Other newspapers	2	1	2	1	3	2	6	−13
County employees	–	–	3	2	1	4	5	−21
Rural homeowners	–	1	–	2	5	4	4	−24
Farmers	–	–	–	–	1	10	4	−33

[1] +3 – A leading, active, unified element for the plan.
   +2 – A unitedly favouring element, but not in a strong or leading role.
   +1 – Predominantly for, but with some splitting or reservations.
    0 – Strong but divergent positions taken by some important components of group.
   −1 – Predominantly against, but with some splitting or reservations.
   −2 – A unitedly opposing element, but not in a strong or leading role.
   −3 – A leading, active, united element against the plan.
[2] Opposed metropolitan reforms in some recent campaigns.
[3] Favoured metropolitan reforms in some recent campaigns.

Source: Advisory Commission on Intergovernmental Relations, *Factors Affecting Voter Reactions to Governmental Reorganization in Metropolitan Areas* (Washington, DC, US Government Printing Office, 1962, 69–70)

While metropolitan reform is comparatively unusual in the United States, this is not the case elsewhere. Several major examples of reorganization have been established in Canadian cities, where there are close similarities with the US in terms of metropolitan structure. Apart from the federal-type reform of Metro Toronto (A. Rose, 1972), the other important metropolitan reorganization was the creation in 1971 of Winnipeg Unicity. The Unicity has centralized legal powers within the metropolitan-wide council while establishing a network of community committees that would act as the link between the citizen and the council. Not unexpectedly the proposal met vociferous opposition from the threatened municipalities, though, according to Axworthy (1974), they failed to mobilize sufficient opposition because most citizens felt closer affinities with the city than they did with the local municipalities. Ironically, then, while the municipalities claimed that the change would mean a 'loss of local identity', suburban political leaders found that events had already overtaken them.

In contrast to these Canadian reforms (and also those of England, including London), metropolitan reorganization in the United States is more incremental and gradualist. Several reasons account for this (Birkhead, 1974; Honey, 1981). The relationships between state and local governments in the United States differ markedly from provincial–state relations in Canada or central–local relations in Britain. The decentralization ethos permeates American life far more than it does the other countries. Finally, integration would bring different 'costs': because central city impoverishment and racial problems in the American city are more pronounced, these costs are likely to be greater and consequently will generate greater suburban opposition.

New metropolitan institutions have emerged, sometimes following the intervention of the federal government. The noteworthy development here has been the councils of government (COGs) set up in response to federal aid requirements. Because of their consensual nature, they have been unable to tackle the controversial equity issues associated with the fragmented city — instead they have concentrated on Williams' system-maintenance functions — but their significance lies in the integration they achieve. Territorial self-interests are difficult to counteract, particularly where they are institutionally recognized, so that adapting to new areal institutions will be a slow and painful process. These integrative experiments may also help implant the seed to legitimize the metropolitan-wide institution for, whatever other values structural change establishes, it must meet the test of legitimacy.

CONCLUSIONS

Our approach in this chapter has been largely empirical and orthodox, in the sense that the discussion has been preoccupied with the factors commonly considered as underlying the need to restructure the territorial framework of the state.

At the outset it was argued that the process of territorial reorganization was a politically and administratively hazardous road for governments to embark upon, if only because it is a process in which there are 'winners' and 'losers'. Put in this way, another basic question that reorganization (or its failure) raises is 'who gains and who loses' as a result of change. Dunleavy (1980b) suggests that (looking at the case of Britain) the predominantly pluralist accounts of the reorganization process — and much of the earlier discussion in this chapter has looked at the nature of these — overlook the questions of class conflict and the redistributive consequences of change. He goes on to show that

> the provincial changes in England and Wales effected a massive transfer of some sixteen per cent of the population involved from potentially Labour (or at least two-party) county boroughs to overwhelmingly Conservative controlled shire counties, a change with critical implications for millions of working people, for levels of public expenditure and for the political viability of the Labour Party. (1980b, 129)

The new system left some 58 per cent of the population of England and Wales in 'safe' Conservative areas, and less than 20 per cent in 'safe' Labour territory, a form of change (or manipulation?) that led Dunleavy to argue,

> whether or not an outcome of this kind can be shown to have been the conscious goal of any individual decision maker, it is difficult to imagine an outcome which could be more functionally appropriate for the interests of capital in the current British semi-continuous recession. (1980b, 130)

This outcome has already been commented upon, though from a different perspective, namely the differences between the two major parties in their preferred local government map. Because Conservative party interests were so favoured within the reformed system, particularly with the loss of separate status by the county boroughs, it is hardly surprising that lobbying by county boroughs to regain their position was supported by the Labour government of 1974–79 and that a policy of 'organic change' was proposed to redress the situation.

If there is one single factor that underlies the reorganization question it is that of self-interest. Central governments of a particular party hue will see the 'ideal' map in their own way; the interests of capital will be served by a territorial map whose electoral configuration will help ensure administrations that will reduce public spending and the local tax burdens that industry will need to shoulder; middle-class suburbs will fight attempts by the city to annex them; militant working-class groups or ethnic minorities will strive for community control or some meaningful degree of participation within the new system; existing local jurisdictions will resist attempts to dissolve them and, if this is 'inevitable', will attempt to ensure some measure of separate status within the new jurisdictional map. Examples of each of these are legion and must be common to all, or certainly most, attempts at reorganization.

In any specific case the political geographer might tackle the question of which are the dominant factors at play. Much of the debate in Britain and elsewhere among the advanced capitalist nations has been expressed in terms of the quest for greater efficiency and economy. No doubt this relates to a more general objective of 'escaping from the fiscal crisis' (Dearlove, 1979, 245). But it also tended to circumscribe the debate to questions that, as we have seen, have no easy, or really satisfactory, solution. Rhodes (1980) suggests that one reason why reform should have been couched in terms mainly of efficiency or better service provision is that, by focusing on this as the main issue, the other factors that reorganization should properly discuss — particularly, from our point of view, the optimum areal division of power between the centre and the localities — could be avoided, while at the same time raising the probabilities that a consensus could be achieved. If 'losers' are to be identified here, they are the separate jurisdictions.

The study of the territorial reorganization of the state is a fascinating field of enquiry for the political geographer. Inevitably, it will draw him back to a point emphasized within the first chapter — the question of frameworks within which to operate. Whatever the approach adopted, he will find the issue of reorganizing the territorial state focuses on those key questions of power, conflict and consensus that form the backbone to his discipline.

Bibliography

Adams, R.F. (1965) 'On the variation in the consumption of public services', *Review of Economics and Statistics*, 47, 400–5.

Advisory Commission on Intergovernmental Relations (1963) *Performance of Urban Functions: Local and Areawide*. Washington: Government Printing Office.

Advisory Commission on Intergovernmental Relations (1967) *Fiscal Balance in the American Federal System* Vol. 2. Washington: Government Printing Office.

Advisory Commission on Intergovernmental Relations (1973a) *Regional Decision-making: New Strategies for Substate Regionalism*. Vol. I of *Substate Regionalism and the Federal System*. Washington: Government Printing Office.

Advisory Commission on Intergovernmental Relations (1973b) *Regional Governance: Promise and Performance*. Vol. II of *Substate Regionalism and the Federal System*. Washington: Government Printing Office.

Advisory Commission on Intergovernmental Relations (1974a) *The Challenge of Local Government Reorganisation*. Vol. III of *Substate Regionalism and the Federal System*. Washington: Government Printing Office.

Advisory Commission on Intergovernmental Relations (1947b) *Governmental Functions and Processes: Local and Areawide*. Vol. IV of *Substate Regionalism and the Federal System*. Washington: Government Printing Office.

AGPS (1976) 'Local government and regions', in *Habitat*. Canberra: Australian Government Publishing Service, 253–6.

Aitken, M. and Depré, R. (1980) 'Policy and politics in Belgian cities', *Policy and Politics*, 8(1), 73–106.

Akzin, B. (1964) *State and Nation*. London: Hutchinson University Library.

Alesch, D.J. and Dougharty, L.A. (1971) *Economies of Scale in State and Local Government*. Santa Monica: Rand Corporation.

Almond, G.A. and Verba, S. (1963) *The Civic Culture: Political Attitudes and Democracy in 5 Nations*. Princeton: Princeton University Press.

Alt, J.E. (1971) 'Some social and political correlates of county borough expenditures', *British Journal of Political Science*, 1, 49–62.

Alternatives to Domestic Rates (1981). London: HMSO.

Anderson, J. (1973), 'Ideology in geography: an introduction', *Antipode*, 5(3), 1–6.

Anon (1982) 'Editorial essay: political geography — research agendas for the nineteen eighties', *Political Geography Quarterly*, 1(1), 1–17.

Antunes, G.E. and Mladenka, K. (1976) 'The politics of local services and service distribution', in L. H. Masotti and R. L. Lineberry (eds), *The New Urban Politics*. Cambridge, Mass.: Ballinger, 147–71.

Arnaud, N. (1979) 'Colonialisme intérieur et centralisme d'état: Le Cas de l'Occitaine, *Plural Societies*, 10(2), 49–79.

Arnstein, S.R. (1969) 'A ladder of citizen participation', *Journal of the American Institute of Planners*, 35(4), 216–24.

Ashford, D.E. (1976) *The Limits of Consensus: The Reorganization of British Local Government and the French Contrast*. Western Societies Program Occasional Paper No. 8. New York: Western Societies Program, Center for International Studies, Cornell University.

Ashford, D.E. (1980) 'Introduction: political choice and local finance', in D. E. Ashford (ed.) *Financing Urban Government in the Welfare State*. London: Croom Helm, 9–27.

Ashford, D.E. (1982) *French Dogmatism and British Pragmatism*. London: Routledge and Kegan Paul.

Axworthy, T. (1974). 'Winnipeg Unicity', in ACIR (1974) *Substate Regionalism and the Federal System, Vol. V. A Look to the North: Canadian Regional Experience*. Washington: ACIR, 83–108.

Bachrach, P. and Baratz, M. (1963) 'Decisions and non-decisions: an analytical framework', *American Political Science Review*, 57, 641–51.

Bachrach, P. and Baratz, M. (1970) *Power and Poverty: Theory and Practice*. New York: Oxford University Press.

Banks, A.S. and Textor, R.B. (1963) *A Cross-Polity Survey*. Cambridge, Mass.: MIT Press.

Banks, J.C. (1971) *Federal Britain? The Case for Regionalism*. London: Harrap.

Barlow, I.M. (1981) *Spatial Dimensions of Urban Government*. Chichester: John Wiley (Research Studies Press).

Baron, H.M. (1971) 'Race and status in school spending: Chicago 1961–66', *Journal of Human Resources*, 6, 1–24.

Beard, C. (1965) *An Economic Interpretation of the Constitution of the United States*. New York: Free Press. Third edition.

Beer, S. (1974) 'The modernization of American federalism', *Publius*, 4, 49–95.

Beer, S.H. (1977) 'A political scientist's view of fiscal federalism', in W. E. Oates (ed.), *The Political Economy of Fiscal Federalism*. Lexington, Mass.: D. C. Heath.

Bennett, R.J. (1980) *The Geography of Public Finance*. London: Methuen.

Benson, C.S. and Lund, P.B. (1969) *Neighborhood Distribution of Local Public Services*. Berkeley: Institute of Governmental Services, University of California Press.

Benson, G.C.S. (1961) 'Values of decentralized government — 1961', in G. C. S. Benson, M. Diamond, H. F. McLelland, W. S. Stokes and P. Thompson, *Essays in Federalism*. Claremont College: Institute for Studies in Federalism, 1–18.

Bercuson, D.J. (1977) 'Canada's burden of unity: an introduction', in D. J. Bercuson (ed.), *Canada and the Burden of Unity*. Toronto: Macmillan, 1–18.

Berger, S. (1977) 'Bretons and Jacobins: reflections on French regional ethnicity', in M. J. Esman (ed.), *Ethnic Conflict in the Western World*. Cornell University Press, 159–78.

Bergman, E.F. (1975) *Modern Political Geography*. Dubuque, Iowa: Wm. C. Brown Co.

Binder, L., Coleman, J.S., LaPalombara, J., Pye, L.W., Verba, S. and Weiner, M. (1971) *Crises and Sequences in Political Development*. Princeton: Princeton University Press.

Birch, J.V. (1977) *Political Integration and Disintegration in the British Isles*. London: George Allen and Unwin.

Birgersson, B.A., Forsell, H., Odmark, T., Strömberg, L. and Örtendahl, C. (1971) *Medborgarna Infromeras: Den Kommnnala Självstyrelsen*. Stockholm.

Birkhead, G.S. (1974) 'Introduction', in ACIR (1974), *Substate Regionalism and the Federal System. Vol. V. A Look to the North: Canadian Regional Experience*. Washington: ACIR, 1–12.

Bish, R.L. (1971) *The Public Economy of Metropolitan Areas*. Chicago: Markham.

Bish, R.L. and Ostrom, R.V. (1973) *Understanding Urban Government: Metropolitan Reform Considered*. Washington: American Enterprise Institute for Public Policy Research.

Blake, D.E. (1967) 'The measurement of regionalism in Canadian voting patterns', *Canadian Journal of Political Science*, 5, 55–81.

Blondel, J. (1969) *An Introduction to Comparative Governments*. London: Weidenfeld and Nicolson.

Boaden, N. (1971a) 'Innovation and change in English government', *Political Studies*, 19, 416–29.

Boaden, N. (1971b) *Urban Policy-Making*. London: Cambridge University Press.

Boaden, N. and Alford, R. (1968) 'Sources of diversity in English local government', *Public Administration*, 47, 203–24.

Bogdanor, V. (1979) *Devolution*. London: Oxford University Press.

Bollens, J.C. and Schmandt, H.J. (1975) *The Metropolis, Its People, Politics and Economic Life*. New York: Harper and Row. Third edition.

Booth, D.A. (1963) *Metropolitics: The Nashville Consolidation*. East Lansing: Institute for Community Development, Michigan State University.

Boots, A. *et al.* (1972) *Inequality in Local Government Services: A Case Study in Local Roads*. Washington: The Urban Institute.

Bourne, L.S. (1975) *Urban Systems: Strategies for Regulation: A Comparison of Policies in Britain, Sweden, Australia and Canada*. Oxford: Clarendon Press.

Bowie, R.R. and Friedrich, C.J. (eds) (1954) *Studies in Federalism*. Boston: Little, Brown.

Boyle, L. (1966) *Equalisation and the Future of Local Government Finance*. Edinburgh: Oliver and Boyd.

Bradford, D. and Kelejian, H. (1973) 'An econometric model of the flight to the suburbs', *Journal of Political Economy*, 81 (May–June), 566–89.

Brand, J. (1974) *Local Government Reform in England 1888–1974*. London: Croom Helm.

Brand, J. (1978) *The National Movement in Scotland*. London: Routledge, Kegan and Paul.

Brazer, H.E. (1959) *City Expenditures in the United States*. National Bureau of Economic Research, Occasional Paper 6. New York: National Bureau of Economic Research.

Break, G. (1967) *Intergovernmental Fiscal Relations in the United States*. Washington: Brookings Institution.

Brecht, A. (1945) *Federalism and Regionalism in Germany. The Division of Prussia*. Cornell University Press.

Brown, A.J. (1972) *The Framework of Regional Economics in the United Kingdom*. London: Cambridge University Press.

Brunn, S. (1974) *Geography and Politics in America*. New York: Harper and Row.

Brunn, S. (1975) *Towards a More Perfect Union*. New York: Oxford University Press.

Buchanan, J.M. (1950) 'Federalism and fiscal equity', *American Economic Review*, 40 (4), 583–99.

Budge, I. and Unwin, D. (1966) *Scottish Political Behaviour: A Case Study in British Homogeneity*. London: Longmans.

Bulpitt, J. (1971) 'Territory and power: some problems of analysis', *The New Atlantis*, 3(2), 7–21.

Burgess, T. and Travers, T. (1980) *Ten Billion Pounds*. London: Grant McIntyre.

Burkhead, J. (1967) *Input and Output in Large City High Schools*. Syracuse: Syracuse University Press.

Burnett, A.D. (1978) 'Political demands and public services: geographical aspects of petitioning and protesting over Portsmouth's public services'. Portsmouth Polytechnic, Discussion Paper.

Burnett, A.D. (1981) 'The distribution of local political outputs and outcomes in British and North American cities: a review and research agenda', in A. D. Burnett and P. J. Taylor (eds), *Political Studies from Spatial Perspectives*. Chichester: John Wiley, 201–35.

Burnett, A. D. (1982) 'Protesting and petitioning in Portsmouth', in K. R. Cox and R. J. Johnston (eds), *Conflict, Politics and the Urban Scene*. London: Longmans.

Burnett, A. D. and Hill, D.M. (1982) 'Neighborhood organisations and the distribution of public service outputs in Britain', in R. C. Rich (ed.), *The Politics of Urban Public Services*. Lexington: Lexington Books, 189–206.

Butler, D.E. and Stokes, D. (1974) *Political Change in Britain: the evolution of electoral choice*. London: Macmillan. Second edition.

Buttimer, Sr. A. (1974) *Values in Geography*. Commission on College Geography, Resource Paper No. 24. Washington: Association of American Geographers.

Cameron, D. R. and Hofferbert, R.I. (1974) 'The impact of federalism on education finance: a comparative analysis', *European Journal of Political Research*, 2, 225–58.

Careless, J.M.S. (1969) 'Limited identities in Canada', *Canadian Historical Review*, 25, 1–10.

Carroll, B.A. and Carroll, T.G. (1980) 'Britain: Northern Ireland', in D. C. Rowat (ed.), *International Handbook on Local Government Reorganisation*. London: Aldwych Press, 286–301.

Castells, M. (1977) *The Urban Question*. London: Edward Arnold.

Castells, M. (1978) *City, Class and Power*. London: Macmillan.

Chubb, B. (1971) *The Government and Politics of Ireland*. Stanford, California: Stanford University Press.

CIPFA (1980) *Financial, General and Rating Statistics, 1980–81*. London: The Chartered Institute of Public Finance and Accountancy.

Clark, G.L., and Dear, M.J. (1981) 'The state in capitalism and the capitalist state', in M. J. Dear and A. Scott (eds), *Urbanization and Urban Planning in Capitalist Societies*. London: Methuen.

Clark, T. N. (ed.) (1968) *Community Structure and Decision-Making: Comparative Analyses*. San Francisco: Chandler, 15–126.

Clark, T.N. (1971) 'Community structure, decision-making, budget expenditures and urban renewal in 51 American communities', in C. M. Bonjean, T. N. Clark and R. L. Lineberry (eds), *Community Politics: A Behavioral Approach*. New York: The Free Press, 293–313.

Clark, T.N. (1974) 'Community autonomy in the national system: federalism, localism and decentralization', in T. N. Clark (ed.), *Comparative Community Politics*. New York: John Wiley, 21–51.

Clarke, J.W. (1969) 'Environment, process and policy: a reconsideration', *American Political Science Review*, 63, 1172–82.

Cobban, Sir A. (1945) *National Self-Determination*. London: Oxford University Press.

Cockburn, C. (1977) *The Local State*. London: Pluto Press.

Cohen, S.B. and Rosenthal, L.D. (1971) 'A geographical model for political systems analysis', *Geographical Review*, 61, 5–31.

Commission on the Constitution (1973a) *Devolution and other Aspects of Government: An Attitudes Survey*. Research Papers 7. London: HMSO.

Commission on the Constitution (1973b). *Financial and Economic Aspects of Regionalism and Separatism*. Research Papers 10. London: HMSO.

Commission on the Constitution (1973c) *Report of the Royal Commission*. Cmnd 5460. *Memorandum of Dissent*. Cmnd 5460–1. London: HMSO.

Committee for Economic Development, Research and Policy Committee (1966) *Modernizing Local Government*. New York: CED.

Committee for Economic Development (1970) *Reshaping Government in Metropolitan Areas*. New York: CED.

Confederation of Irish Industry (1971) 'Report on local government reform'. Dublin: Confederation of Irish Industry. Mimeo.

Connor, W. (1972) 'Nation-building or nation-destroying?', *World Politics*, 24, 319–55.

Connor, W. (1977) 'Ethnonationalism in the first world: the present in historical perspective', in M. J. Esman (ed.), *Ethnic Conflict in the Western World*. Cornell University Press, 19–45.

Conradt, D.P. (1978) *The German Polity*. London: Longman.

Coppieters, F. (1974) *The Community Problem in Belgium*. Brussels: Institut Belge d'Information et de Documentation.

Coulter, P.B. (1970) 'Comparative community politics and public policy: problems in theory and research', *Polity*, 3 (Autumn), 22–43.

Cox, E. and Howard, P. (1973) 'Conflict and changes in the Sydney rocks', *Australian and New Zealand Journal of Sociology*, 9(2), 55–8.

Cox, K.R. (1973) *Conflict, Power and Politics in the City*. New York: McGraw Hill.

Cox, K.R. (1978) 'Local interests and urban political processes in market societies', in K. R. Cox (ed.), *Urbanization and Conflict in Market Societies*. London: Methuen, 94–108.

Cox, K.R. (1979) *Location and Public Problems. A Political Geography of the Contemporary World*. Oxford: Basil Blackwell.

Cox, K.R. (n.d.) 'The spatial evolution of national voting response surfaces, theory and measurement'. Discussion Paper No. 9. Columbus, Ohio: Department of Geography, Ohio State University.

Cox, K.R. and Johnston, R.J. (eds) (1982) *Conflict, Politics and the Urban Scene*. London: Longman.

CPRS (1977) *Relations between Central Government and Local Authorities*. Report by the Central Policy Review Staff. London: HMSO.

Craven, E. (1975) 'Introduction', in E. Craven (ed.), *Regional Devolution and Social Policy*. London: Heinemann, 1–35.

Crenson, M. (1971) *The Unpolitics of Air Pollution*. Baltimore: Johns Hopkins Press.

Cripps, F. and Godley, W. (1976) *Local Government Finance and its Reform*. Cambridge: Department of Applied Economics.

Crouch, W.W. and Dinnerman, B. (1963) *Southern California Metropolis: A Study in Development of Government in a Metropolitan Area*. Berkeley: University of California Press.

Cuneo, C.J. (1978) 'A class perspective on regionalism', in D. Glenday, H. Guindon and A. Turoweitz (eds), *Modernization and the Canadian State*. Toronto: Macmillan, 132–56.

Dahl, R.A. (1957) 'The concept of power', *Behavioural Science*, 2, 201–15.

Dahl, R.A. (1961) *Who Governs?* New Haven: Yale University Press.

Dahl, R.A. (1968) 'Power', *International Encyclopedia of the Social Sciences*, Vol. 12. New York: Macmillan, 405–15.

Dahl, R.A. (1971) *Polyarchy*. New Haven: Yale University Press.

Dahl, R.A. and Tufte, E. (1973) *Size and Democracy*. Stanford: Stanford University Press.

Danielson, M.N. (1972) 'Differentiation, segregation and political fragmentation in the American metropolis', in the Commission on Population Growth and the American Future, Research Report 4, *Governance and Population: The Governmental Implications of Population Change*. Washington, DC: US Government Printing Office, 143–76.

Danielson, M.N. (1976) 'The politics of exclusionary zoning in suburbia', *Political Science Quarterly*, 91, 1–18.

Danielson, M.N., Hershey, A.M. and Bayne, J.M. (1977) *One Nation, So Many Governments*. Lexington: Lexington Books.

Danziger, J.N. (1976) 'Twenty-six outputs in search of a taxonomy', *Policy and Politics,* 5, 210–12.

Danziger, J.N. (1978) *Making Budgets: Public Resource Allocation.* Sage Library of Social Research Vol. 63. Beverly Hills, California: Sage.

Danziger, J. (1980) 'California's Proposition 13 and the fiscal limitations movement in the United States', *Political Studies,* 29, 599–612.

Davies, B. (1968) *Social Needs and Resources in Local Services.* London: Joseph.

Davies, B. *et al.* (1971) *Variations in Services for the Aged: A Causal Analysis.* London: Bell.

Davies, J.G. (1972) *The Evangelistic Bureaucrat.* London: Tavistock.

Davis (1978) *The Federal Principle.* Berkeley, California: University of California Press.

Dawson, R.E. and Robinson, J.A. (1963) 'Inter-party competition, economic variables and welfare policies in the American states', *The Journal of Politics,* 25, 265–89.

Day, G. (1980) 'Wales, the regional problem and development', in G. Rees and T. L. Rees (eds), *Poverty and Social Inequality in Wales.* London: Croom Helm, 230–51.

Dear, M. (1981) 'A theory of the local state', in A. D. Burnett and P. J. Taylor (eds), *Political Studies from Spatial Perspectives.* Chichester: John Wiley, 183–200.

Dear, M. and Clark, G. (1978) 'The state and geographical process: a critical review', *Environment and Planning,* A, 10, 173–83.

Dearlove, J. (1979) *The Reorganisation of British Local Government.* Cambridge: Cambridge University Press.

Dennis, N. (1972) *Public Participation and Planners' Blight.* London: Faber.

Department of the Environment (1972) *Survey of the Transport of Goods by Road.* London: HMSO.

Deutsch, K. (1953) 'The growth of nations: some recurrent examples of political and social integration', *World Politics,* 5(2), 168–95.

Deutsch, K. (1966) *Nationalism and Social Communication.* Cambridge, Mass.: MIT Press.

Deutsch, K. (1979) *Tides among Nations.* New York: The Free Press.

Deutsch, K.W. *et al.* (1957) *Political Community and the North Atlantic Area: International Organisation in the Light of Historical Experience.* Princeton, NJ: Princeton University Press.

De Vree, J.K. (1972) *Political Integration: The Formation of Theory and its Problems.* The Hague: Mouton.

Dicey, A.V. (1885) *Introduction to the Study of the Law of the Constitution.* London: Macmillan. 9th edition 1939.

Dikshit, R. (1975) *The Political Geography of Federalism.* London: Macmillan.

Duchacek, I.D. (1970) *Comparative Federalism: The Territorial Dimension of Politics.* New York: Holt, Rinehart and Winston.

Duchacek, I.D. (1975) 'External and internal challenges to the federal bargain', *Publius,* 5(2), 41–76.

Duchacek, I.D. (1977) 'Antagonistic cooperation: territorial and ethnic communities', *Publius,* 7(4), 3–29.

Duncan, S.S. and Goodwin, M. (1982) 'The local state: functionalism, autonomy and class relations in Cockburn and Saunders', *Political Geography Quarterly*, 1(1), 77–96.

Dunleavy, P. (1980a) *Urban Political Analysis*. London: Macmillan.

Dunleavy, P. (1980b) 'Social and political theory and the issues in central–local relations', in G. Jones (ed.), *New Approaches to the Study of Central–Local Government Relationships*. Farnborough: Gower Press, 116–36.

Durkheim, E. (1964) *The Division of Labor in Society*. New York: Free Press.

Dye, T.R. (1962) 'Metropolitan integration by bargaining among sub-areas', *American Behavioral Scientist*, 4, 11–13.

Dye, T.R. (1966) *Politics, Economics and the Public: Policy Outcomes in the American States*. Chicago: Rand McNally.

Dye, T.R. (1967) 'Governmental structure, urban environment and educational policy', *Midwest Journal of Political Science*, 11, 353–80.

Easton, D. (1965) *A Framework for Political Analysis*. Englewood Cliffs, NJ: Prentice-Hall.

Eisenstadt, S.E. and Rokkan, S. (eds) (1973) *Building States and Nations*. Beverly Hills, California: Sage.

Elazar, D. J. (1962) *The American Partnership: Intergovernmental Coordination in the United States*. Chicago: Chicago University Press.

Elazar, D.J. (1966) *American Federalism: A View from the States*. New York: Thomas Crowell.

Elazar, D.J. (1973) 'Cursed by bigness or toward a post-technocratic federalism', *Publius*, 3(2), 239–98.

Elazar, D.J. (1975) 'Urbanism and federalism: twin revolutions of the modern era', *Publius*, 5(2), 15–39.

Elazar, D.J. (1978) *Israel: From Ideological to Territorial Democracy*. New York: General Learning Press.

Elazar, D.J. (1979) 'The role of federalism in political integration', in D. J. Elazar (ed.), *Federalism and Political Integration*. Ramat Gan: Turtledove Publishing, 13–59.

Ellis, U. (1933) *New Australian States*. Sydney: The Endeavour Press.

Enloe, C.H. (1973) *Ethnic Conflict and Political Development*. Boston: Little Brown and Company.

Enloe, C.H. (1974) 'Central governments' strategies for coping with separatist movements', in W. Morris-Jones (ed.), *The Politics of Separatism*. London: Institute of Commonwealth Studies, Collected Seminar Papers, 79–84.

Esman, M.J. (ed.) (1977) *Ethnic Conflict in the Western World*. Cornell University Press.

European Community (1973) No. 167.

European Economic Community (1977) *Report of the Study Group on the Role of Public Finance in European Integration*, Vol. I *General Report*; Vol. II *Individual Contributions and Working Papers*. Brussels: Commission of the European Communities.

Eversley, D. (1975) 'Regional devolution and environmental planning', in E. Craven (ed.), *Regional Devolution and Social Policy*. London: Heinemann, 35–58.

Fabricant, S. (1952) *The Trend of Government Activity in the United States Since 1900*. New York: National Bureau of Economic Research.

Farkas, S. (1971) *Urban Lobbying*. New York: New York University Press.

Fawcett, C.B. (1919) *Provinces of England*. London: Hutchinson.

Fesler, J.W. (1949) *Area and Administration*. University, Ala.: University of Alabama Press.

Fesler, J.W. (1965) 'Approaches to the understanding of decentralisation', *Journal of Politics*, 27, 536–66.

Fifer, J.V. (1976) 'Unity by inclusion: core area and federal state American independence', *Geographical Journal*, 142, 402–10.

Finer, S.E. (1975) 'State and nation-building: the role of the military', in C. Tilly (ed.), *The Formation of National States in Western Europe*. Princeton, NJ: Princeton University Press, 84–163.

Finifter, A.W. (1970) 'Dimensions of political alienation', *American Political Science Review*, 64, 389–410.

Firn, J.P. (1978) 'Devolution — an exit–voice model of regional policy', in E. Nevin (ed.), *The Economics of Devolution*. Proceedings, Section F of the British Association for the Advancement of Science, Aston University, 1977. Cardiff: University of Wales Press, 112–29.

Fischer, C.S. (1975) 'The city and political psychology', *American Political Science Review*, 69, 559–71.

Fletcher, J. and Wanhill, S. (1978) 'Devolution and local government finance', in E. Nevin (ed.), *The Economics of Devolution*. Proceedings, Section F of the British Association for the Advancement of Science, Aston University, 1977. Cardiff: University of Wales Press, 39–55.

Foster, C.D., Jackman, R.A. and Perlman, M. (1980) *Local Government Finance in a Unitary State*. London: George Allen and Unwin.

Franck, T.M. (ed.) (1968) *Why Federations Fail: An Inquiry into the Requisites for Successful Federalism*. New York: New York University Press.

Frank, A.G. (1972) *Capitalism and Underdevelopment in Latin America*. London: Penguin.

Freeman, T.W. (1968) *Geography and Regional Administration*. London: Hutchinson.

Frey, R.L. (1977) 'The inter-regional income gap as a problem of Swiss federalism', in W. E. Oates (ed.), *The Political Economy of Fiscal Federalism*. Lexington, Mass.: Lexington Books, 93–104.

Fried, R.C. (1974) 'Politics, economics and federalism: aspects of urban government in Mittel-Europa', in T. N. Clark (ed.), *European Communities*. Beverly Hills, California: Sage Publications.

Fried, R.C. (1975) 'Comparative urban performance', in F. I. Greenstein and N. W. Polsby (eds), *The Handbook of Political Sciences, Policies and Policymaking*. Reading, Mass.: Addison-Wesley. Vol. 6, 305–79.

Friedman, J. (1966) *Regional Development Policy: a case study of Venezuela*. Cambridge, Mass.: MIT Press.

Friedrich, C.J. (1968) *Trends of Federalism in Theory and Practice*. London: Pall Mall Press.

Galtung, J. (1971) 'A structural theory of imperialism', *Journal of Peace Research*, 8, 81–117.

Gilbert, C.E. and Clague, C. (1962) 'Electoral competition and electoral systems in large cities', *Journal of Politics*, 24, 323–49.

Glenn, N.D. and Simmons, J.L. (1967) 'Are regional differences diminishing?' *Public Opinion Quarterly*, 31, 176–93.

Godley, W. and Rhodes, J. (1972) *The Rate Support Grant System*. Cambridge: Department of Applied Economics.

Gold, J.R. (1976) 'Neighbourhood, territory and identity in the city', in J.R. Gold (ed.), *Neighbourhood Planning and Politics: A Geography Seminar Series*. Oxford Polytechnic: Discussion Paper in Geography, 1–17.

Goldsmith, M. (1980) *Politics, Planning and the City*. London: Hutchinson.

Gonzales-Casanova, P. (1965) 'Internal colonialism and national development', *Studies in Comparative International Development*, 1.

Good, M.H. (1978) 'The policy-making autonomy of the Italian regions: A study of legislation and central controls, 1970–75', *Planning and Administration*, 5(1), 7–19.

Gottman, J. (1952) *Le Politique des états et leur géographie*. Paris: Colin.

Gottman, J. (ed.) (1980) *Centre and Periphery: Spatial Variations in Politics*. Chichester: Wiley.

Gourevitch, P.A. (1978) 'Reforming the Napoleonic state: the creation of regional governments in France and Italy', in S. Tarrow, P. Katzenstein and L. Graziano (eds), *Territorial Politics in Industrial Nations*. New York: Praeger, 28–63.

Gourevitch, P.A. (1979) 'The re-emergence of peripheral nationalisms: some comparative speculations on the spatial distribution of political leadership and economic growth', *Comparative Studies in Sociology and History*, 21, 303–22.

Gourevitch, P.A. (1980) *Paris and the Provinces*. Berkeley: University of California Press.

Gradus, Y. (1982) 'Power relations in space and regional inequalities — the Israeli case', paper given at International Seminar on Political Geography, University of Haifa, January 1982.

Greene, K., Neenan, W.B. and Scott, C.D. (1974) *Fiscal Interactions in a Metropolitan Area*. Lexington, Mass.: D. C. Heath.

Grew, R. *et al.* (1978) *Crises of Political Development in Europe and the United States*. Princeton, NJ: Princeton University Press.

Grodzins, M. (1966) *The American System: A New View of Government in the United States*. Chicago: Rand McNally.

Gurr, T.R. (1970) *Why Men Rebel*. Princeton: Princeton University Press.

Guthrie, R. and McLean, I. (1978) 'Another part of the periphery: Reactions to devolution in an English development area', *Parliamentary Affairs*, 31(2), 190–200.

Guy, C.M. (1981) *Retail Location and Retail Planning in Britain*. Farnborough: Saxon House.

Hall, R. (1973) 'Regionalism and local government reform', in Open University Urban Development Course. Milton Keynes: Open University Press, Block 5.

Hallman, H.W. (1977) *Small and Large Together*. Beverly Hills: Sage Publications.

Hampton, W. (1970) *Democracy and Community*. London: Oxford University Press.

Hansen, T. (1981) 'Transforming needs into expenditure decisions', in K. Newton (ed.), *Urban Political Economy*. London: Frances Pinter, 27–46.

Hansen, T. and Kjellberg, F. (1976) 'Municipal expenditures in Norway: autonomy and constraints in local government activity', *Policy and Politics*, 4, 25–50.

Harrigan, J. (1976) *Political Change in the Metropolis*. Boston: Little Brown and Co.

Harsthorne, R. (1950) 'The functional approach in political geography', *Annals, Association of American Geographers*, 40(2), 95–130.

Hartle, D.G. and Bird, R.M. (1971) 'The demand for local political autonomy; an individualistic theory', *Journal of Conflict Resolution*, 15, 443–56.

Harvey, D. (1973) *Social Justice and the City*. Baltimore: Johns Hopkins University Press.

Hatry, H.P. (1976) 'Measuring the quality of public services', in W. D. Hawley and D. Rogers (eds), *Improving the Quality of Urban Management*. Beverly Hills: Sage Publications, Ch.2.

Hawkins, B.W. (1966) 'Public opinion and metropolitan reorganisation in Nashville'. *The Journal of Politics*, 28, 408–18.

Hawley, A.H. (1951) 'Metropolitan population and municipal government expenditures in central cities', *The Journal of Social Issues*, 7(1), 100–8.

Hayward, F. (1973) *The One and Indivisible French Republic*. London: Weidenfeld and Nicolson.

Hechter, M. (1975) *Internal Colonialism: The Celtic Fringe in British National Development*. London: Routledge and Kegan Paul.

Hechter, M. and Levi, M. (1979) 'The comparative analysis of ethnoregional movements', *Ethnic and Racial Studies*, 2(3), 260–74.

Hicks, U.K. (1978) *Federalism: Failure and Success*. London: Macmillan.

Hill, D.M. (1974) *Democratic Theory and Local Government*. London: George Allen and Unwin.

Hill, R.C. (1974) 'Separate and unequal: governmental inequality in the metropolis', *American Political Science Review*, 68, 1557–68.

Hill, R.C. (1977) 'State capitalism and the urban fiscal crisis in the United States', *International Journal of Urban and Regional Research*, 1, 76–100.

Hirsch, W.Z. (1970) *The Economics of State and Local Government*. New York: McGraw Hill.

Hirsch, W.Z. (1971) 'The fiscal plight, causes and remedies', in W. Z. Hirsch *et al.* (eds), *Fiscal Pressures on the Central City*. New York: Praeger, 3–40.

Hirschmann, A.O. (1970) *Exit, Voice and Loyalty: Responses to Decline in Firms, Organisations and States*. Cambridge, Mass.: Harvard University Press.

Hodges, M. (1978) 'Integration theory', in T. Taylor (ed.), *Approaches and Theory in International Relations*. London: Longman, 237–56.

Hofferbert, R.I. (1966) 'The relation between public policy and some structural and environmental variables in the American states', *American Political Science Review*, 60, 73–82.

Hoffman, S. (1959) 'The areal division of powers in the writings of French political thinkers', in A. Maass (ed.), *Area and Power*. Glencoe, Ill.: The Free Press, 113–49.

Hogwood, B.W. and Lindley, P. (1980) *Which English Regions?* Studies in Public Policy No. 5. University of Strathclyde, Glasgow: Centre for Studies in Public Policy.

Holden, M., Jr (1964) 'The governance of the metropolis as a problem in diplomacy', *Journal of Politics*, 26, 627–48.

Holmes, J.M. (1944) *The Geographical Basis of Government*. Sydney: Angus and Robertson.

Holmes, J. and Sharman, C. (1977) *The Australian Federal System*. Sydney: George Allen and Unwin.

Honey, R. (1976a) 'Geography and jurisdictional change in England'. University of Iowa, Department of Geography, mimeo.

Honey, R. (1976b) 'Efficiency with humanity: geographical issues in Scotland's local government reform', *Scottish Geographical Magazine*, 92, 109–20.

Honey, R. (1981) 'Alternative approaches to local government change', in A. D. Burnett and P. J. Taylor (eds), *Political Studies from Spatial Perspectives*. Chichester: John Wiley, 245–74.

Humes, S. and Martin, E. (1970) *The Structure of Local Government. A Comparative Survey of 81 Countries*. The Hague: IULA.

Hunter, F. (1953) *Community Power Structure*. Chapel Hill: University of North Carolina Press.

Hunter, T.S. (1977) *Federalism and Fiscal Balance*. Canberra: Australian National University Press and Centre for Research on Federal Financial Relations.

Institute of Public Administration (1971) *More Local Government*. Dublin: Irish Institute of Public Administration.

Jacob, H. (1972) 'Contact with government agencies: a preliminary analysis of the distribution of government services', *Midwest Journal of Political Science*, 16.

Jacob, H. and Lipsky, M. (1968) 'Outputs, structure and power: an assessment of changes in the study of state and local politics', *Journal of Politics*, 30, 510–39.

Jacob, P.E. and Teune, H. (1964) 'The integrative process; guidelines for the analysis of the bases of political community', in P. E. Jacob and J. R. Toscano (eds), *The Integration of Political Communities*. Philadelphia: Lippincott.

Jain, S. (1974) *Size Distribution of Income: A Compilation of Data*. Washington, DC: World Bank.

Janelle, D.G. (1968) 'Central place development in a time–space framework', *Professional Geographer*, 20, 5–10.

Janelle, D.G. (1975) 'Spatial aspects of alienation and the phasing out of bureaucracy', in R. Abler, D. Janelle, A. Philbrick and J. Sommer, *Human Geography in a Shrinking World*. North Scitutate, Mass.: Duxbury Press, 99–107.

Johnston, R.J. (1979) *Political, Electoral and Spatial Systems*. Oxford: Clarendon Press.

Johnston, R.J. (1980) *The Geography of Federal Spending in the United States of America*. Chichester: John Wiley (Research Studies Press).

Johnston, R.J. (1981) 'British political geography since Mackinder: a critical review', in A. D. Burnett and P. J. Taylor (eds), *Political Studies from Spatial Perspectives*. Chichester: John Wiley, 11–31.

Jones, B.D. (1977) 'Distributional considerations in models of government service provision', *Urban Affairs Quarterly*, 12, 291–312.

Jones, B.D. and Kaufman, C. (1974) 'The distribution of urban public services', *Administration and Society*, 6, 337–60.

Jones, E. and Eyles, J. (1977) *An Introduction to Social Geography*. London: Oxford University Press.

Kalk, E. (1971) *Regional Planning and Regional Government*. The Hague: IULA.

Kaplan, H. (1967) *Urban Political Systems: A Functional Analysis of Metro Toronto*. New York: Columbia University Press.

Kasperson, R.E. (1965) 'Towards a geography of urban politics: Chicago, a case study', *Economic Geography*, 11, 95–107.

Katznelson, I. (1976) 'The crisis of the capitalist city: urban politics and social control', in W. D. Hawley and M. Lipsky (eds), *Theoretical Perspectives On Urban Politics*. Englewood Cliffs, NJ: Prentice Hall.

Kaufman, C. (1974) 'Political urbanism: urban spatial organisation, policy and politics', *Urban Affairs Quarterly*, 9, 421–36.

Keating, M. (1975) 'The Scottish Local Government Bill', *Local Government Studies*, New Series, 1(1), 49–61.

Kemp, D.A. (1978) *Society and Electoral Behaviour in Australia*. Brisbane: University of Queensland Press.

Kerner Commission (1968) *Report of the National Advisory Commission on Civil Disorders*. New York: Bantam Books.

Kerr, H.H. (1974) *Switzerland: Social Cleavages and Partisan Conflict*. Sage Professional Papers in Contemporary Political Sociology, Vol. 1, No. 2. London: Sage.

Kesselman, M. and Rosenthal, D. (1974) *Local Power and Comparative Policies*. Sage Professional Papers in Comparative Politics, Vol. 5, No. 49. Beverly Hills, California: Sage.

Key, V.O., Jr (1949) *Southern Politics in State and Nation*. New York: A. A. Knopf.

King, D.N. (1973) 'Why do local authority rate poundages differ?' *Public Administration*, 51, 165–73.

Kjellberg, F. (1979) 'A comparative view of municipal decentralisation: neighbourhood democracy in Oslo and Bologna', in L. J. Sharpe (ed.), *Decentralist Trends in Western Democracies*. London: Sage, 81–118.

Kohr, L. (1957) *The Breakdown of Nations*. London: Routledge, Kegan and Paul. Republished in paperback by C. Davies (1974).

Kolinsky, M. (ed.) (1978) *Divided Loyalties*. Manchester: Manchester University Press.

Kosinski, L. (1970) *The Population of Europe*. London: Longman.

Kotler, M. (1969) *Neighborhood Government: The Local Foundations of Political Life*. Indianapolis: Bobbs Merrill.

Krane, D. (1978) 'Longitudinal patterns of centralisation and decentralisation: testing theories of government organisation', *Journal of Developing Areas*, 12, 297–314.

LaPalombara, J. (1974) *Politics within Nations*. Englewood Cliffs, NJ: Prentice Hall.

Lasswell, H.D. (1936) *Politics: Who Gets What, When, How*. New York: McGraw Hill.

Layfield Committee (1976) *Report of the Layfield Committee of Enquiry into Local Government Finance*. Cmnd 6453. London: HMSO.

Lazer, H. (1977) 'Devolution, ethnic nationalism and populism in the United Kingdom', *Publius*, 7(4), 49–70.

Leemans, A.F. (1970) *Changing Patterns of Local Government*. The Hague: IULA.

LeGrand, J. (1975) 'Fiscal equity and central government grants to local authorities', *The Economic Journal*, 85, 531–47.

Lerner, D. (1966) 'Some comments on centre–periphery relationships', in R. L. Merritt and S. Rokkan (eds), *Comparing Nations*. New Haven: Yale University Press, 259–65.

Levy, F.S., Meltsner, A.J. and Wildavsky, A. (1974) *Urban Outcomes*. Berkeley: University of California Press.

Lijphart, A. (1968) *The Politics of Accommodation*. Berkeley: University of California Press.

Lijphart, A. (1977) *Democracy in Plural Societies. A Comparative Exploration*. New Haven: Yale University Press.

Lindberg, L.N. and Scheingold, S.A. (eds) (1971) *Regional Integration*. London: Oxford University Press.

Lineberry, R.L. (1975) 'Equality, public policy and public services: the underclass hypothesis and the limits to equality', *Policy and Politics*, 4, 67–84.

Lineberry, R.L. (1977) *Equality and Urban Policy*. Beverly Hills, California: Sage.

Lineberry, R.L. and Fowler, E.P. (1967) 'Reformism and public policies in American cities', *The American Political Science Review*, 61, 701–17.

Lineberry, R.L. and Sharkansky, I. (1974) *Urban Politics and Public Policy*. New York: Harper and Row.

Lineberry, R.L. and Welch, R.E. Jr (1974) 'Who gets what: measuring the distribution of urban services', *Social Science Quarterly*, 54, 700–12.

Linge, G.J.R. (1975) *Canberra: Site and City*. Canberra: Australian National University Press.

Lipset, S.M. and Rokkan, S. (1967) 'Cleavage structures, party systems and voter alignments: an introduction', in S. M. Lipset and S. Rokkan (eds), *Party Systems and Voter Alignments*. New York: Free Press, 1–64.

Lipsky, M. (1970) *Protest in City Politics: Rent Strikes, Housing and the Power of the Poor*. Chicago: Rand McNally.

Lipsky, M. (1976) 'Towards a theory of street-level bureaucracy', in W. D. Hawley *et al.*, *Theoretical Perspectives on Urban Politics*. Englewood Cliffs, NJ: Prentice Hall, 100–45.

Livingston, W.S. (1952) 'A note on the nature of federalism', *Political Science Quarterly*, 67, 81–95.

Local Authorities Association (1980) *RSG. Tenth Report*. London: Local Authorities Association.

Lockard, D.S. (1959) *New England State Politics*. Princeton University Press.

Logan, M.I., Maher, C.A., McKay, J., Humphreys, J.S. (1975) *Urban and Regional Australia: analysis and policy issues*. Melbourne: Sorrett Publishing.

Logan, W.S. (1968) 'The changing landscape significance of the Victoria–South Australia boundary', *Annals, Association of American Geographers*, 58, 128–54.

Long, N.E. (1958) 'The local community as an ecology of games', *American Journal of Sociology*, 54, 251–61.

Lonsdale, R. (1972) 'Manufacturing decentralization: the discouraging record of Australia', *Land Economics*, 48 (4), 321–8.

Lovering, J. (1978a) 'The theory of the "internal colony", and the political economy of Wales', *Review of Radical Political Economics*, 10, 55–67.

Lovering, J. (1978b) 'Dependence and the Welsh economy', *Economic Research Papers Reg. 22*. University College of North Wales, Bangor: Institute of Economic Research.

Lupsha, P.A. and Siembieda, W.J. (1977) 'The poverty of public services in the land of plenty: an analysis and interpretation', in D. C. Perry and A. J. Watkins (eds), *The Rise of the Sunbelt Cities*. Urban Affairs Annual Reviews, Vol. 14. Beverly Hills: Sage Publications, 169–90.

Maass, A. (ed.) (1959) *Area and Power: a theory of local government*. New York: The Free Press.

McKenzie, N. (1977) 'Centre and periphery: the marriage of two minds', *Acta Sociologica*, 20(1), 55–74.

Mackintosh, J.P. (1968) *The Devolution of Power: Local Democracy, Regionalism and Nationalism*. London: Penguin.

McRoberts, K. (1979) 'Internal colonialism: the case of Quebec', *Ethnic and Racial Studies*, 2(3), 293–318.

Mansergh, N. (1936) *The Government of Northern Ireland: A Study in Devolution*. London: George Allen and Unwin.

Marando, V.L. (1974) 'An overview of the political feasibility of local government reorganisation', in T. P. Murphy and C. R. Warren (eds), *Organising Public Services in Metropolitan America*. Lexington, Mass.: Lexington Books, 17–52.

Margolis, J. (1961) 'Metropolitan finance: territories, functions and growth', in *Public Finances: Needs, Resources and Utilization*, National Bureau of Economic Research, A Conference of the Universities — National Bureau Committee for Economic Research. Princeton: Princeton University Press, 229–93.

Marshall, D.R. (ed.) (1979) *Urban Policy Making*. Beverly Hills, Calif.: Sage Publications.

Martyn, K.A. (1965) *Report on Education to the Governor's Commission on Los Angeles Riots*. Los Angeles.

Massam, B.H. (1975) *Location and Space in Social Administration*. London: Edward Arnold.

May, R.J. (1969) *Federalism and Fiscal Adjustment*. Oxford: Clarendon Press.

Mayer, K.B. (1968) 'The Jura problem: ethnic conflict in Switzerland', *Social Research*, 35, 707–40.

Mayo, P.A. (1974) *The Roots of Identity: Three National Movements in Contemporary European Politics*. London: Allen Lane.

Meacher, M. (1971) 'Scrooge areas', *New Society*, 2 December, 1084–6.

Meadows, W.J. (1981) 'Local government', in P. M. Jackson (ed.), *Government Policy Initiatives, 1979–80: Some Case Studies in Public Administration*. London: Royal Institute of Public Administration, 42–62.

Mellor, R.E. (1978) *The Two Germanies*. London: Harper and Row.

Merritt, R.L. (1976). *Symbols of American Community, 1735–1775*. New Haven Conn.: Yale University Press.

Miller, W.L. with Sarlvik, B., Crewe, I. and Alt, J. (1977) 'The connection between SNP voting and the demand for Scottish self-government', *European Journal of Political Research*, 5(1), 88–102.

Mladenka, K.R. (1978) 'Citizen demand and bureaucratic response: direct dialing democracy in a major American city', in R. L. Lineberry (ed.), *The Politics and Economics of Urban Services*. Sage Contemporary Social Science Issues, Vol. 43. Beverly Hills, Calif.: Sage Publications, 11–28.

Moore, B. and Rhodes, J. (1978) *Industrial and Regional Policy — the Republic of Ireland*. University of Cambridge, Department of Applied Economics.

Morgan, D.R. and Kirkpatrick, S.A. (eds) (1972) *Urban Political Analysis*. New York: The Free Press.

Muir, R.E. (1975) *Modern Political Geography*. London: Macmillan.

Muir, R.E. and Paddison, R. (1981) *Politics, Geography and Behaviour*. London: Methuen.

Musgrave, R.A. and Musgrave, P.B. (1976) *Public Finance in Theory and Practice*. Tokyo: McGraw-Hill.

Musgrave, R.A. and Polinsky, A. (1970) 'Revenue-sharing — a critical view', in *Financing State and Local Governments*. Boston: Federal Bank of Boston.

Myrdal, G. (1957). *Economic Theory and Underdeveloped Regions*. New York: Methuen; London: Harper and Row.

Nathan, R.P. and Adams, C. (1976) 'Understanding central city hardship', *Political Science Quarterly*, 91, 47–62.

Naustdalslid, J. (1977) 'A multi-level approach to the study of centre–periphery systems and socio-economic change', *Journal of Peace Research*, 14(3), 203–22.

Neenan, W.B. (1972) *Political Economy of Urban Areas*. Chicago: Markham Publishing Co.

Neiman, M. (1975) *Metropology: Toward a More Constructive Research Agenda*. Beverly Hills, Calif.: Sage Publications.

Netzer, D. (1977) 'Public sector investment strategies in the mature metropolis'. Paper given at Symposium on Strategies for the Maturing Metropolis, St Louis, Missouri, 6–8 June.

Newton, K. (1972) 'Democracy, community power and non-decision making', *Political Studies*, 20(4), 484–7.

Newton, K. (1975) 'Social class, political structure and public goods in American public politics', *Urban Affairs Quarterly*, 11, 241–64.

Newton, K. (1976a) *Second City Politics*. London: Oxford University Press.

Newton, K. (1976b) 'Community performance in Britain', *Current Sociology*, 22, 49–86.

Newton, K. (1976c) 'Feeble governments and private power: urban politics and policies in the United States', in L. H. Masotti and R. L. Lineberry (eds), *The New Urban Politics*. Cambridge, Mass.: Ballinger.

Newton, K. (1978) *Is Small Really so Beautiful? Is Big Really So Ugly?* Studies in Public Policy No. 18. University of Strathclyde, Glasgow: Centre for Studies in Public Policy.

Newton, K. (1979) 'Central place theory and local public expenditure in Britain'. Paper given at the Moscow IPSA Congress, 12–18 August, 1979. International Political Science Association.

Newton, K. (1980) 'Cities and their services'. Paper given at SSRC Urban Political Geography Meeting, Exeter, 1980.

Newton, K. (1981) *Urban Political Economy*. London: Frances Pinter.

Newton, K. and Sharpe, L.J. (1977) 'Local outputs research: some reflections and proposals', *Policy and Politics*, 5(3), 61–82.

Northwest Interprofessional Group (1974) *Local Authority Needs and Resources — The Effect of the Rate Support Grant in the North West*. London: Centre for Environmental Studies.

Oakland, W.H. (1979) 'Central cities: fiscal plight and prospects for reform', in P. Mieszkowski and M. Straszheim (eds), *Current Issues in Urban Economics*. Baltimore: Johns Hopkins University Press, 322–58.

Oates, W.E. (1972) *Fiscal Federalism*. New York: Harcourt Brace Jovanovich.

O'Connor, J. (1973) *The Fiscal Crisis of the State*. New York: St Martin's Press.

Offe, C. (1975) 'The theory of the capitalist state and the problem of policy formulation', in L. N. Lindberg, R. Alford, C. Crouch and C. Offe, *Stress and Contradiction in Modern Capitalism*. Lexington, Mass.: Lexington Books.

Oliver, F.R. and Stanyer, J. (1969) 'Some aspects of the financial behaviour of county boroughs', *Public Administration*, 47, 169–84.

Olson, M. (1965) *The Logic of Collective Action: Public Goods and the Theory of Groups*. Cambridge, Mass.: Harvard University Press.

Orridge, A.W. (1981) 'Uneven development and nationalism', *Political Studies*, 29, 1–15 and 181–90.

Orridge, A.W. and Williams, C.H. (1982) 'Autonomist nationalism: a theoretical framework for spatial variations in its genesis and development', *Political Geography Quarterly*, 1(1), 19–39.

Ostrom, E. (1974) 'Exclusion, choice and divisibility: factors affecting the measurement of urban agency output and impact', *Social Science Quarterly*, 54, 691–9.

Ostrom, V., Tiebout, C.M. and Warren, R.O. (1961) 'The organization of government in metropolitan areas: a theoretical inquiry', *American Political Science Review*, 55, 831–42.

Paddison, R. (1977) *The Political Geography of Regionalism*. Armidale, NSW: University of New England Press.

Paddison, R. (1978) 'The Green Ban Movement: a case study of an urban social movement'. Unpublished discussion paper.

Paddison, R. (1981) 'Identifying the local political community: a case-study of Glasgow', in A. D. Burnett and P. J. Taylor (eds), *Political Studies from Spatial Perspectives*. Chichester: John Wiley, 341–55.

Paddison, R. (1982) 'Intergovernmental relations and the federal state: territorial stability in Australia'. Paper read at International Seminar on Political Geography, Haifa, January.

Paddison, R. (forthcoming) *Delimiting an Urban Political Geography*.

Page, E.C. (1978) 'Michael Hechter's internal colonial thesis: some theoretical and methodological problems', *European Journal of Political Research*, 6, 295–317.

Page, E.C. (1981) 'An alternative view of the Scottish bill', in *Public Expenditure Policy and the Rate Support Grant*. CURR Discussion Paper No. 2. University of Glasgow, Centre for Urban and Regional Research.

Page, E.C. and Midwinter, A. (1979) *Remote Bureaucracy or Administrative Efficiency? Scotland's New Local Government System*. Studies in Public Policy No. 38. University of Strathclyde, Glasgow: Centre for Studies in Public Policy.

Pahl, R.E. (1970) *Whose City?* London: Longman.

Parsons, T. (1966) *Societies, Evolutionary and Comparative Perspectives*. Englewood Cliffs, NJ: Prentice Hall.

Pascal, A.H. and Menchik, D. (1979) *Fiscal Containment: Who Gains? Who Loses?* Rand Report R-2494/I-FF/RC. Santa Monica, California.

Peirce, N. (1975) 'Public worker pay emerges as a growing issue', *National Journal*, 7 (23 August), 1198–206.

Peterson, G. (1976) 'Finance', in G. Gorham and R. Glazer (eds), *The Urban Predicament*. Washington, DC: The Urban Institute.

Phillips, P. (1977) 'National unity, continental economics and national disintegration', in D. J. Bercuson (ed.), *Canada and the Burden of Unity*. Toronto: Macmillan, 19–43.

Pickvance, C.G. (1976) 'On the study of urban social movements', in C. G. Pickvance (ed.), *Urban Sociology: Critical Essays*. London: Tavistock.

Polsby, N. (1963) *Community Power and Political Theory*. New Haven, Conn.: Yale University Press.

Pommerehne, W.W. (1977) 'Quantitative aspects of federalism: a study of six countries', in W. E. Oates (ed.), *The Political Economy of Fiscal Federalism*. Lexington, Mass.: Lexington Books, 275–355.

Potter, D. (1975) 'Communication, nation and politics', in *D101 Making Sense of Society*, Block 3: Communication. Milton Keynes: The Open University Press, 161–83.

Poulantzas, N. (1973) *Political Power and Social Classes*. London: New Left Books.

Pounds, N.J.G. and Ball, S. (1964) 'Core areas and the development of the European states system', *Annals, Association of American Geographers*, 54(1), 24–41.

Pratt, J. (1980) 'A sense of place', in R. D. Grillo (ed.), *'Nation' and 'State' in Europe*. London: Academic Press, 31–43.

Pratt, L. (1977) 'The state and province-building: Alberta's development strategy', in L. Panitch (ed.), *The Canadian State: Political Economy and Political Power*. Toronto: University of Toronto Press.

Prest, A.R. (1978) *Intergovernmental Financial Relations in the United Kingdom*. Canberra: Centre for Research on Federal Financial Relations, Australian National University.

Prud'homme, R. (1977) 'France: central government control over public investment expenditures', in W. E. Oates (ed.), *The Political Economy of Fiscal Federalism*. Lexington, Mass.: Lexington Books, 65–74.

Puchala, D.J. (1974) *International Politics Today*. New York: Dodd Mead.

Rae, D.W. and Taylor, M. (1970) *The Analysis of Political Cleavages*. New Haven, Conn.: Yale University Press.

Rallings, C.S. and Lee, A. (1977) 'Politics of the periphery — the case of Cornwall'. Paper presented to the Conference of the PSA Work Group on The Politics of the United Kingdom, Aberystwyth, September 1977.

Rawls, J. (1972) *A Theory of Justice*. Oxford: Clarendon Press.

Reagan, M. (1972) *The New Federalism*. New York: Oxford University Press.

Redcliffe-Maud (Lord) and Wood, B. (1976) *English Local Government Reformed*. London: Oxford University Press.

Reece, J.E. (1979) 'Internal colonialism: the case of Brittany', *Ethnic and Racial Studies*, 2(3), 275–92.

Reischauer, R.D. (1977) 'Governmental diversity: bane of the grants strategy in the United States', in W. E. Oates (ed.), *The Political Economy of Fiscal Federalism*. Lexington, Mass.: Lexington Books, 115–28.

Rich, R.C. (1977) 'Equity and institutional design in urban service delivery', *Urban Affairs Quarterly*, 12, 383–410.

Rich, R.C. (1979) 'Distribution of services. Studying the products of urban policy making', in D. R. Marshall (ed.), *Urban Policy Making*. Beverly Hills, Calif.: Sage, 237–59.

Rich, R.C. (1980) 'The roles of neighborhood organizations in urban service delivery'. *NASPAA Urban Affairs Papers*.

Ridley, F.F. (1973) *The French Prefectoral System: An Example of Integrated Administrative Decentralisation*. Commission on the Constitution, Research Papers 4. London: HMSO.

Riker, W.H. (1964) *Federalism: Origin, Operation and Significance*. Boston: Little, Brown and Company.

Riker, W.H. (1969) 'Six books in search of a subject, or does federation exist and does it matter?' *Comparative Politics*, 2(1), 135–46.

Robinson, K.W. (1961) 'Sixty years of federation in Australia', *Geographical Review*, 51, 1–20.

Robson, W. (1966) *Local Government in Crisis*. London: Allen and Unwin.

Rokkan, S. (1975) 'Dimensions of state-formation and nation-building: a possible paradigm for research on variations within Europe', in C. Tilly (ed.), *The Formation of National States in Western Europe*. Princeton, NJ: Princeton University Press, 562–600.

Ronen, D. (1980) *The Quest for Self-Determination*. New Haven, Conn.: Yale University Press.

Rose, A. (1972) *Governing Metropolitan Toronto: A Social and Political Analysis 1953–1971*. Berkeley: University of California Press.

Rose, G. (1971) 'Local councils in metropolitan areas', *Fabian Research Series*, 296.

Rose, R. (1970) *The United Kingdom as a Multi-National State*. Occasional Paper No. 6. University of Strathclyde, Glasgow: Survey Research Centre.

Rose, R. (1971) *Governing without Consensus*. London: Faber.

Rose, R. and Urwin, D.W. (1970) 'Persistence and change in Western party systems since 1945', *Political Studies*, 18, 287–319.

Rose, R. and Urwin, D. (1975) *Regional Differentiation and Political Unity in Western Nations*. Sage Professional Papers in Contemporary Political Sociology, 06-007. Beverly Hills, Calif.: Sage Publications.

Rowat, D.C. (ed.) (1977) *The Government of Federal Capitals*. Toronto: University of Toronto Press.

Rowat, D.C. (ed.) (1980) *International Handbook on Local Government Reorganization*. London: Aldwych Press.

Royal Commission on Local Government in England (1969a) *Report*. Vols I and II. Cmnd 4040. London: HMSO.

Royal Commission on Local Government in England (1969a) *Community Attitudes Survey — England*. Research Study 9. London: HMSO.

Royal Commission on Local Government in Scotland (1969a) 'The Wheatley Report', 2 vols. Edinburgh: HMSO.

Royal Commission on Local Government in Scotland (1969b) *Community Survey: Scotland*. Research Studies 2. Edinburgh: HMSO.

Rubinfeld, D.L. (1979) 'Judicial approaches to local public-sector equity: an economic analysis', in P. Miezkowski and M. Straszheim, *Current Issues in Urban Economics*. Baltimore: Johns Hopkins University Press, 542–76.

Rudolph, J.R. (1977) 'Ethnic sub-states and the emergent politics of tri-level interaction in Western Europe', *Western Political Quarterly*, 30(4), 537–58.

Runciman, W.G. (1966) *Relative Deprivation and Social Justice*. London: Routledge, Kegan and Paul.

Rustow, D.A. (1967) *A World of Nations*. Washington DC: The Brookings Institution.

Ryerson, S. (1968) *Unequal Union: Confederation and the Roots of Conflict in the Canadas 1815–1873*. Toronto: Progress Books.

Saunders, P. (1979) *Urban Politics: a Sociological Interpretation*. London: Hutchinson.

Saunders, P. (1980) 'The problem of space in urban sociology/politics'. Paper given at PSA Work Group on UK Politics, 5th annual conference, Cardiff, 16–19 September 1980.

Savage, R.L. (1973) 'Patterns of multilinear evolution in the United States', *Publius*, 3(1), 75–108.

Sawer, G. (1969) *Modern Federalism*. Carlton, Vic.: Pitman.

Saywell, J. (1977) *The Rise of the Parti Québecois, 1967–1976*. Toronto: University of Toronto Press.

Scharpf, F.W., Reissart, B., and Schnabel, F. (1978) 'Policy effectiveness and conflict avoidance in intergovernmental policy formation', in K. Harf and F. W. Scharpf (eds), *Intergovernmental Policy Making*. London: Sage.

Schuman, H. and Gruenberg, H. (1972) 'Dissatisfaction with city services; is race an important factor?' in H. Hahn (ed.), *People and Politics in Urban Society*. Beverly Hills, Calif.: Sage, 369–92.

Schwartz, M.A. (1974) *Politics and Territory. The Sociology of Regional Persistence in Canada*. Montreal: McGill–Queen's University Press.

Scott, A.D. (1952) 'Federal grants and resource allocation', *Journal of Political Economy*, 60, 534–8.

Senior, D. (1965) 'The city region as an administrative unit', *Political Quarterly*, 36, 82–91.

Sharkansky, I. (1976) *The United States: A Study of a Developing Country*. New York: Longman.

Sharkansky, I. and Hofferbert, R.I. (1969) 'Dimensions of state politics, economics and public policy', *American Political Science Review*, 63, 867–80.

Sharpe, L.J. (1970) 'Theories and values of local government', *Political Studies*, 18, 153–74.

Sharpe, L.J. (1978) 'Reforming the grass roots: an alternative analysis', in D. Butler and A. H. Halsey (eds), *Policy and Politics*. London: Macmillan, 82–110.

Sharpe, L.J. (ed.) (1979) *Decentralist Trends in Western Democracies*. London: Sage Publications.

Sharpe, L.J. (1981) 'Is there a fiscal crisis in Western European local government? A first appraisal', in L. J. Sharpe (ed.), *The Local Fiscal Crisis in Western Europe*. London: Sage Publications, 5–28.

Sherwood, F.P. (1969) 'Devolution as a problem of organization strategy', in R. T. Daland (ed.), *Comparative Urban Politics*. Beverly Hills, Calif.: Sage Publications, 60–87.

Simeon, R. (1972) *Federal–Provincial Diplomacy. The making of recent policy in Canada*. Toronto: University of Toronto Press.

Smallwood, F. (1965) *Greater London: The Politics of Metropolitan Reform*. Indianapolis: Bobbs-Merrill.

Smiley, D.V. (1974) 'Federal–provincial conflict in Canada', *Publius*, 4(3), 7–24.

Smith, A.D. (1981) *The Ethnic Revival*. Cambridge: Cambridge University Press.

Smith, B.C. (1965) *Regionalism in England. Its Nature and Purpose*. London: Acton Society Trust.

Smith, B.C. (1980) 'Measuring decentralisation', in G. Jones (ed.), *New Approaches to the Study of Central–Local Government Relationships.* Farnborough: Gower Press.

Smith, C.J. (1980) 'Neighbourhood effects on mental health', in D. Herbert and R. J. Johnston (eds), *Geography and the Urban Environment.* Vol. III. Chichester: Wiley, 363–415.

Smith, D. (1977) 'Western politics and national unity', in D. J. Bercuson (ed.), *Canada and the Burden of Unity.* Toronto: Macmillan, 142–68.

Smith, D.M. (1974) 'Who, what, where and how: a welfare focus for human geography', *Geography,* 59, 289–97.

Smith, D.M. (1977) *Human Geography: a Welfare Approach.* London: Edward Arnold.

Smith, G. (1972) *Politics in Western Europe.* London: Heinemann.

Soja, E.W. (1968) 'Communications and territorial integration in East Africa: an introduction to transaction flow analysis', *East Lakes Geographer,* 4, 39–57.

Soja, E.W. (1971) *The Political Organization of Space.* Commission on College Geography, Resource Paper No. 8. Washington: Association of American Geographers.

Sommer, R. (1969) *Personal Space: The Behavioral Basis of Design.* Englewood Cliffs, NJ: Prentice-Hall.

Southron, D.W.D. (1972) 'Finance', in G. Rhodes (ed.), *The New Government of London: The First Five Years.* London: Weidenfeld and Nicolson, 347–98.

Stacey, M. (1969) 'The myth of community studies', *British Journal of Sociology,* 20, 134–46.

Stanyer, J. (1976) *Understanding Local Government.* Glasgow: Fontana/Collins.

Steinberg, J. (1976) *Why Switzerland?* Cambridge: Cambridge University Press.

Stephens, G.R. (1974) 'State centralization and the erosion of local autonomy', *Journal of Politics,* 36, 44–76.

Stevens, A.R. (1974) 'State boundaries and political cultures: an exploration in the tri-state area of Michigan, Indiana and Ohio', *Publius,* 4(1), 111–25.

Stevens, R.M. (1977) 'Asymmetrical federalism: the federal principle and the survival of the small republic', *Publius,* 7(4), 177–203.

Stevenson, G. (1977) 'Federalism and the political economy of the Canadian state, in L. Panitch (ed.), *The Canadian State: Political Economy and Political Power.* Toronto: University of Toronto Press, 71–100.

Stevenson, G. (1979) *Unfulfilled Union.* Toronto: Gage.

Stewart, J. (1980) 'The Bill and central–local relations', in *The Local Government Planning and Land Bill.* Birmingham: Institute of Local Government Studies.

Stokes, D. (1967) 'Parties and the nationalization of electoral forces', in W. N. Chambers and W. O. Burnham (eds), *The American Party Systems: Stages of Political Development.* New York: Oxford University Press, 182–202.

Stokes, D. (1969) 'A variance components model of political effects', in J. M. Clannch (ed.), *Mathematical Applications in Political Science,* Vol. 1. Dallas, Texas: Southern Methodist University, 61–85.

Strayer, J. (1970) *On the Medieval Origins of the Modern State.* Princeton: Princeton University Press.

Tarlton, C.D. (1965) 'Symmetry and asymmetry as elements of federalism: a theoretical speculation', *Journal of Politics,* 27, 861–74.

Tarrow, S. (1977) *Between Center and Periphery.* New Haven, Conn.: Yale University Press.

Tarrow, S. *et al.* (eds) (1978) *Territorial Politics in Industrial Nations.* London: Praeger.

Taylor, A.H. (1973) 'Journey time, perceived distance and electoral turnout — Victoria Ward, Swansea', *Area,* 5, 59–63.

Taylor, P.J. and Johnston, R.J. (1979) *The Geography of Elections.* London: Penguin.

Thompson, R. (1973) 'Planners, motorways and people'. University of Canterbury, Department of Psychology and Sociology.

Thornhill, W. (1972) *The Case for Regional Reform.* London: Nelson.

Tiebout, C.M. (1956) 'A pure theory of local expenditures', *Journal of Political Economy,* 64, 416–24.

Tilly, C. (ed.) (1975) *The Formation of National States in Western Europe.* Princeton: Princeton University Press.

Tocqueville, A. de (n.d.) *Democracy in America.* Translated by Henry Reeves. New York: A. S. Barnes.

Tyne and Wear County Council (1977) *Is this a United Kingdom?* Newcastle: Conference Proceedings.

Van Loon, R.J. and Whittington, M.S. (1976) *The Canadian Political System.* Toronto: McGraw-Hill Ryerson. Second edition.

Verba, S. (1971) 'Sequences and developments', in L. Binder *et al., Crises and Sequences in Political Development.* Princeton: Princeton University Press, 283–316.

Verba, S. and Nie, N.H. (1972) *Participation in America: Political Democracy and Social Equality.* New York: Harper and Row.

Viera, P.R. (1967) 'Towards a theory of decentralization: a comparative view of forty-five countries'. PhD dissertation, University of Southern California, Los Angeles.

Vile, M.J.C. (1977) 'Federal theory and the new federalism', *Politics,* 12(2), 1–14.

Vincent, P.E. (1971) 'The fiscal impact of commuters', in W. Z. Hirsch *et al., Fiscal Pressures on the Central City.* New York: Praeger, 41–143.

Walsh, A. (1969) *The Urban Challenge to Government.* New York: Praeger.

Warren, C.R. (1974) 'Developing alternative models for servicing metropolitan America', in T. P. Murphy and C. R. Warren (eds), *Organizing Public Services in Metropolitan America.* Lexington, Mass.: Lexington Books, 3–14.

Warren, R.O. (1964) 'A municipal services market model of metropolitan organisation', *Journal of American Institute of Planners,* 30, 193–204.

Waterman, S. (1981) 'Electoral reform in Israel: a geographer's view', Geographical Research Forum No. 3, Occasional Papers. Beer-Sheba: Ben Gurion University of the Negeb, Department of Geography, 16–24.

Watts, R.L. (1966) *New Federations: Experiments in the Commonwealth.* Oxford: Clarendon Press.

Webber, M.M. (1963) 'Order in diversity: Community without propinquity', in L. Wingo (ed.), *Cities and Space.* Baltimore: Johns Hopkins University Press, 23–56.

Weber, E. (1977) *Peasants into Frenchmen.* Stanford: Stanford University Press.

Weber, M. (1948) *From Max Weber* (eds H. H. Gerth and C. Wright Mills). London: Routledge and Kegan Paul.

Webster, B.A. (1977) 'Distributional impacts of local government policy'. Paper given at IBG Urban Geography Study Group Conference, Leicester.

Weisbrod, B.A. (1964) *External Benefits of Public Education: An Economic Analysis.* Princeton: Princeton University Press.

Wettenhall, R.L. and Power, J.M. (1974) 'The administrative side of regionalism within states. Australian national report'. Paper tabled at 16th Annual Congress of Administrative Sciences, Mexico City.

Wheare, K.C. (1963) *Federal Government.* London: Oxford University Press, 4th edition.

Whebell, C.F. (1973) 'A model of territorial separatism', *Proceedings, Association of American Geographers Conference,* 295–8.

Whitlam, E.G. (1969) 'An urban nation', First Annual Leslie Wilkinson Lecture, University of Sydney, 2 July 1969, 10. Repeated in E. G. Whitlam, 'A new federalism', *Australian Quarterly,* 43(3), September 1971, 11.

Whittlesey, D. (1939) *The Earth and the State.* New York, Holt.

Wilken, W.H. (1974a) 'The impact of centralization on effectiveness, economy and efficiency', in T. P. Murphy and C. R. Warren (eds), *Organizing Public Services in Metropolitan America.* Lexington, Mass.: Lexington Books, 107–26.

Wilken, W.H. (1974b) 'The impact of centralization on access and equity', in T. P. Murphy and C. R. Warren (eds), *Organizing Public Services in Metropolitan America.* Lexington, Mass.: Lexington Books, 127–38.

Williams, C.H. (1980) 'Ethnic separatism in Western Europe', *Tijdschrift voor Economische en Social Geographie,* 71, 142–58.

Williams, C.H. (ed.) (1981) *National Separatism.* Cardiff: University of Wales Press.

Williams, G. (ed.) (1978) *Social and Cultural Change in Contemporary Wales.* London: Routledge and Kegan Paul.

Williams, H.H., Liebman, C. and Dye, T.R. (1965) *Suburban Differences and Metropolitan Policies: A Philadelphia Story.* Philadelphia: University of Pennsylvania Press.

Williams, O.P. (1971) *Metropolitan Political Analysis: A Social Access Approach.* New York: Free Press.

Williams, O. and Adrian, C. (1963) *Four Cities: A Study of Comparative Policy-Making.* Philadelphia: University of Pennsylvania Press.

Williamson, J.G. (1965) 'Regional inequality and the process of national development', *Economic Development and Cultural Change,* 13, 1–84.

Wilson, J.Q. and Banfield, E.C. (1964) 'Public-regardingness as a value premise in voting behavior, *American Political Science Review,* 58, 876–87.

Wolfinger, R. (1971 'Non-decisions and the study of local politics', *American Political Science Review*, 65, 1063–80.

Wood, B. (1974) *The Process of Local Government Reform 1966–74.* London: George Allen and Unwin.

Wood, R.C. (1961) *1400 Governments.* Cambridge, Mass.: Harvard University Press.

Woolmington, E.A. (1966) *A Spatial Approach to the Measurement of Support for the Separatist Movement in Northern New South Wales.* Armidale, NSW: University of New England.

Wright, D. (1978) 'The River Murray: microcosm of Australian federal history', in B. W. Hodgins, D. Wright and W. H. Heick, *Federalism in Canada and Australia: The Early Years.* Waterloo, Canada: Wilfred Laurier University Press, 278–86.

Ylsivaker, P. (1959) 'Some criteria for a "proper" areal division of government powers', in A. Maass (ed.), *Area and Power.* Glencoe, Ill.: The Free Press, 27–49.

Young, K. and Kramer, J. (1978) *Strategy and Conflict in Metropolitan Housing.* London: Heinemann.

Ziegler, D.J. and Brunn, S.D. (1980) 'Geopolitical fragmentation and the pattern of growth and need: defining the cleavage between sunbelt and frostbelt metropolises', in S. D. Brunn and J. O. Wheeler (eds), *The American Metropolitan System.* London: Edward Arnold, 77–92.

Index